Another Slice of
Arkansas Pie

Another Slice of
Arkansas Pie

A Guide to the Best Restaurants, Bakeries, Truck Stops and Food Trucks for Delectable Bites in The Natural State

Kat Robinson

TONTI
PRESS

Published by Tonti Press
Little Rock, Arkansas

Cover image of pecan pie a la mode at Local Flavor Café in Eureka Springs
Back cover image a fried pie from Flywheel's Pies in Prescott
Front page image of butter chess pie at Paul's Bakery in Van Buren

All photography by Kat Robinson except where noted

First published 2018

Manufactured in the United States of America

ISBN-13: 978-0-9998734-0-3

Library of Congress Control Number: 2018901400

Notice: The information in this book is true and complete to the best of our knowledge. It is offered without guarantee on the part of the author. The author disclaims all liability in connection with the use of this book.

For Grav

Table of Contents

FOREWORD

"As American as apple pie" is a common expression that pays homage to the most traditional and beloved of all American desserts, but a historical search reveals that pie started out as a savory affair. The crust was only a vehicle for the filling that had to be cracked open to get to the crow or rabbit or pigeon inside. Indeed, the crust was referred to as a "cofyn." It wasn't until the 1700's when the sugar colonies developed in the Caribbean did we see the birth of sweet pies. Still, savory pies ruled, and it wasn't until the 1800's when the sugar refining industry of the American South turned a once rare resource into something commonplace and inexpensive. With sugar production came a kind of intoxication according to Michael Pollan in his book, *The Botany of Desire*. This sensory delight of sweet along with the proliferation of fruit orchards across the country resulted in pie being permanently imprinted on American tastes.

Fast forward to the modern culinary landscape of endless sweet pie possibilities where the "cofyn" is as varied as the filling it holds. Crusts made of crackers, cookies, butter and flour combinations, filo, cornmeal, nuts, puff pastry and more. Fruit pies, chess pie, chocolate pies, custard filled, vinegar pies, meringue topped, whipped cream crowned, simple and complex, the combinations are limitless.

My earliest pie memories come from The Hotel Sam Peck which my family owned for decades in downtown Little Rock, Arkansas. Mattie Jackson's Bavarian Cream Pie with cinnamon still ranks high in my pie dreams. Franke's makes a similar pie, and it tugs on my heartstrings periodically, flooding me with nostalgic memories of my once favorite dessert. I'm the fourth generation Peck to have served pie to Arkansans and visitors to the Natural State. My family has served countless slices of different kinds of this American staple. At Trio's Restaurant, which I co-created in 1986, we are renowned for our desserts, and our dessert repertoire is heavy on the pie side for obvious reasons. We love pie!

Kat Robinson, queen of Arkansas pie and author of *Arkansas Pie: A Delicious Slice of the Natural State* published in 2012, lives her passion to explore and honor this culinary gem. If she ever needs someone to help her sample the hundreds of different pies served across our state, sign me up!

Capi Peck

With thanks to Rachel E. Gross of Slate, *March 13, 2015*

INTRODUCTION

It all started with a fried pie.

The year was 2007. I had a few months earlier left the morning show I'd produced for eight years, Today's THV This Morning. I'd been saving up things I wanted to do when I finally left TV on a list, and on that list was a little pie shop in DeValls Bluff.

A short time earlier, Viv Barnhill, her brother Carl Rice and his wife Betty all came up to Little Rock in the wee hours of the morning to appear on the morning show. They brought with them the pies that had put their mama's pie shop on the map, overstuffed fried pies with an amazing crispy dough, packed with a variety of fruits and custards. Those pies were phenomenal, and everyone in that newsroom that morning tried a bite or several. I promised myself I'd get out there and go at some point in time.

Here it was, the first day of December 2007, and I was keeping that promise, hitting the road to drive just over an hour to get to the shop just off US 70 at Arkansas 33, a little pie shop inside little house. I spent my morning talking with Viv and taking a few photographs and procuring pies, which came back with me in the backseat of my car. At home I shot a few photos more and wrote several words about it on my still rather new website and thought no more about it.

We were having dinner on the 7th, a birthday dinner for my brother Zack at Cregeen's Irish Pub in North Little Rock's Argenta District, when I got the news – there were a lot of people looking at Tie Dye Travels. My website that had been getting maybe a dozen visits a day suddenly had 1200 hits. I would find out in the next few hours that the *Arkansas Times'* Eat Arkansas blog had picked up the piece and shared it out.

That was the day I decided pursuing Arkansas food as a niche topic was a good idea, under the idea that if I wrote about food, I'd never starve. There is substantial truth to that idea, as my waistline can attest. Starvation has indeed never quite entered the picture.

Ten years on, I'm sitting in the dining room of Mrs. Rhoda Adams, asking questions and allowing her to spin out her tale of how she came to be in the restaurant business. It's taking a little while. She intersperses her answers with calls to her husband James and her daughter Dorothy as they prep for the day. "I need some more pecans!" she hollers, before diving into how people used to just show up at her house so she had to get a place, this place, this restaurant where she sells her famous hot tamales, fried chicken, soul food, burgers and indeed pies – but never on Sunday, because that's when she's at church. "You need to get this tray from me," she yells back, having filled a cookie sheet with rows of tiny pie shells now filled with pecan and sweet potato filling.

"Someone should write a book about this," I thought to myself, not for the twentieth time. Oh yeah, I already did, my mind reminds me. That was *Arkansas Pie: A Delicious Slice of the Natural State*, which I pounded out in August of 2012 on a 30-day deadline set by a publisher who wanted to get a book about Arkansas food,  any Arkansas food, into consumer hands as quickly as possible. I don't remember much of that month. It was a blur of working a day job, writing every weeknight and getting on the road every single weekend to go shoot pies and collect stories. From the moment it left my hands I kept thinking of how much better I could make it.

It did well enough. These past five years I have encountered it again and again, with a food lover seeking me out or finding me at an event or a signing, showing me their copy. You see, the book took on a life of its own. Readers took their books on the road, kept them in the glove compartment, dragged them into restaurants and asked the owners and the piemakers to sign them. I could never in my wildest dreams have seen what was going to happen.

Five years is a lot of water under the bridge, and in that time we've lost a lot of pie restaurants, some new, some classic. Some of the bastions of pie, such as Ed and Kay's in Benton, The Village Wheel in Bull Shoals, Ray's Dairy Maid in Barton, and

Chip's Barbecue in Little Rock, have disappeared. Even as this book came together, the magnificent Jenny Lind Country Café at Gate Nine closed shop.

What's happened, though, is a growing knowledge of pie across the state. The first book listed 180 restaurants; this one covers more than 400. They're not just restaurants that offer a smattering of pie choices at the end of a meal but a selection of bakeries and panaderias where you can get your pies to take home; food trucks that share the pie love; antique malls where the pies are good as the rare find; walk-up outdoor lunch counters; and truck stops that cater to the most discerning of road diners. Pie can be extraordinarily fancy, such as the buttermilk pie with pear brandy cream and volcano salt caramel at Modern Ozark Dining in Bentonville. Or it can be as simple as the local apples sliced and spiced and wrapped in a rustic dough and baked on a sheet at Big Springs Trading Company in St. Joe. It can meet a high price point or a low one, and contain anything from fruit to cream to custard to meringue to nuts to, well, whatever your heart desires. Events have been sparked celebrating pie. Arkansas's population has claimed pie as its own, reveling with it, rejoicing in it.

Now, with the introduction of *Make Room for Pie: A Delicious Slice of the Natural State with Kat Robinson*, a special produced by Emmy award-winner Larry Foley and directed by Hayot Tuychiev, and with the publishing of this book, I hope pie lovers can once again journey out into the regions of the Natural State, wandering the highways in search for their favorite slice.

Kat Robinson
February 21, 2018
Little Rock

GRANDMA'S HOUSE CAFÉ

In 1991, Ernestine Shepherd opened the Blue Bird House Café right next to a scenic overlook on US Highway 71. The richly blue painted building drew drivers off the road for good country-style vittles. For ten years it was a Razorback fan staple.

Bad health forced Mrs. Ernestine to close the place down in 2001, two years after the lack of traffic following the opening of the interstate took its bite out of business. She decided to put the Blue Bird House Café up for sale.

She had a buyer right off the bat – her own daughter, Elaine Bowlin. Elaine and her husband Jerry renamed it Grandma's House Café. Elaine wanted the place to feel like eating at your grandparent's home. The Bowlins painted the building gray and opened shop.

Gray Weldon

The Bowlins serve up the foods of the Ozarks four days a week on a classic country-style buffet – breakfasts of baked ham, fried bacon, sausage, eggs, fried potatoes, biscuits, white and chocolate gravy and pancakes cooked to order. The lunch buffet always includes ham and pan fried chicken along with other items such as meatloaf, pork chops, barbecue chicken breast, dumplings, cream gravy and potatoes, brown and green beans, and huge fluffy yeast rolls.

Diners are welcomed in and shown to a table, a real dining table of some sort or another. The restaurant is packed with them, all mismatched, in-between china cabinets and hutches. These hungry customers are then set loose upon the buffet to fend for themselves.

No one says you cannot start with the pie buffet. After all, your choice of whatever six or eight pies are offered for the day are right there for the choosing, and you are not limited to one. Each pie is sliced into sixteen slices, which means you can give yourself a sample of half a slice instead of settling for just one whole one. Every whole pie is handmade. You can poke your head in the kitchen door, right off the front room, and watch them being pulled out of the oven or topped with cream on a counter. You can get run out of that kitchen, too, if you're too nosy.

The pies that are walked from that kitchen to the pie buffet, located in front of an old fireplace mantle, vary according to the preferences of the cooks. There's usually a no- sugar-added pie of some sort, usually apple. Then there will be cream pies — chocolate and coconut, banana, pineapple. A fruit pie, like cherry. A peanut butter pie. A real variety.

Once you take your plate to the table, you can enjoy the company of your fellow diners or gaze out into one of the deepest valleys of the Ozarks, where in summer verdant ridges call in the sunshine and in winter the blues and grays and browns of the quiet months prove the clarity of the arctic air.

I have heard there is a menu — actually been offered one every time I come through the door — but I can't imagine why. Every homemade item seems to be right there on one of the wheeled bars right in the front room.

Pie lovers and buffet diners alike take note: Grandma's House Café is one of those throwback restaurants in the state that only takes cash, so be sure to bring your money along. The nearest ATM is 13 miles away in West Fork.

21588 South US Highway 71
Winslow, Arkansas 72959
(479) 634-2128

LETHA'S FRIED PIES

Handpies are a way of life across Arkansas, and no matter whether they're actually fried or baked, Arkansawyers tend to call them fried pies. Many are made in the restaurants that serve them – but for many, many other locations, the pies are made by one of three or four companies.

In northern and western Arkansas, a goodly number of those pies come from Letha's Pies in West Fork. It's named for Letha Glenn, who started the business along with her husband Tom in 1990 in their home in Fayetteville. Letha made several different desserts at the time. Tom would deliver them to different businesses in northwest Arkansas and southwest Missouri.

They moved into a small bakery in Branson a while later and built a clientele. But the bakery burned in November 2008. The Glenn's son Tim and daughter-in-law Rhonda wanted to keep it going, and in 2009 with their parents, reformed the business into Letha's Pies, offering nothing but fried pies, They moved the operation to West Fork and built it up from its mom-and-pop roots. Today, it's a bakery creating a dozen different flavors of fried pies that are distributed through eight states.

They're commercially distributed, so you can't just walk up and buy a pie. Most restaurants that serve the dessert proudly display a card advertising Letha's. They're also the official fried pie of the Arkansas State Fair.

Website: LethasPies.com

CHESTER COUNTRY CAFÉ

In the little town of Chester, a couple of blocks northwest of the I-49 on-ramp, you'll find this L-shaped building that looks like anyone's house, complete with tomato plants and flower baskets in the front yard. The homestyle eatery offers daily plate lunch specials, an unhurried late breakfast, a selection of pizzas and an offering of desserts. Most days, that includes pie, some of which are unusual – take, for instance, the White Christmas pie, with its cranberries and white fluff, or the Aussie lime pie. Each day's desserts are on the sideboard.

315 East Front Avenue
Chester, Arkansas 72934
(479) 369-4900

WORKMAN'S HILLTOP TRAVEL CENTER

The Workman's Hilltop Travel Center north of Alma off I-49 offers a mess of double-handed fried pies right by the register in a number of flavors – amongst them cherry, blueberry, apple and chocolate. The fat pastries are wrapped in plastic and can be heated if you ask nicely. Sliced pie is available at the Red Hog Café, within the truck stop.

8265 Arkansas Highway 282 at Interstate 49
Alma, Arkansas 72921
(479) 632-1356
WorkmansTravelCenters.com

PIRATE'S COVE CAFÉ

The community of Greenland lies just south of Fayetteville along the Boston Mountain Scenic Byway, not far from the Arkansas Air and Military Museum. The local standby is Pirate's Cove Café, a breakfast-and-hot-lunch joint named for the local high school football team, the Greenland Pirates. Each day a collection of different desserts is offered. Of note, the Dutch apple pie is rather tasty.

201 North Main Avenue
Fayetteville, Arkansas 72701
(479) 435-6540

RICK'S BAKERY

It didn't take a rocket scientist to create Fayetteville's most iconic bakery. It took a NASA engineer. Rick Boone had a full-ride scholarship with the Air Force. After jobs in the space industry dried up with the end of the Apollo program, he needed something to do. That something came in the form of a tiny doughnut shop he and his wife Susan opened in a strip mall in 1980.

Though they quickly blasted the business up to seven locations, the Boones realized they weren't making money, so they pulled back to the original store on College Avenue and focused hard to make it good.

It's not just good, it's out of this world. Today, Rick's Bakery has taken over a 12,500 square foot mall with wings of bakers, decorators and designers, an eat-in restaurant and pastries galore.

Rick's regularly offers three solid flavors of whole cream pies. The chocolate silk is absolutely a must if you can only have one - a nice, deep, darker chocolate than most cream pies, smooth and satisfying. The Key lime and coconut pies are equally satisfying. Slices are also packaged and ready to go.

The bakery also makes double-crusted cherry and peach pies, a triple chocolate pie and good old fashioned buttermilk, too.

1220 North College Avenue (Across from the Veteran's Hospital)
Fayetteville, Arkansas 72703
(479) 442-2166
RicksBakery.com

THE ROLLING PIN CAFÉ

Fayetteville is a booming college city, growing by leaps and bounds in innovation, population and a bubbling food scene. But you can still find an old-fashioned country-style café inside the city limits.

Out on the Huntsville Road, in a large facility that houses the local Area Agency on Aging, the Rolling Pin Café is tucked into a back corner away from the road. Don't let the plain Jane façade outside fool you; within you'll find conversations a-bub at mismatched tables under country décor.

The Rolling Pin Café was opened in 1993 by Travis and Devona Freeman who, on their own website, describe themselves as a "quirky husband and wife team." The website also divides its feature sections into breakfast, lunch and pie – the only such site where I've ever seen "bootscoot" in reference to a restaurant. The lunch menu's three specialties are brown beans, Northern beans with ham and a vegetable plate.

To my knowledge and experience, The Rolling Pin is the only place in Fayetteville (and most of Arkansas) that offers a straight-on rhubarb pie, untinged with strawberries. The double-crusted pie, just like other fruit pies such as blueberry and peach, is butter-kissed and hand pinched, just like a good crispy crusted pie should be. Other flavors on the menu include banana, peanut butter, cherry cream; and egg custard. Sugar-free versions are available.

The Rolling Pin Café
2565 East Huntsville Road
Fayetteville, Arkansas 72701
(479) 521-3855
RollingPinCafe.net

PENGUIN ED'S HISTORIC B&B BARBECUE

Barbecue and pie go hand-in-hand so often in Arkansas, something you're bound to notice as you go through this book. At Penguin Ed's Historic B&B in Fayetteville, that's no exception. What's unusual is that famed Betty's fried pies aren't offered at the other two locations of the barbecue shop.

That's because the B&B spot is the continuation of an entirely different barbecue shop, the vaunted B&B Barbecue, which Bill and Betty Basset opened in 1960. It was the first barbecue-priority restaurant in the city of Fayetteville, a city that came late to the smoked meats game, perhaps due to Ozark isolation, perhaps due to the prevalence of traditional smoked meats without the sauce and seasoning. For whatever reason, B&B was the start of something good.

Ed Knight, the penguin-loving restaurateur who has already gotten his beak wet in the barbecue business with the first Penguin Ed's in 1993, shared the Basset's desire to keep a Fayetteville landmark going, and so when the family bowed out of the business in 1998, Knight purchased it and added Penguin Ed's name to the title. But he didn't change much. The original wood paneled interior remains, as does the cadre of red phones at the table where one places one's order. And the Knights continue to offer Betty's fried pies, but only at this location.

These handheld wonders must be ordered 15 minutes in advance. The overstuffed doughy pockets come sprinkled with cinnamon and sugar and are filled with your choice of apple, peach, apricot or chocolate.

230 South East Avenue
Fayetteville, Arkansas 72701
(479) 521-3663
PenguinEds.com

I will never come out and say there's a singular best pie in Arkansas. But I have told many people over these past five years about my favorite – a decadent Bourbon Chocolate Chunk Pecan pie offered by Chef Jerrmy Gawthrop at the Greenhouse Grille in Fayetteville. The farm-to-fork restaurant is well known for its use of hyperlocal produce, meats and fungi – including the magnificent shiitake fries with magic catsup.

To my dismay, during the compilation of this book, the Greenhouse Grille closed. However, Chef Gawthrop did share the recipe for this magnificent pie.

BOURBON CHOCOLATE CHUNK PECAN PIE

6 medium eggs
2 cups brown rice syrup
or corn syrup
2 cups brown sugar
1/3 cup bourbon (Jack
Daniels)
4 ounces semi-sweet
chocolate chunks
2 pie crusts, blind-baked
2 2/3 cups toasted
pecans

Grav Weldon

Beat eggs until smooth. Slowly add syrup and brown sugar. Pour in bourbon and mix thoroughly.

Place chocolate chunks across bottom of pie shells. Pour batter over the chocolate. Top with pecans.

Place on sheet pan and bake in preheated 350° oven for 45 to 50 minutes or until center is firm.

Makes two pies.

POWERHOUSE SEAFOOD AND GRILL

The Key lime pie comes on a chocolate cookie crust for a twist on the old favorite, which seems very fitting with the upscale Cajun fare for which the restaurant is best known.

112 North University Avenue
Fayetteville, Arkansas 72701
(479) 442-8300
PowerhouseSeafoodandGrill.com

ROLANDO'S RESTAURANTE

Key lime pie is also a specialty at Rolando's Restaurante, where the rich custard is served on a thick, moist graham cracker crust and topped with hand whipped cream and raspberry couli (see page 237).

509 West Spring Street
Fayetteville, Arkansas 72701
(479) 251-1650
RolandosRestaurante.com

SASSY'S RED HOUSE

Traditional possum pie comes in two basic varieties – that which is served in a pie pan, and that which is cut from a 13" x 9" casserole dish. The latter is the sort you'll be served when you order the delicacy at Sassy's Red House in Fayetteville. The popular bar and grill along College Avenue is often packed with Razorback fans. This is a pie for sharing – two to four people is advised.

708 North College Avenue
Fayetteville, Arkansas 72701
(479) 856-6366
SassysBarBQ.com

APPLE BLOSSOM BREWING COMPANY

In 2013, the craft brew scene took off in northwest Arkansas, a frothy development that lead to the creation of the Fayetteville Ale Trail. There are eleven breweries on the list. Pinnacle Car Services offers two tours (north and south) for those who which to partake at a number of the locations along the trail without getting behind the wheel.

Of these, the Apple Blossom Brewing Company deserves a special note. The ten-barrel brewery on Zion Road is attached to its companion 200+ seat restaurant, a cavernous edifice divided by honest-to-goodness woodworked bars and barbacks from Ireland. The brewery has already received notice for a deep house list with such entries as Nitro Hazy Morning Coffee Stout, Bourbon Barrel Aged Old Boggy Stock Ale Bomber, and the unique and spicy Soulless Ginger.

The menu unabashedly brags on the brews, with a menu centered around a beer queso created from its Fayetteweisse American-style lager, tempura-battered fish and chips, and a range of comforting pastas. The sandwich menu is deep, too, thanks to house-baked breads created from cultured yeasts kept on-site, many of which are made from locally-produced organic War Eagle Mill flours, all overseen by executive pastry chef Cody Johnson. That's right – this is a brewery with a pastry chef.

The bourbon chocolate chip pecan pie is a melding of chocolate chip cookie and pecan pie, with both the goo of such a pie and a conglomeration of chocolate throughout. This is a rich but irresistible pie that cries for a stout rather than a cup of milk, a sweet slice drizzled with a buttery chocolate sauce and served with a wicked grin.

1550 East Zion Road
Fayetteville, Arkansas 72703
(479) 287-4344
appleblossombrewing.com

THE GREEN GOAT

At the corner of Martin Luther King Jr. Drive and Wood Avenue on Fayetteville's side, you'll find this colorful food truck in a garden yard serving up Cuban food for breakfast and lunch. Of note is the Nutella and salted caramel empanadas, a particularly delectable sweet-and-salty handpie. Guava and cream cheese empanadas are also available.

583 South Wood Avenue
Fayetteville, Arkansas 72701
(479) 310-5444
GreenGoatGourmet.com

NELLIE B's BAKERY

California natives Priscilla and Danielle Wright opened Nellie B's Bakery in December 2014 in the Elkins community (east of Fayetteville) with a combination of recipes derived from generations of family from different heritages – including English, Italian and Native American.

The Wrights specialize in cake but their pies are of note – traditional flavors with a twist, such as pumpkin with butterscotch sauce and zest-topped Key lime. They also love fresh-fruit double crusted pies and build them with whole fresh strawberries, blackberries, peaches, bananas or what's available, topping each crust with an ample coating of sugar crystals.

2421 North Center Street
Fayetteville, Arkansas 72701
(479) 305-3735
Facebook.com/NellieBsBakery

CATFISH HOLE

The Gazzola family still runs Catfish Hole in Alma and Fayetteville. The original Alma location was purchased in 1993 Pat and Janie Gazzola, who had spent 24 years working in the oil and gas industry beforehand. Dinners are served family style, with catfish, hush puppies, pickle relish and such passed around. Dessert, though, is a personal thing. The house pie is Key lime, though fried pies are made available on Friday and Saturday nights.

4127 West Wedington Drive
Fayetteville, Arkansas 72704
(479) 521-7008
TheCatfishHole.com

24 Collum Lane West
Alma, Arkansas 72921
(479) 632-9718

THE FARMER'S TABLE CAFÉ

On the south end of Fayetteville, an old Craftsman style home houses one of the most hep new eateries in the area – a farm-to-fork gathering place packed with people gathering for a bite. That'd be The Farmer's Table Café, which focuses on locally sourced organic and handmade dishes for breakfast, lunch and dinner.

Pies at The Farmer's Table are as rustic as you'd expect from the name, in traditional varieties such as pumpkin, pecan and chocolate mousse. The apple pie in particular has that glow to it, the sort of glow you get when your apples are just-ripe when picked. This particular pair of slices was made from Granny Smith and Arkansas Blackapples out of the A&A Orchard operation nearby, and those lattice strips and crust came crafted from War Eagle Mill flour.

The pies are sometimes more elaborate but within the same comfortable scope of local foods, such as blackberry rosemary vanilla pie or lemon lavender cream pie. They all come crafted with an artisan's eye, flawed but perfect, just like you'd find on the counter in the farmhouse of your dreams.

In many ways, The Farmer's Table Café is the beautiful realization of the sort of food- crafting places like Grandma's House Café represents – comfortable surrounds, comfortable food and pie. I long to see what this Fayetteville upstart looks like in 30 years.

1079 South School Avenue
Fayetteville, Arkansas 72701
(479) 966-4125
TheFarmersTablecafe.com

MOCKINGBIRD KITCHEN

The mockingbird is the state bird of Arkansas. It's also the name of an elevated pie derived from a longtime Arkansas favorite. Such is the mockingbird pie at Mockingbird Kitchen in Fayetteville, a high-concept yet airy version of what we have come to know as the possum pie.

Chef Chrissy Sanderson started out at longtime Fayetteville staple Bordino's in 1998 after graduating with a degree in political science from the University of Arkansas. Two years later, she headed north to Hyde Park, New York to train at the prestigious Culinary Institutes of America before returning to Arkansas and taking the reins at Bordino's for another eight years. She began teaching culinary classes at the Northwest Arkansas Community College in 2007 (now home to the Brightwater School for Arkansas Food) and spent time in the years in-between at Bentonville Butcher and Deli and at Tusk and Trotter. In 2016, she opened Mockingbird Kitchen in the corner pocket of a sprawling shopping center, right next to Arcadia Retrocade, where gamers can pay $5 to enjoy dozens of console and videogames, unlimited, to their heart's content.

Within Mockingbird Kitchen, the walls bear simple drawings: Audubon-style sketches of birds, reflecting co-owner and partner Leigh Helm's love of bird- watching, and illustrations of herb and spice plants, all under red-orange drums of light over mahogany tables.

The menu could be froufrou. Instead, it's populated with comfort foods to love, presented gorgeously and made with local ingredients, like Crystal Lake Farms birds in its crispy fried chicken; beef from Grass Roots Farmers Cooperative in the meatloaf and Kent Walker Artisan Cheese in the queso.

The pie – the starring feature on Mockingbird Kitchen's dessert menu – eschews the trappings of a traditional possum pie while echoing its best attributes. From the bottom, the "sandy crust" of flour and pecans prevalent in other versions is elevated to a salted pecan crust here. The bottom layer is a delectably delicious, light vanilla-tinged cream spread with magnificent chocolate pastry cream and dolloped with hand-whipped cream and candied pecans. Chef Chrissy's creation is light enough for a single dessert but appears much larger in size and scope. This mockingbird plays possum on its own terms.

1466 North College Avenue
Fayetteville, Arkansas 72703
(479) 435-6333
MockingbirdKitchen.com

HARVEST MOON PIES

Fayetteville's new devotion to pie, evidenced by the many new restaurants that have embraced the dessert, isn't limited to the traditional brick and mortar restaurant. It's the sole focus of Harvest Moon Pies, an Airstream trailer turned into the sweetest little business you'll find in the city.

Its proprietor and pie genius is Amanda Harrison Robinson. She didn't start out as a chef. She started out as an opera singer. In fact, Amanda's early career traces through the Metropolitan Opera in New York City. She spent years singing there and in Europe. But she came to a point where she had to make a choice – stay in opera and live that career, or begin a family.

Family won out. After a brief stint at the Kansas City Conservatory, she moved home to northwest Arkansas, where she cared for her mother through cancer treatments, and where she taught choir for a short while at Gravette Schools. One day she got a call – a youth minister position had opened up at St. Paul's Episcopal Church in Fayetteville.

She's been in that job twelve years now. Her work there with the youth program caught the eye of the Fuller Institute, which named it one of the top 40 Youth Ministry programs across the United States. She and her husband Dan have two girls, Isabelle and Lillian, who are now in their teenage years.

I've saved her story for the last of those from the city, because, well, it left me speechless. One late morning in January 2018, Amanda invited me to shoot a pie and tell me a story.

You see, Amanda's had an auspicious life. But she wanted something more. And she found that in an odd way – in the checkout line at the Walgreen's at MLK and School Street on the south side of Fayetteville.

"I went to get dental floss, and right there at the checkout line was this book," she told me as she went back to her office. When she set the book down on the table where I was photographing her cranberry crumble, I had no words.

The book was *Arkansas Pie: A Delicious Slice of the Natural State*.

The next day, Amanda went to her banker and asked for a loan. She also asked if she was crazy. Her loan officer told her to go for the idea – of opening up her own pie food truck. She bought an Airstream trailer. Her nephew rebuilt her house into a commercial kitchen and away she went, opening Harvest Moon Pies in 2017.

The adorable restored 1962 Airstream is open eleven months of the year, offering whole pies and slices and handpies with all-organic ingredients and unusual combinations, such as the cranberry crumble Amanda shared with me, full of cranberries and almonds, peanuts and oatmeal. There's the popular Moonapple pie, with its fat lattice. Amanda also makes a laudable coconut cream pie, coconut cream, lemon meringue... and even savory handpies full of ground beef and vegetables or curried chicken. Harvest Moon Pies also does "pie-io-li" – tiny sweet pockets of toasted apple-filled ravioli served with ice cream.

418 South Government Avenue (at the Quick Town Food Truck Court)
Fayetteville, Arkansas
HarvestMoonPies.com

COMBS STORE AND CAFÉ

This comfortable general store offers all the things you need for being in the outdoors in the Ozarks – from hunting and fishing licenses to motorcycle parts to gas, RV spots and even a good hot meal. Pies are often on the dessert menu, and if you happen in on a day when the skillet caramel apple pie is fresh out of the oven, forget lunch and get dessert first.

10342 Arkansas Highway 16
Combs, Arkansas 72721
(479) 677-2783

BRIAR ROSE BAKERY

You don't expect to see an English cottage alongside an Arkansas highway, but that's exactly what you'll discover in Farmington. Briar Rose Bakery, a peaked-roof structure with Tudor styling, stucco and half-timbering and exposed stonework, looks like the sort of thing you might discover in a fairy tale. Inside, beams cross over a yellow and white bakery that covers items from cinnamon rolls to woodfired pizza, savory danishes and baskets of rustic breads.

It was meant to be whimsical. The structure was built over a former termite exterminator's office. The unique edifice was modeled and named after the Brothers Grimm fairy tale about a sleeping princess and the prince that came to rescue her (which we know better as Sleeping Beauty). It's owned by Diane and Larry Bowden, the couple's son Brett and daughter Nicole, along with Nicole's husband Brad Brekelbaum, who's also the lead pastry chef.

Funny thing is, the Bowdens got started in the operation with a barbecue trailer. They bought the property to use as a parking lot for Damon's BBQ, where they started out selling California-style tri-tip barbecue. The bakery came along later, with construction beginning in 2009 and the doors opening in April 2011.

The coconut cream personal mini pies are of particular note. These cloud-like not-too-sweet poofs hover in puff pastry crust filled with a mild custard, with texture provided by toasted bits of coconut throughout. These are pies meant for tea and china, exactly the sort of pie you should enjoy in a fairy tale.

28 East Main Street
Farmington, Arkansas 72730
(479) 300-6027
nwacottage.com

KT AND SONS CAFÉ

KT and Sons Café sits roughly 1000 feet away from the Oklahoma border. The eatery began life as KT's Café in 1989, but in December 2015 it reopened under the new name, when Kaye Trentham brought in her two sons to help run the only restaurant in the town of Evansville. Clint Trentham serves as pastor for Calvary Assembly

of God in Fort Smith, while Tim Trentham is a cattle farmer and retired mechanic. The three operate the café Tuesday through Saturday for lunch and dinner, with breakfast also being offered on Saturdays.

Kaye has been making pies as long as she can remember. At 77 years old, she still creates gorgeous meringues and rich nut pies, including the only Almond Joy pie I've found that's a baked coconut, chocolate and almond pie instead of a cream pie. She also makes a marvelous apple walnut pie, noted by its gorgeously golden baked crust, crunchy walnuts and apple filling.

The restaurant's location on Arkansas Highway 59 about 30 miles north of Van Buren is remote, but those marvelous pies are worth the drive.

20674 South Arkansas Highway 59
Evansville, Arkansas 72729
(479) 848-3022

E & L's CAFÉ

If you're looking for pies in Siloam Springs, head to E and L's Café and Homestyle Cooking – where homemade pies are advertised right on the window. Check the case on the counter for such pies as sweet potato, chocolate cream, strawberry rhubarb, apple, Almond Joy cream, banana cream, pecan and Elvis varieties. At the time of this writing, the restaurant housed at the Super 7 Inn is in the process of merging with Taqueria Jaliscos, a local food truck operation, to create an American/Mexican blended menu.

1951 East Highway 412
Siloam Springs, Arkansas 72761
(479) 373-3999

NEAL'S CAFÉ

Neal's Café opened along old US Highway 71 in Springdale back in 1944. Toy and Bertha Neal started with the premise of serving "The Best of Better Foods" and the fourth generation of Neals continue to do so today.

The bright pink restaurant with its iconic neon still sits along Thompson Avenue today. Within, you can still order pulleys – the center cut of the chicken breast, fried in a skillet – with your meat-and-three meal. Neal's also serves a classic apple-and-cheese salad, turkey and dressing, red hot apples and more on its standard list of side items.

The décor is eclectic – hailing back to the Neals' original compromise. Bertha wanted her restaurant to be pink, so Toy obliged. It IS pink – and decorated with guns, arrowheads and taxidermy between its mirrored flat slab fireplaces. The restaurant retains its original concrete-block bones and chrome-edged tabletops, though the pink walls are occasionally painted… pinker.

The pies, of course, are a major draw. Meringue pies come topped with twirls of whipped peaks, one per slice. They're almost always available, lofty slices of lemon, chocolate and coconut meringue. Neal's also does a very respectable job of cut-lattice fruit pies, including a gooey cherry pie straight out of the 1950s.

806 North Thompson Street
Springdale, Arkansas 72764
(479) 751-9996

SUSAN'S RESTAURANT

Along Sunset Avenue, a tall sign stands in front of a brown-roofed building. It proudly states "Home of Susan's World Famous Here Locally (Open 6 a.m.-2 p.m. Breakfast) Restaurant." The building itself is often packed with locals, Razorback fans on their way south to Fayetteville, and of course pies.

Within, the Mhoon family has established an eatery that maintains a mid-century style, complete with lunch counter, family-style seating and wood paneling. A tall case to the left of the bar holds pie slices. When in season, the must-acquire pie is strawberry icebox, with light and tart berries suspended in an equally light cream.

No matter what time of year you come, though, the upside-down apple pie is a must-try. The caramel-swathed pecan top crust covers perfect, firm slices of apple below.

1440 West Sunset Avenue
Springdale, Arkansas 72764
(479) 751-1445

SPRING STREET GRILL & CAFÉ

Since 1987, diners have been able to get a grand meal at this block-wide eatery in downtown Springdale, best known for casseroles, salads and an outstanding orange roll. The meringue pies are not to be overlooked.

101 Spring Street
Springdale, Arkansas 72764
(479) 751-0323
Facebook.com/SpringStreetGrill

ESPIGA DE ORO PANADERÍA Y PASTELERÍA

Located in downtown Springdale across from the post office, Panaderia La Espiga de Oro's gorgeous gold-walled establishment includes cases upon cases of fine Mexican breads, pastries and desserts. The strawberry empanada is a brightly filled, beautifully crafted delight.

428 Holcomb Street
Springdale, Arkansas 72764
(479) 717-9969
Facebook.com/EspigaDeOroPasteleria

PATRICK'S BURGERS

Originally opened in 1971, Springdale's version of the local dairy bar, with great burgers and milkshakes ordered at the counter and served in a dining room painted with bright apparitions of paradoxical classic paintings. Patrick's also offers Glenn's fried pies right on the counter.

3976 Elm Springs Road
Springdale, Arkansas 72762
(479) 751-9245
PatricksBurgers.homestead.com

T&T DINER

This dairy bar attached via roof to a convenience store and gas station alongside US Highway 412 on the east side of town is popular for its burgers. It also offers fried pies from Glenn's Bakery in more than a dozen flavors.

17440 US Highway 412
Springdale, Arkansas 72764
(479) 751-4797

WAGON WHEEL COUNTRY CAFÉ

On the north side of Springdale, right near the Lowell border, there's an old wooden structure with a tree growing through its front porch. The edifice has been around for decades, and in a previous life was known as Hobo Joe's. Today it's the Wagon Wheel Country Café, and it's been serving up homestyle food since 2009. Linda Bryant, who served as cafeteria manager at George Junior High School for 15 years before the restaurant opened, runs the place alongside her husband, Larry.

When you pass through the double doors, you enter an enormous oversized dining room with a fireplace hearth that spans the entire north wall. Dining tables just like you'd find in any country kitchen are surrounded by spoke-backed chairs. There's always a lunch or dinner special posted alongside the day's sides and pies.

The small pie case up front can be deceptive. The Wagon Wheel offers, from time to time, varieties of more than two dozen different pies – including four that are sugar-free. On one visit I had the opportunity to shoot ten different sorts of pies – including chocolate silk, German chocolate, pecan, coconut, peanut butter, fresh strawberry, even possum pie from a casserole pan.

If you contact the restaurant in advance, they can have a sugar-free pie ready to go when you arrive. And they don't look at you like you're crazy if you order two slices.

4080 North Thompson Street
Springdale, Arkansas 72764
(479) 927-1510

MAMA Z's CAFÉ

The tradition of pasta brought to northwest Arkansas more than a century ago continues at this eatery alongside US Highway 412 in Tontitown on the road to Siloam Springs. The Zulpo family continues the tradition of mild but hearty sauces and fresh pasta handmade in a shop out behind the restaurant.

Pies and cobblers are the desserts offered, and if it's pie you're seeking, it's pie you'll get – fluffy meringue pies of coconut or chocolate cream. That is, if you're not too full after a meal of pasta. Don't worry, you can get it to go.

357 West Henri De Tonti Boulevard (US Highway 412)
Springdale, Arkansas 72762
(479) 361-2750

PIPPIN APPLE PIES

Kelli Maestri's budding pie catering business has drawn a lot of attention. Her Springdale-area service offers the same pies that Kelli learned how to make from her Grandma Flossie. The pies - which include peach, pecan, coconut cream, lemon meringue and apple – can be ordered by phone at (479) 236-8514. Kelli's pies can be viewed and requested via Instagram @pippinapplepies.

TATER'S FRESH GRILL

Lowell sits between the larger communities of Springdale and Rogers, a town built twice – once in the early 19th century along the Old Wire Road, then again after it was destroyed in the Civil War. It's home to trucking giant J.B. Hunt.

Lowell's standout pie restaurant is Tater's Fresh Grill. Momma Tater creates desserts that cause tongues to wag – massive cookies the size of hats, unusual cakes with bacon embedded between layers of chocolate, and spiky-topped meringue pies. Meringue isn't the only pie served here – the pies range from the perfectly straight fresh straw- berry and cream cheese pie to a delectable blueberry and walnut crumb pie.

109 North Bloomington Street
Lowell, Arkansas 72745
(479) 361-8800
Facebook.com/TatersFreshGrill

PANADERIA VEGA

Admonishing customers on social media with the frequent whisper of "no hay dieta hoy" (no diet today!) is common for the folks at Panaderia Vega, who have served Rogers and the surrounding area for more than 15 years. This orange-interior bakery is full of cases of delicious pastries, including an admirable enpanadas de piña (pineapple empanadas) along with vanilla cream, pumpkin and strawberry versions.

115 North Dixieland Road
Rogers, Arkansas 72756
(479) 636-4059

FORK AND CRUST

Lori Rae didn't start out looking for a life of pie. The pies found her. The Harrison stay-at-home mother of four was wrapped up in a life of soccer matches and family activities. But when her third daughter was diagnosed with a heart condition, it set Lori on a different course.

"She was my child who always thinks on her feet, in control of her emotions," Lori tells me, "but this sent her over the edge, because so much was happening to her. She was 17 at the time. One day, we were watching a show about hand splitting cherries for pies and she said 'let's do that,' and when you're trying to get her out of worrying what would happen, you just do it. It was June, and there were fresh cherries available but we didn't have a cherry pitter so we went to the store to get what we needed. The whole process was amazing. Making the cherry pie was exactly what we needed. I know people say this all the time about pie – but it's magic. After we'd

tried different treatments and diagnoses and traveled the U.S., pie healed my family." Lori started making little ones to sell at a farmers market in south Missouri. Four months later, she leased a commercial kitchen and offered pies to area grocery stores. In 2010, those pies went on the board at Neighbor's Mill in Harrison.

In 2016, Lori opened Fork and Crust, a pie-based restaurant in Rogers. There were people waiting for pies before the shop even opened. In 2017 she added a second store in Bentonville, and in 2018 a third in Fayetteville. The pies are widely varied – from standards such as caramel apple, lemon chess and chocolate cream to raspberry chiffon, chocolate oatmeal and whiskey bacon pecan. But she doesn't stop there. In the case you might find cookie dough pie, cinnamon roll pie or chocolate banana tof-fee; other days it might be packed with carrot cake pie, lemon curd with raspberry or pear ginger with cranberry (which, I must say, is divine). And the cherry crumb that Lori made with her daughter is still on the menu.

"I never thought I'd ever do pie," Lori says. "If you'd told me when my kids got out of the house I'd be living away from my husband with three shops in two years, I would never have guessed it."

5208 West Village Parkway #11   Tiny Pie Bar at Remedy Road Boutique
Rogers, Arkansas 72758   112 West Central Avenue
(479) 268-6634   Bentonville, Arkansas 72712
ForkAndCrust.com   (479) 321-1316

FOSTER'S PINT AND PLATE

What do you share for dessert at the largest pub in northwest Arkansas? Go for the triple crème banana pie – a disc of graham cracker cookie crust topped with fresh bananas, banana cream, hot dulce de leche drizzle and a dolloped of whipped cream. Or try the peanut butter chocolate pie with toasted peanuts and caramel glaze.

2001 South Bellview Road Suite #2
Rogers, Arkansas 72758
(479) 621-0093
FostersPintAndPlate.com

LUCY'S DINER

You can get pie 24 hours a day at Lucy's Diner in Rogers. One of a couple of locations (the other being in Fort Smith, read more page 232), the bright café with the teal interior will serve you a cream or fruit pie any hour of the day.

511 West Walnut Street
Rogers, Arkansas 72756
(479) 230-5829

LOG CABIN RESTAURANT

Out towards Beaver Lake on Highway 12, the Wright family opened this breakfast, lunch and pizza joint in 2007 Its list of pies is substantial and includes such unusual offerings as blackberry cheese pie, cherry supreme and banana cream pies.

14550 Arkansas Highway 12 East
Rogers, Arkansas 72756
(479) 925-7222
LogCabinEat.com

SAM'S OLD TYME HAMBURGERS

A tall revolving case of pies stands by the en- trance to the dining room at Sam's Old Tyme Hamburgers in Rogers. Selections such as cherry cream cheese, possum, chocolate meringue and the lattice-topped cinnamon loaded apple pie are often available.

223 East Locust Street
Rogers, Arkansas 72756
(479) 986-9191
SamsHamburgers.com

THE STATION CAFÉ

A standard for traditional dairy-diner fare in Bentonville since 1977, this burger, fries and pie joint originally opened by Betty and Cecil Turner was once called The Filling Station. Today The Station is best known for an Angus burger called the Steakburger

that's cited as one of northwest Arkansas's best burgers. Amongst the pies offered daily in the restaurant's case, you will often find such favorites as chocolate cream, coconut cream or walnut.

SE D Street and Sixth Street
Bentonville, Arkansas 72712
(479) 273-0553
TheStationCafeInc.com

GOOSEBERRY HANDMADE PIES

The shop is unassuming – a simple bar along one wall, a small case in a corner on the other, a counter to pick up and pay for your orders and two blackboards with flavors of the day. The pies at Gooseberry Handmade Pies require no pretension.

One afternoon in early January, I found myself leaned against the counter in this space, talking over a small Ozark Mountain Grape pie with Jerry Leding. He had insisted I try the pies I was shooting, and for good reason, too. I was already enamored with the gorgeous violet grapes within the sugar-touched crust. He mentioned they were a special varietal. I immediately asked him if they were Saturn grapes, one of the cultivars from the University of Arkansas Fruit Station at Clarksville grown at Dahlem Vineyards in Wiederkehr Village, and he stopped.

"You're close – but these are seeded grapes." Jerry started, then looked at me a moment and started again. "I'm from Altus." He then proceeded to tell me about how his mother apparently once made grape pies herself, but because they're so time consuming, she'd stopped doing it before he got of an age to enjoy them. I in turn told him about my daughter's spell at the Altus Grape Festival (read it on page 246). We both agreed, those grape pies are cherished. It takes up to an hour to seed enough grapes for a pie.

Leding used to work for Walmart, while his Sarah daughter had a job at a pharmacy. They opened Gooseberry Handmade Pies in October 2014 with, you guessed it, gooseberry pies. The Ledings found a supplier and are bringing the old Ozark pie favorite back to the table. The pies, baked from recipes Jerry's cultivated and created in the crust Jerry's mother-in-law used to bake, come from locally sourced ingredients – grapes from the Altus region, pecans from across the border in Oklahoma, peaches and apples from nearby orchards.

You can tell a Gooseberry Handmade Pie when you see it. Sarah's a genius when it comes to creating art with dough, from a plaid strawberry rhubarb to the goose-foot mullet piercings of the gooseberry to the hand-placed perfect bunch of grapes atop the Ozark Mountain Grape pie. She also custom decorates pies for birthdays, weddings and events with a cutter and a little dye, for undeniably artistic edibles. Gooseberry Handmade Pies are also available at several JJ's Grill locations in the Bentonville area. The maple walnut is available at Leverett Lounge in Fayetteville.

2210 South Walton Boulevard
#12 Bentonville, Arkansas 72712
(479) 224-1318
GooseberryPies.com

MODERN OZARK DINING

High-end, high-concept pie? Indeed, it's one of the many desserts that rotate into and out of the prix fixe menu at Modern Ozark Dining. Those who come to eat have their dinner choices made for them – and those who are lucky may encounter the restaurant's precisely plated buttermilk pie – a gorgeous, buttery blade of pie topped with the most delicate of cream, whipped together with pear brandy, atop a small pool of volcano salt caramel. It may look like the future, but the flavor of all three together is extraordinarily evocative of an Ozark spring.

110 NW Second Street Suite 110
Bentonville, Arkansas 72712
(479) 544-9455
Mod.Restaurant

BIZZY B'S BAKERY

Beate McChristan and Barbi Sand's Bizzy B's Bakery specializes in wedding cakes, but her operation also offers a fine selection of marvelous pies, including pecan, cherry crumb, chocolate cream and coconut.

1501 SE Walton Boulevard #101
Bentonville, Arkansas 72712
(479) 657-2557
BizzyBBakery.com

MARKHAM & FITZ

"Are you craving chocolate? It's totally normal," explains the website for Markham & Fitz, a fine chocolatier that's taken up residence at the Brightwater School for Arkansas Food. Amongst the delicate truffles, confections and chocolate beverages offered at the dessert shop, you'll find a chocolate raspberry tart, consisting of a dark chocolate base and fresh raspberries in a pastry shell. Markham and Fitz is a true bean-to-bar chocolatier, sourcing from Haiti, Dominican Republic, Bolivia and Nicaragua.

801 SE 8th Street., Suite 45
Bentonville, Arkansas 72712
(479) 235-6236
MarkhamAndFitz.com

THE HIVE AT 21c MUSEUM HOTEL

Chef Matthew McClure is a five-time James Beard Award nominee, named to ump-teen uppity chef lists across the United States, lauded for innovations in the kitchen and some BMF (buttermilk fried) chicken and charged with uniting with other Bentonville chefs to mentor a new generation of culinarians... but his pecan pie is exactly what pecan pie should be. That's to say, humble, just like Matt.

Mind you, the slab of pie that comes to your table at The Hive at 21c arrives in a rectangular slab, carried in a hot but tiny cast iron casserole. It's still the same sort of Karo nut pie your grandparents probably had on the table at Thanksgiving.

McClure's dedication to preserving the melody of Ozark foods while joining in new notes of innovative tweaks to classic restaurants results in chords of augmented flavor in most every dish he creates. With the pie, those notes come in the buttermilk ice cream made in-house, a tangy note against the lightly salted pecan meat and the sweet but firm goo below. Still, the choir of flavor in each bite sings just as honestly as if it'd just come out of your mamma's oven.

200 NE A Street
Bentonville, Arkansas 72712
(479) 286-6575
TheHiveBentonville.com

ONYX COFFEE LAB

This pie is Doughp. That's not a poor attempt at spelling "dope," (though the two words are pronounced the same). It's the actual spelling of the bakery associated with Onyx Coffee Lab, the top suave coffee roaster and java-lover hotspot in downtown Bentonville. Onyx has other locations in Fayetteville, Springdale and Rogers, but this one is of particular visual interest – a cacophony of white hexagonal tile, reclaimed wood and white neon. The coffee bar at this location sits in the center of the room, rather than at its end, which brings the barista staff into the conversation.

Doughp provides the pastries – including the pies, in particular a rich, deep salty chocolate custard meant to pair exquisitely with Onyx coffee blends. Its resonant cocoa notes against a touch of sea salt pair well with a frothy, milk-endowed coffee beverage – while its color magnificently echoes the palette of the facility. Definitely an after- dinner pie.

100 NW Second Street #106
Bentonville, Arkansas 72712
(479) 715-6492
OnyxCoffeeLab.com

VENTRIS TRAIL'S END RESORT

Ventris Trail's End Resort near Garfield is best known for a private fireworks display, the likes of which are rarely seen outside major cities. Jody Simrell and his folks carefully plan out the Independence Day celebration each year, down to undergoing specialty training to handle the complicated pyrotechnic munitions required to properly illuminate the night sky over Beaver Lake and the hundreds of watchers who gather on pontoon boats, party barges, bass boats and kayaks at Marker 8.

The fireworks are a once-a-year extravaganza. The restaurant, which is open most of the year, serves pizza and burgers and dinner each night. Jan Simrell, Jody's mom, makes the pies – gorgeous fruit pies with hand- stripped lattice. The peach pie in season is made from fresh local peaches, still pink from the area around the pit, is textured and delightful.

9484 Simrell Drive
Garfield, Arkansas 72732
(479) 359-3912
BeaverLakeResorts.com

HIWASSEE HILTON/DAIRY FREEZE/DINER

No one really knows where the Hiwasse Hilton got its name, but it's certainly a popular spot for those who live in the far-northwest Arkansas community. The burger and ice cream joint is called everything from the Hiwasse Dairy Freeze to the Hiwasse Diner to the Hiwasse Café. It serves excellent home cooking and pie.

13548 Arkansas Highway 72
Hiwasse, Arkansas 72739
(479) 787-6809

JUDY'S CAFÉ

Judy Becker's most popular dish at Judy's Café in Sulphur Springs is the beans and cornbread. The restaurant, opened in November 2017, offers breakfast, lunch and dinner as well as a pie or two each night. Call ahead for flavors.

116 South Hibler Avenue
Sulphur Springs, Arkansas 72768
(479) 298-0068

THE GALLERY CAFÉ

The Gallery Café takes up a double storefront in downtown Decatur. Within, a varied collection of old tools from spears to saws adorn the walls. The restaurant is best known for its meringue pies – in particular, unusual flavors such as German chocolate meringue and peanut butter chocolate chip meringue. Its chocolate, butterscotch, banana, coconut, butterscotch, lemon, and peanut butter meringue pies are all quite popular. The Gallery Café offers pumpkin, buttermilk, raisin, cherry, apple and sugar-free apple pies as well.

167 North Main Street
Decatur, Arkansas 72722
(479) 752-3577

THE WOODEN SPOON

There's a barn on the side of the highway in Gentry. Every weekday at lunchtime and every Friday night, there are people on the porch, waiting to enter. And every day, before the first customer walks through the door, a lady in a cap, dress and apron writes the specials on the board. Those specials always include at least half a dozen different pies. Welcome to The Wooden Spoon.

Cam and Jane Klassen didn't plan to get into the restaurant business. The folks at the Spavinaw Stove Shop across the street from where the eatery is today, asked them if they'd come in and sell sandwiches at a counter inside. The counter was so popular that the Klassens decided to make it a family affair. They had a massive mortise-and-tenon horse barn constructed before 1870 in Michigan taken apart, brought to Gentry and reassembled, peg-by-peg. From the inside out they finished it with wooden floors, stout walls and a lot of love.

The Klassens and many of their employees are members of the Church of God in Christ, commonly referred to as the Mennonites. The waitresses, cooks and hostesses wear beautiful dresses and aprons and small caps. Every surface in the building, from the stone fireplaces to the exposed hand-hewn beams to the delicate green walls, is evocative of a country home. And for regulars who live in and near Gentry, it has become just that – a second home of sorts.

"We have people that come in so regularly that if they don't show up, that they've either told us the week before, or we check on them." Cam tells me. "In some cases, we actually call them to make sure that they're all right because if they don't show up, something's not good."

"Our customers become friends," Jane shares. "It's the best part of running a restaurant."

Jane says the pies at The Wooden Spoon have gained their good reputation because of the girls who make them. Since the restaurant opened, there have always been pies offered, and the family members and the employees who become like family to the Klassens bring their enthusiasm to the kitchen.

Coconut is the most popular flavor, but others have their own fans, such as the butterscotch praline and the caramel pecan cream cheese I adore. There's the Bumblebee: four different berries baked into a traditional double crust pie. There's also pumpkin coconut pecan, which tastes a bit like the holidays. Traditional flavors such as lemon meringue, chocolate rhubarb and French silk rotate through the lineup as well.

Pies are available every day The Wooden Spoon is open, but the day before Thanksgiving, close to 500 pies pass out of the kitchen into the waiting hands of customers who want to take those restorative, familiar sweet flavors at their own familial table.

1000 South Gentry Boulevard
Gentry, Arkansas 72734
(479) 736-3030
WoodenSpoonGentry.com

CROSSBOW RESTAURANT

Wilma Ledbetter will tell you, "pie will you keep you young." Back in the 1960s, Wilma and her sister Betty Lee bought the Crossbow Restaurant from a local resident and began running it as their own. They ran it together for 11 years before Betty Lee got out.

Today, Wilma's daughter Theresa Dubberly owns and runs the operation, but at the age of 84, Wilma still makes the pies every single day as they are needed: apple, cherry, coconut or chocolate, still made from the same 1960s recipe from the day the Ledbetters opened the shop. Go for the pie, stay to marvel at the cleanly preserved S shaped lunch counter, the Mid-Century Medieval touches and the collection of crossbows still on display from the restaurant's first owner.

537 North Parrott Drive
Huntsville, Arkansas 72740
(479) 738-2422

HUNTSVILLE PANTRY

Across the street and up the hill from the Crossbow Restaurant, there's a wooden facility filled with just about every dry food good you can imagine. This is Huntsville Pantry, a specialty shop and bakery that offers every sort of sundry you might find in the Ozarks. In addition to Amish products from Ohio, there are aisles of local honey, flour and cornmeal, jellies and jams and canned fruits and vegetables. The bakery commonly offers cookies, cakes and pies – and, if you're looking for a particular variety of pie, there are several take-and-bakes you can purchase to cook up at home, including one of the few black raspberry pies offered in the state. The Huntsville Pantry also offers a selection of sugar-free take and bake pies in apple, blueberry and cherry.

562 North Parrott Drive
Huntsville, Arkansas 72740
(479) 738-6414
Facebook.com/
HuntsvillePantry

GRANNY'S KITCHEN

Kathy Bolinger has been taking on good pie for decades in the Huntsville area. She's the "granny" behind Granny's Kitchen, a tin-topped eatery serving homestyle cooking. Bolinger's pies are of many styles and many flavors. Her caramel apple pie has won pie contests in the region, while other offerings such as her Reese's and Mississippi mud pies receive good notice as well. The cream pies are what get most of the attention, but any pie in the case is worthy. Get the fresh strawberry if it's in season.

215 North Parrott Drive
Huntsville, Arkansas 72740
(479) 738-2838

GLENN'S BAKERY

Many of the fried pies found across the northwest corner of the state come from a little bakery in Huntsville. The tiny bakery along Parrott Drive produces hundreds of pies in an assortment of flavors. Call ahead to pick up your favorites.

Glenn's Bakery
497a Parrott Drive
Huntsville, Arkansas 72740
(479) 325-8344
Facebook.com/GlennsFriedPies

HINDSVILLE CAFÉ

Years of bypasses and four-laning have taken US Highway 412 away from downtown Hindsville, which sits between Springdale and Huntsville just north of a long ridge. There's a building that dates to 1908 in its tiny downtown, and at the north end of that building you'll find the Hindsville Café.

The restaurant was opened in October 2017 by Faye Keller and Cathy Eddy. It's become known for its large breakfasts and for a one pound ribeye offered Friday and Saturday nights, seared over a woodflamed grill. The Hindsville Café does offer a variety of traditional pies, including pecan, cherry, lemon and Grandma DeDe's coconut meringue. Find yours in the case at the front when you enter and reserve a slice.

4304 South Main Street
Hindsville, Arkansas 72740
(479) 789-6033

LOW GAP CAFÉ

A solitary building hugging a hillside along a remote Arkansas highway, ten miles from civilization seems an odd place to find a graduate of the Culinary Institutes of America, but that's what you'll find when you visit the Low Gap Café. The address says Jasper, but this stone edifice sits closer to Ponca and its excellent elk watching near the headwaters of the Buffalo National River.

Nick Bottini went to California after finishing his degree at the CIA in New York. On visiting family in Arkansas, he decided this was where he wanted to be so he and his family relocated to the Ozarks. The restaurant itself seems to have suddenly found a great following in 2012, partly because of its extraordinarily fine menu and partly because of generous, flaky slices of pie.

The pies are the dominion of Nick's wife, Mary. Every one, from fruit pies to conservatively lofty meringues, comes plated as gorgeously as you'd find in a five-star restaurant, paired with a specialty high-dollar coffee blend. I highly recommend the decadent caramel apple pecan pie, with a balanced texture of fresh pecans against Ozark apples under a thick lattice top.

Highway 64 in Low Gap (HC 70 Box 287)
Jasper, Arkansas 72641
(870) 861-5848
LowGapCafe.com

BOARDWALK CAFÉ AT ARKANSAS HOUSE

It may seem hard to believe, but the first all-organic restaurant in Arkansas didn't open until 2005 – and not in a bustling city like Little Rock, but in a tiny burg in the Ozarks.

The Boardwalk Café is owned and operated in an old dairy bar, rewired for solar power, next door to the historic bed and breakfast, the Arkansas House. Everything on the menu is sourced organically – much of it from the Morgan's own farm, and from 35 area farmers who work with the Morgans to bring in all of the produce. While a few items, such as the shrimp from the Gulf, come from further afield, all of the dishes are prepared as naturally and health-consciously as possible.

The house pie is black walnut pie, baked from Ozark black walnuts and English walnuts from within Newton County. The pie has darker notes than what you might expect from your average nut pie, thanks to the sorghum molasses and cane syrup in its filling. Do get yours with a scoop of ice cream to cut the bite.

215 Court Street
Jasper, Arkansas 72641
(870) 446-5900
TheArkHouse.com

BLUE MOUNTAIN BAKERY

The local bakery is also doing its best to keep things natural. At Blue Mountain Bakery, two blocks away, Dawn Dulle and her crew are creating muffins, cakes, pecan rolls and even pies utilizing non-GMO, organic flour and local ingredients.

Frances and Scott Zemlik, formerly of Belle Chasse, Louisiana, purchased the bakery in 2015. Today, you can walk into the blue-and-stone patchworked interior and find a host of good scents to envelope your senses. Of note are fresh-cut local apple lattice pies in the fall and syrupy, tangy fresh strawberry pies when the berries are first ripe in late spring.

207 North Stone Street
Jasper, Arkansas 72641
(870) 446-2345
Facebook.com/BlueMountainBakeryAndCafe

OZARK CAFÉ

The Ozark Café in Jasper is the second oldest restaurant in the state. Originally started in 1909, it's been in continuous operation with the exception of a brief period of time during World War II. The restaurant is best known for its ridiculous burgers, including the towering Excaliburger (a large beef patty between two grilled cheese sandwiches) and the Cheese Volcano (a burger on the griddle topped with a mountain of Cheddar cheese, which melts through the burger and onto the griddle to create a disc of hot molten cheese). The restaurant serves all sorts of Arkansas favorites, from chocolate gravy to fried pickles. It also offers a fried apple pie, which you really should get a la mode.

107 East Court Street
Jasper, Arkansas 72641
(870) 446-2976
OzarkCafe.com

SHARON K'S CAFÉ

It's hard to go looking for pies and pass a place that proudly declares its own home-made pies on the sign out front. Sharon K's Café proudly announces those pies, and any lunchtime you can find coconut cream pie on the counter.

205 Arkansas Highway Seven
Jasper, Arkansas 72641
(870) 446-2789

CLIFF HOUSE INN

A few miles south of town is where you'll find the pie of the Arkansas Sesquicenten-nial. The Cliff House Inn is a restaurant , gift shop and bed and breakfast perched on the edge of what's called the Arkansas Grand Canyon – at a point on a ridge a thousand feet above the city of Jasper, six miles away.

The Cliff House Inn originally opened in 1967. Among its early owners were Bob and Francis McDaniel, who owned the place for nearly 18 years. Francis wanted a couple of things for the restaurant there: a signature biscuit and a signature pie.

"Francis tried different pies and hit on it," says Becky McLaurin, one of the current owners, "because people would call ahead and ask 'you know that pie you make? The one with the pineapple? We're heading that way and wanted to make sure you had it.' " Hence the name of the pie she stuck with, Company's Comin' Pie.

The pie is singular in Arkansas because of its crust. "(It's) sorta like a Divinity crust," McLaurin continues, "made with egg whites and sugar. It takes about an hour to make. You beat the egg whites and the sugar for about 25 minutes, and then you add crushed saltine crackers and a cup of pecan pieces, then you stir that in and it's a thick gooey mixture. You divide it into two pie tins. You form the crust with a spatula and bake it for 25 minutes. When you get ready to serve a pie, you take a pint of real whipping cream and put a little sugar in, and then you add a bit of crushed pineapple. Fill your pie crust with that. It's kind of an unusual pie but people love it."

Jim Berry, the next owner after the McDaniels, was very active in the tourism com-munity. In 1986, a new campaign to celebrate 150 years since Arkansas statehood, was born – "Company's Comin', Let's Get Ready." The suggestion was made to have the pie at the Cliff House Inn named the state pie of Arkansas. There's no record that the Legislature actually made it official, but it's the closest thing Arkansas has ever had as a state dessert. Here's how to make it yourself.

COMPANY'S COMIN' PIE
from the Cliff House Inn

Gray Weldon

6 egg whites
1 tsp cream of tartar
2 cups sugar
1 tsp vanilla
1 sleeve saltine crackers, crushed
1/2 cup chopped pecans

Topping:
1 small container whipped topping
3 Tbsp sugar
2 Tbsp crushed pineapple

Beat egg whites until fluffy. Add cream of tartar and sugar. Beat 25 minutes or until stiff. Stir in vanilla. Stir in crackers and pecans by hand. Spray two pie pans with nonstick spray. Divide mixture evenly between pans. Spread mixture in pan, forming a crust. Bake at 285 degrees for 25 minutes or until done. Combine topping ingredients. Pour into pie shell. Serve and enjoy. Refrigerate leftovers.

6 Arkansas Highway 7
Jasper, Arkansas 72641
(870) 446-2292
CliffHouseInnAR.com

OARK GENERAL STORE

The Oark General Store in Oark is not the oldest restaurant in Arkansas. The general store opened in 1890 but it wasn't a restaurant. The Eiseles, who run the place, acknowledge that their store has only served food a short portion of its 125+ year history. Its location, not far from the Mulberry River atop an Ozark National Forest plateau, has always been rather isolated. Even today, there's no cellphone signal. The store has changed hands multiple times over the years but, thanks to a grateful community, it has never shut down.

Its current owners, Brian and Reagan Eisele, bought it in 2012. The former congressional staffers, who met on a trip to their respective congressfolk, were taking in Azerbaijan in 2010 and came back to Arkansas to be married at Boxley Valley – and three weeks later, purchased the Oark General Store.

Neither Brian nor Reagan knew how to make pie when they started, but necessity (especially with booming motorcycle tourism that brings thousands through the community each year) has lead them both to learn how to cook for a restaurant and, in turn, recreating great dishes from the area their store now serves.

Go for the robust burgers and homemade onion rings and the only public WiFi in a 30 mile radius. Stay for the pie – Brian is likely to talk you into a slice. They include chocolate and coconut meringue, pecan, peanut butter, cherry, and oatmeal. The Eiseles have been good enough to share that oatmeal pie recipe in this book – a recipe straight out of the Great Depression.

OATMEAL PIE
from the Oark General Store

3 eggs
1 cup brown sugar
1 cup corn syrup (Pride of Dixie brand preferred)
1 1/2 cup old-fashioned rolled oats
2 teaspoons vanilla extract
2 tablespoons melted salted butter
1 pie crust
9" pie pan

Preheat oven to 350 degrees. Place uncooked pie crust into pie pan. Scatter the oats in the bottom, making sure to cover the bottom well (if you need a few extra oats, that's okay and will not affect outcome).

Add eggs, corn syrup, brown sugar, vanilla extract to bowl and mix until blended. Try not to overmix. Add butter slowly while stirring to avoid cooking the eggs. Slowly pour mixture on top of oats. Place pie in oven and bake for 45 minutes. After 45 minutes, check pie to see if it's set. You want the pie to be jiggly, not runny. If after 45 minutes, the pie is still too liquid, put back in oven for another 10-15 minutes.

Remove from oven and allow to cool 15 minutes or until the bottom of the pan is cool enough to touch.

10360 County Road 5440
Oark, Arkansas 72852
(479) 292-3351
OarkGeneralStore.com

CATALPA CAFÉ

Five miles beyond the Oark General Store, you'll find the Catalpa Café,. Four days a week it offers surprisingly upscale yet downhome meals and amazing pie.

Randy Atkins and his family bought the existing café (referenced in *Arkansas Pie: A Delicious Slice of the Natural State*) in 2013. Gone are the artifacts of the old Ozarks. Today the interior is a bright green and red, the grill is always going and the case is full of pie – if you get there early enough. Randy's mom makes the pies: chocolate mousse, peach oatmeal, cherry lattice and pecan. Chicken pot pies are also frequent visitors to the menu, as is prime rib, chili verde and a host of delectable pasta dishes.

255 County Road 5351
Oark, Arkansas 72854
(479) 292-3292
Facebook.com/CatalpaCafe

LOCAL FLAVOR CAFÉ

You might find yourself hard pressed to find the most successful restaurant in Eureka Springs, but when it comes to most beloved, I'm almost certain that'd fall to Local Flavor Café. Originally a coffeehouse opened in 1991 by Janice and Kirby Murray in a former art studio, it changed hands several times before Britt Evans, a longtime employee, came to own it. Britt's a sixth-generation native to the area. His family came to Eureka Springs way back in 1820. He learned how to cook in his grandparents' kitchen starting at the age of five and his mother, Brenda, once owned the popular Brenda and Lanta's on Center Street. His first stint at Local Flavor came in its second year, 1992 – but after a short time he moved away. A need to raise money to attend the New England Culinary Institute in Vermont drove him back to town in 1998, where he waited tables at Local Flavor and another restaurant, Ermilio's, and picked up some construction odd jobs.

However, Britt ended up purchasing Local Flavor for his own a few months later when the most recent owners offered it to him for a fair price. In the beginning, he would run breakfast and lunch at Local Flavor and then wait tables at Ermilio's. His mom ended up coming on board and worked side-by-side with her son until 2012. He's expanded both the kitchen and the floorspace of the restaurant several times over, even building out a patio that overhangs Main Street.

Local Flavor does have a semi-pie in its Chocolate Decadence, a rich make-its-own-crust chocolate custard. But its star pie is a simple pecan pie on a shortbread crust, a perfect and satisfying end to any dinner.

71 South Main Street
Eureka Springs, Arkansas 72632
(479) 253-9522
LocalFlavorCafe.net

MUD STREET CAFÉ

Main Street in Eureka Springs is built over a long spring that runs the length of the valley. Before the asphalt and concrete of the current street, the avenue would flood from time to time. Locals called it Mud Street, and it stuck.

Below street level today lies one of Eureka Springs' most iconic restaurants, accessible by a long staircase that brings you into a grotto underneath a building. This original Mud Street Café, with its windowless, theater-ended subterranean cavern, is housed in the lowest level of a building constructed in 1888. It's a gorgeous place to enjoy a lingering breakfast or brunch.

Recently, Bobbi Fisher has opened a street-level addition to the restaurant, a smaller space perfect for the winter months when tourists haven't arrived and the locals have the town to themselves. The Mud Street Annex sits in a storefront on Main Street, a long hall filled with tables and a long bar. Diners chat under the original restored Ozarka water sign, and visitors can peer down at a specially-made glass floor, below which one can see the water running in the spring that gave the restaurant its name.

There's always some sort of pie in the case, sometimes blueberry cream, sometimes peanut butter cream, sometimes chocolate truffle. The light pies are great paired with the coffeehouse's famed blends, roasted by local company Fresh Beanz.

Mud Street Café
22 South Main Street Suite G
Eureka Springs, Arkansas 72632
(479) 253-6732
MudStreetCafe.com

Mud Street Café Annex
28 South Main Street
Eureka Springs, Arkansas 72632
(479) 253-5399

BALCONY RESTAURANT

The 1905 Basin Park Hotel has two unique claims to fame in Arkansas. The first is a recognition by the Ripley Foundation (best known for "Ripley's Believe It Or Not!") for the unusual structure and placement of the hotel. Each of the hotel's floors has its own ground level entrance, thanks to its spot on the side of a mountain.

The second is on the menu at The Balcony Restaurant one floor above the hotel's lobby. Alongside the Arkansas mud pie and the Southern Derby pie, you'll find a fried huckleberry pie made on-site with locally grown huckleberries, partnered with a scoop of custom made huckleberry ice cream. The delectable pairing brings the nostalgia of rural Arkansas back to the table.

12 Spring Street Suite 112
at the Basin Park Hotel
Eureka Springs, Arkansas 72632
(479) 253-7837
BasinPark.com

With a population of around 2000, Eureka Springs may have the greatest concentration of restaurants to residents of any city I've ever visited. With more than 100 different restaurants and another 20 bars, there's an establishment for eating or drinking for every 17 people. There are also over 200 lodging options in town, ranging from one and two unit bed and breakfasts to hundred room hotels to the 72 rooms at the historic 1886 Crescent Hotel, considered the most haunted hotel in America.

THE BAKER'S TABLE

Up the hill from Local Flavor Café, Balcony Restaurant and Mud Street Café, sits one of the newer eateries in town. The Baker's Table is owned by Karin Emde, a pastry chef who spent time working in Canadian restaurants and oil field camps and in military camps in Afghanistan. After a brief stint out of the business, working as a power engineer Emde returned home to Eureka Springs and bought the spot next to Nibbles Eatery. She opened The Baker's Table in 2017. You may sometimes see her mom, Judy Holden, in the shop.

The pie star of this showcase is Emde's tiny lemon curd tarts, a particular specialty evocative of a perfect English-style teatime treat.

77 Spring Street
Eureka Springs, Arkansas 72632
(479) 981-6490
The-Bakers-Table.business.site

SWEET AND SAVORY CAFÉ

Ann Naumann and Trey Merritt opened the Sweet and Savory Café on the east side of town in 2014. The blue building houses two bright dining rooms and a counter full of pastries that changes from day to day. Alongside the orange rolls, sweet breads and dark chocolate covered macaroons that share the surface, there's almost always a pie – chocolate meringue, coconut cream, even an old-fashioned Crack Pie.

2076 East Van Buren
Eureka Springs, Arkansas 72632
(479) 253-7151
TheSweetAndSavoryCafe.com

MYRTIE MAE'S RESTAURANT

One of the most famous possum pies in the state is offered every day at Myrtie Mae's Restaurant inside the Best Western Inn of the Ozarks. The restaurant claims a heritage that goes back to the old Sam Leath motor camps created in the 1910s, through the legend of Myrtie Mae Barrett, a woman who was reported to have nailed a sign to a tree offering chicken dinners to tourists. She was said to have been able to welcome travelers into her living room, go out back and kill a chicken, butcher it, fry it up and serve it with all the sides in less than an hour – on roughly the same spot where the restaurant is located today.

The possum pie here is a favorite, topped with dairy whipped cream and pecans and a drizzle of chocolate and served with a diner-worthy cup of coffee.

207 West Van Buren
Eureka Springs, Arkansas 72632
(479) 253-9768
MyrtieMaes.com

The possum pie may have been created at Cagle's Mill in Russellville (see page 252) or at Myrtie Mae's – or it may have simply been adapted from some home cook's card file. Here's the recipe for the version originally sold at Myrtie Mae's.

MYRTIE MAE'S HOME STYLE DINING POSSUM PIE
from Myrtie Mae's Restaurant

6 ounces cream cheese, softened
3/4 cup confectioners' sugar
1 (9-inch) graham cracker crust
1/4 cup chopped pecans
1/3 cup instant chocolate pudding mix
1/4 cup instant vanilla pudding mix
2 cups cold milk
3/4 teaspoon vanilla extract
1/2 cup whipping cream, whipped
12 to 16 pecan halves

In a mixing bowl, beat cream cheese and sugar until smooth. Spread onto bottom of crust. Sprinkle with chopped pecans.

In another mixing bowl, combine pudding mixes. Add milk and vanilla extract; beat on low speed for two minutes. Spoon over the pecans. Refrigerate at least two hours. Top with whipped cream and pecan halves.

Yields 8 servings.

ROCKIN' PIG SALOON

The Rockin' Pig Saloon may sound like a dirty biker bar, but the bar on the bypass is spotlessly clean, smells like roasting meat and has one of the best jukeboxes in town. Every day, the Rockin' Pig offers smoked meats, gourmet pizzas, a wide selection of craft beer and a single choice of fried pie. The handpie is always served piping hot with vanilla bean ice cream, and it's always a good bet.

Rockin' Pig Saloon
2039 East Van Buren
Eureka Springs, Arkansas 72632
(479) 363-6248
RockinPigSaloon.com

OSCAR'S CAFÉ

The best front porch for pie in Eureka Springs has to be at Oscar's Café, where the pies come in combinations of fresh fruits and custards or gorgeous little hand tarts. Salvatore Wilson and Hana Maufe both met while working as chefs on yachts in Spain. In 2013, they opened Oscar's Café along the Historic US 62 loop that circles around the heart of the town. The bright cottage is full of Hana's beautiful wall hangings, while the menu is an eclectic blend of everything, from mangoes lassi to English and French influenced breads to a delectable variety of soups and sandwiches.

17 White Street
Eureka Springs, Arkansas 72632
(479) 981-1436
EurekaSprings.org/Oscars-Cafe

The Victorian Sampler was a gorgeous tearoom housed in the old Ellis mansion near the 1886 Crescent Hotel in Eureka Springs. Though gone, its recipes live on in its eponymous cookbook, including that of its famed coconut cream layer pie.

COCONUT CREAM LAYER PIE

2 baked pie shells
4 ounces cream cheese, softened
1 package non-dairy topping
½ cup milk
1 teaspoon vanilla
1 cup shredded coconut
2-3 ounce packages instant vanilla pie mix
1 teaspoon vanilla
1 cup toasted coconut
Whipped cream

Combine cream cheese, sugar, topping mix, milk and vanilla. Beat until light and fluffy. Pour into pie shells. Spread ½ cup coconut on each pie and chill several hours or overnight.

Prepare instant pie filling according to package instructions, adding one teaspoon vanilla, and pour over cream cheese layer. Chill until set. Garnish with whipped cream and toasted coconut. Makes two pies.

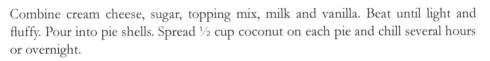

CRAVINGS BY ROCHELLE

The only grocery store in Eureka Springs is Hart's, where you're likely to run into anyone from around town. Hart's doesn't' have its own bakery. Instead, when you want fresh baked breads, cookies, cakes or pies, you can order what you need at the window looking right into Craving's By Rochelle. The bakery (which also has a parking lot entrance and a handful of tables) offers a number of gorgeously decorated baked goods. Pies are usually in the cooler and vary depending on the day, but usually come in such flavors as lemon, chocolate and pumpkin.

137 East Van Buren
Eureka Springs, Arkansas 72632
(479) 363-6576

Grav Weldon

TOP ROCK DRIVE IN

The Top Rock Drive In in Alpena is the home of the Leopard Burger (the Leopard is the local football team mascot). This community hotspot offers a large variety of homemade fried pies in a variety of flavors – chocolate, cherry, and apple plus chocolate peanut butter, lemon, and banana cream. Sugar free apple and sugar free apricot are also available. A second location at Ridgeway recently opened inside the Cattleman's Sale Barn in Ridgeway in the former G's Feed and Seed.

314 US Highway 62
Alpena, Arkansas 72611
(870) 437-5238
Facebook.com/TopRockDriveIn

1417 Ridgeway Loop
Harrison, Arkansas 72601
(870) 416-0056
Facebook.com/TopRockOfRidgeway

COUNTRY ROOSTER

Throughout this book, you'll see pies offered in restaurants and bakeries, from food trucks and truck stops and out of catering kitchens, too. In Green Forest, the best pie in town comes from The Country Rooster – a lunchroom housed within the heart of an antique store and flea market. The eclectic diner-meets-dining-room luncheonette offers different desserts every day, depending on what the cooks want to make. There are usually a couple of choices, including layer cakes, cookies, and a variety of pies. Blueberry and apple are good, as are the coconut and chocolate meringue pies that show up about once a week each.

101 Tommy Ratzlaff Avenue
Green Forest, Arkansas 72638
(870) 438-5710
CountryRooster.Net

CHARLIE'S CAFÉ

Over the years, expansion and construction has changed the route of US Highway 65, which has shortened the commute from folks who travel between Harrison, Arkansas and Branson, Missouri. The changes, cut-throughs and bypasses have meant many of the businesses that once thrived along the highway have disappeared.

Not in Omaha, where Charlie's Café is still going strong. This eatery, beloved to the community, still offers great home cooking throughout the week. Once a week, "doughnut day" is a special treat. But for any customer, any time, there's bound to be a pie made from fresh local peaches, cherry pies, or one of Charlie's Café's specialties – a coconut cream pie with a huge pile of whipped cream and coconut on top. Make sure you bring cash, though – Charlie's does not accept credit or debit.

23783 Old Highway 65
Omaha, Arkansas 72662
(870) 426-4663

DeVITO'S RESTAURANT

This long-running classic eatery sits across what once was US 65 (now DeVito's Loop) from the trout farm gifted from Albert Raney to his son-in-law Jim and daughter Mary Alice DeVito when they returned to the area from DeVito's stint in the armed services in 1970. Jim and Mary Alice fiddled with the idea of opening an Italian restaurant – which they did, in November 1986, with the help of their four sons – James, Steve, Chris and Joe. James would go on to open DeVito's of Eureka Springs two years later.

Despite a fire that destroyed the original DeVito's in 2000, the family rebuilt and continued on, still serving Italian food and catch-your-own trout specialties today. Son Chris is the baker of the family, and his flaky layered apple pie with its two-or-three apple filling (depending on what's in season locally) is always a good bet, as is the chocolate pecan pie.

350 DeVito's Loop North
Harrison, Arkansas 72601
(870) 741-8832
DeVitosRestaurant.com

RANCH HOUSE RESTAURANT

To find pie in Harrison, look for the rampant stallion that sits outside Ranch House Restaurant on the main drag. Crissie Lineberger practically grew up at the restaurant (her best friend's family owned it), and after she married her husband Bobby, they bought it in 2007.

Don't let the old-fashioned country diner décor fool you. Bobby (originally from Polk City, Florida) attended the Disney Culinary Academy and spent years in the restaurant business before settling in Harrison. He cooks, while she manages the restaurant.

The coconut cream and chocolate cream pies are the stars of the menu, soft and sweet, a perfect wrap-up to a meal. Pumpkin and pecan are also sometimes available.

805 US Highway 62
Harrison, Arkansas 72601
(870) 741-3026
RanchHouseHarrison.com

NEIGHBORHOOD DINER

From the highway, Neighborhood Diner looks like one part Streamliner, two parts carhop drive-in. The bright red and yellow building originally opened in 1952 backs up to a hill. Inside, you'll get an excellent roadside diner breakfast or burger. The edifice hasn't changed much since it opened in 1952. Classic car aficionados like to drop in for the nostalgia, and many stay for a slice of chocolate or lemon meringue pie.

1112 North Main Street
Harrison, Arkansas 72601
(870) 743-9493

NEIGHBOR'S MILL

Yes, there is a large, stone mill-type building sitting alongside US Highway 65 on the north side of Harrison. But it's only been there a couple of decades. It was built in homage to the Graue Mill in Oakbrook, Illinois.

Mike and Karin Nabors have been dreaming of a bakery for a very, very long time. Mike bought a 100-year-old gristmill way back in 1974, and it's still in use today at Neighbor's Mill Bakery and Café. The couple started compiling plans to build the facility it's in back in the mid-nineties, with a desire to produce made-from scratch breads and pastries. In 1999, ground was broken on a lot littered with sugar maples and, in August 2000, it opened.

The breads are the star at the restaurant, served alongside soups, on both ends of sandwiches and even on their own at an extra counter on the far end of the shop.

Pies, however, weren't a big draw for the eatery. The first substantial showing of pie at the bakery came in 2010 when Lori Rae began making her handmade rounds for Neighbor's Mill (Lori now owns Fork and Crust, which you can read about on page 36).

You can still pick up one of several different pies at Neighbor's Mill, by the slice or whole, six days a week, in flavors ranging from Dutch apple to Oreo, chocolate peanut butter, coconut and chocolate meringue.

1012 Highway 65 North
Harrison, Arkansas 72601
(870) 741-6455
NeighborsMill.com

LISA'S LEAD HILL CAFÉ

The building where Lisa's Lead Hill Café lives today may have once been part of a motorcourt hotel. The unusual angles of the exterior, how it bends along the curve of the road with just enough space for a single row of cars, plus the old vestibule in the front, just have that call of an old-time traveler's café.

Lisa's interior is packed with golden-studded pleather chairs, formica-wood tables and photographs of classic cars. It's rare not to find slices of pie on the counter – peach is popular, as is apple. There's also always some form of sugar-free pie available – lemon icebox and banana cream are favorites – for those trying to watch their calories.

155 Arkansas Highway 14
Lead Hill, Arkansas 72644
(870) 436-2866

A HOUSE FURTHER

Diamond City is located at the very north end of Arkansas's longest state highway, Scenic Arkansas Highway Seven. The highway itself ends at a marina on Bull Shoals Lake, the major tourism draw for the area.

For those who are hungry for pie, A House Further obliges any appetite. Tony Marks opened the restaurant in March 2017. The name comes from something his parents used to tell him – if he didn't like what was put on the table, he was cordially invited to go "a house further" down the road to try his luck for something better. The whole family is involved in the upstart operation, which does breakfast, sandwiches, salads and such. There are usually a couple of pies offered – pecan, chocolate cream and coconut being amongst the most popular.

1010 Diamond Boulevard
(Scenic Arkansas Highway Seven)
Diamond City, Arkansas 72630
(870) 422-4833

Arkansas has 75 counties. Some are mountainous and some are flat. Some are metropolitan and some are rural. And some are magical.

Searcy County's claim to dessert fame is the chocolate roll, created in Marshall or Leslie or both in the early part of the 20th century. I have my own ties to its creators in the form of my brother's blood family – and I spent more than my share of time over the years in the area.

The span of area between the south side of Leslie and the north end of Pindall, betwixt Cozahome and Ben Hur, is roughly mountainous – in as far as mountains go in Arkansas. This may not be the sort of mountains you expect in the Rockies, but for us here in The Natural State they are a magical land of hollows, show caves, good hiking and camping, getting back to nature and getting to our routes.

The western part of the county is part of the Ozark National Forest, while the Buffalo National River crosses on its north end. Rustic beauty aside, there are outstanding reasons as a traveler to visit the expanse, be the reasons related to nostalgia or to a budding new agritourism industry. There's no other place in Arkansas where you can (with an appointment) visit buffalo roaming free on a 400-acre farm like the 180+ year old Ratchford Farms, no other place in the state to overnight or spend a weekend on a working farm where you can lend a hand milking a cow or working the land like at Dogwood Hills Bed and Breakfast, no other place to enjoy a 50+ year old year-round drive-in like the Kenda Drive In. Searcy County is magical. And of course it has its share of great pies.

DRY CREEK MERCANTILE

Lou and Rose Marie Brandt moved to the Ozarks to raise their kids and enjoy life. He spent time teaching school, and she worked at a Western Sizzlin'. When it came time to retire, the couple decided to create something great – that, for a few months each year, includes pies.

The Brandts bought an old service station along US Highway 65 in Pindall, Arkansas

in 2010 and set about renovating it into a good old-fashioned country store. It has taken several years, a goodly amount of lumber and labor, but the Brandts today have a unique location full of antiques, camping gear, convenience store items and a deli – at the edge of an old homestead. Dry Creek Mercantile, the store the Brandts run, serves only one kind of pie and only for a few months out of the year. The Brandts are committed to making that homemade strawberry pie only when the strawberries are ripe, plentiful and affordable, which means the pie appears in late April or March each year and is gone by the end of summer. But boy is it a doozy, a sweet and tart assertion that summer has reclaimed the area for another season.

21595 US Highway 65
Pindall, Arkansas 72669
(870) 439-8190
DryCreekHomestead.com

BIG SPRINGS TRADING COMPANY

St. Joe sits on one hill overlooking where US Highway 65 crosses the Buffalo National River. Silver Hill sits on the other. For those planning to put in at Gilbert or Tyler Bend or any of the spots along the unspoiled natural beauty of this stream, there's just one get-it-all place for provisions and pie.

Big Springs Trading Company is housed in a colorful shop north of the river. Often-painted metal pigs greet you when you head up the wooden steps, while a lingering whisper of smoked meats greets you the moment you open the door.

The girls at Big Springs are known for more than smoked meats. There's an extraordinary level of service offered to patrons here – especially those who aim to grab and be gone. Smoked ham, turkey and handmade sausages straight out of the smoke

cabinet are sliced and wrapped alongside smoked cheddar, Colby jack, Swiss or provolone cheeses in care packages for the trip. Sometimes that comes with bread. Sometimes it comes with pie. It all comes by request – a message via Facebook to let them know you're on the way, or a quick phone call. Having that sort of service gives travelers a chunk of time they didn't have to spend packing the picnic basket.

I was happily surprised on a recent visit to find not one but two pies available to enjoy. The first, a molasses pecan pie, spoke to my rural roots – a pecan pie not filled with the nougat-like decoupage of Karo nut syrup but simple, straightforward sorghum molasses and pecans picked and delivered by a local woman named Sue Gray.

The other, though, is the perfect picnic pie, a rustic apple pie that falls somewhere between the fried pies seen across the state and a traditional apple pie. This flat hulk was simply hand-rolled dough with a little butter and sugar wrapped around locally harvested apples with just a touch of cinnamon. It's the perfect take-along-and-share pie for a float on the Buffalo or a hike through the Ozarks – or, as far as I'm concerned, for break-and-eat car dining on a scenic drive.

14237 North US Highway 65
St. Joe, Arkansas 72675
(870) 439-2900
BigSpringsRestaurant.com

DAISY QUEEN

No one's really sure how long the restaurant has sat along US Highway 65 in the heart of Marshall, but the Mays have owned the dairy bar there from 1966 until 2003, when their son Jeff and his wife Robin bought the well-loved Daisy Queen. Robin manages the iconic eatery today; the couple's two daughters work there seasonally. Robin says in all those years, the Daisy Queen has gone from being a local favorite to a must-stop for travelers.

"It's still brings people in from the area," she tells me. "But in the past several years we have become known as a tourist stop for people going to Branson, going to the river... in the fall, retired folks swing in."

The restaurant has more than 70 items on the menu, including Angus beef burgers, salads, chicken, the house coleslaw (150 pounds a week!), and an array of soft serve ice cream shakes, sundaes and banana splits. Of course, there's pie – in this case, handmade fried pies filled with apples, a good pairing for soft-serve a la mode.

614 US Highway 65
Marshall, Arkansas 72650
(870) 448-2180

MARSHALL RESTAURANT

One of the few raisin pies available in Arkansas comes from the Marshall Restaurant, in front of the Marshall Motel. This double-crust raisin pie is dark and dense, a traditional funeral pie. Other pies are often available as well.

251 US Highway 65 North
Marshall, Arkansas
72650
(870) 448-3357

CARL'S RESTAURANT

On the east side of town at the foot of the ridge that divides Marshall from southern Searcy County, a family restaurant sits. This is Carl's Restaurant, where pulled pork is hickory smoked for up to 16 hours in an old woodfired pit and every Friday there's catfish on the buffet. Carl's is just now getting a little recognition from outsiders that folks in town have known about for years – the unusual pies. Any particular evening, you can find such creations as Almond Joy, peanut butter Butterfinger, salted cara-

mel, and even spumoni pie in the case by the register. The ever-changing array goes quick, so consider ordering your pie when you get started on the buffet at dinner.

100 Arkansas Highway 27
(at US Highway 65)
Marshall, Arkansas 72650
(870) 448-2122

MISTY'S SHELL

On the other side of the ridge, the hills start to roll a bit, with tops rounded from a century of farming. The next community on the route is Leslie – which, for its population of just 421, manages to hold onto three places to get good pie.

The one by the road happens to be Misty's Shell Station, a convenience store and restaurant best known for being the easiest way to procure a chocolate roll to take

home with you. Misty's also makes its own fried pies in a variety of flavors, including the rather unusual offering of pineapple as a filling. Pies are right by both registers and in a case close to the hot food, so you really can't miss them.

6542 US Highway 65
Leslie, Arkansas 72645
(870) 447-2544

LESLIE CAFÉ

Leslie isn't a big town. Its tiny downtown has seen a renaissance in recent years, with new paint and new tenants transforming the small burg into an artists' community.

The one thing that hasn't changed is the Leslie Café. Originally opened in 1948, the restaurant serves lunch four days a week and dinner on Friday and Saturday night. Colly and John Magruder bought the restaurant in 1999 and take turns working the eatery and their 150-acre cattle farm nearby. While they don't have children of their own, they've adopted a family of employees that are always eager to chat about what's going on around the county.

Pies, especially cream and meringue pies, are available whenever the restaurant is open. Social media folks got into a stir the night I came through to shoot the evening's available pie at the Leslie Café – a dark chocolate cream pie that was almost pitch black under its toasted, chocolate chip-dotted top. The pie is made with Hershey's Special Dark cocoa for a splendidly rich pie.

408 Main Street
Leslie, Arkansas 72645
(870) 841-0326

SKYLARK CAFÉ

Country chic and local foods cross paths at the adorable Skylark Café, just outside of downtown on Walnut Street (Arkansas Highway 66). The almost-teal cottage is as adorable as its owners, Denver and Joy Ellis. Joy bought the house when she was still a teenager, spent seven months renovating it, then opened it for service in 2009. She'd already met Denver, but it would be another five years before she'd join him in Austin, where he was attending the Cordon Bleu Cooking School, in 2014. However, fates converged to bring Joy back to Leslie, and she brought Denver with her.

The menu is dotted with herbs from the acre garden by the café and with local fruit and produce. While pies such as the chocolate walnut are offered year-round, it's the seasonal cream cheese pies, such as strawberry in June and peach in July, that truly draw attention. Each slice is served on a darling mismatched plate.

401 High Street
Leslie, Arkansas 72645
(870) 447-2354

DOGWOOD HILLS GUEST FARM

Searcy County's wonders are best experienced over a sojourn. At Dogwood Hills Guest Farm in the community of Cozahome, the Peplers welcome those who want to experience life in the hills surrounding the Buffalo National River. The first overnight agritourism stay location in Arkansas offers its guests the chance to interact at their own level on a real, working farm – which means, if you'd like, you can milk cows or work in the high tunnel on winter crops, care for goats and sheep and see how an Ozark farm works from the inside out.

Ruthie, Thomas and Gracie also offer specialty dinners once a month where diners can enjoy delectable meals made from organic and ethically-raised ingredients sourced from nearby. One of the many desserts that might be on the menu is pie – such as this locally-sourced apple pie made with fruit from Sue Gray's orchard. This is also a great location to enjoy a vacation for those who are gluten-free; Ruthie and Gracie both are experienced in cooking for the special diet.

544 Cozahome Road
Harriet, Arkansas 72639
(870) 448-4870
TheFarmEx.com

JUNE'S CAFÉ

June and Sid Latture opened June's Café along US Highway 65 all the way back in the 1940s. The long spot along the highway provided sandwiches, June's home cooking and Sid's popular fried chicken to the locals for generations. June ran the shop through the 1970s. The Arkansas Department of Transportation re-routed Highway 65, bypassing the downtown area, and business slowed. But June's has managed to hang on through a series of different owners over the years.

Today, Teena and David Ferrier run the restaurant, keeping the historical aesthetic while offering a locally pleasing menu. Try the coconut cream pie.

614 US Highway 65B
Clinton, Arkansas 72031
(501) 745-4321

L'ATTITUDE BISTRO

Street tacos and North Atlantic seafood isn't the sort of thing you'd expect to see on a small-town menu, but both happen to be featured regularly at L'Attitude Bistro, Tammy Gunn's restaurant just off US Highway 65 in Clinton. The veteran area caterer's restaurant opened in 2014 with a well-received Black Angus New York Strip steak. Today, it offers upscale eats and re-envisioned ideas of downhome treats, such as the often-available coconut, pecan and strawberry pies on its dessert menu.

1303 US Highway 65 South
Clinton, Arkansas 72031
(501) 745-4888
LAttitudeBistro.com

SNAPPY FOOD MART

Fried pies of all sorts can be obtained at the Snappy Food Mart in Bee Branch, where on-the-go hungry folks can also grab Jo Jo potatoes and chicken fingers on the run.

11111 US Highway 65 South
Bee Branch, Arkansas 72013
(501) 654-2285

WAGON WHEEL RESTAURANT

Larry Nelson bought the Wagon Wheel Restaurant in Greenbrier in 1991 after the place he had worked at for years before, Kirkwood Industries, up and relocated. He and his wife Bonnie have been serving some of the most lauded home cooking in central Arkansas ever since. I can vouch for that, since I've been visiting several times a year for more than a decade.

The restaurant on the east side of US Highway south of Greenbrier's core is always packed at breakfast and lunch, does catfish on Fridays and showcases one of the best chicken fried steaks I've ever had. The mushroom omelet has more cheese than egg (which, hey, I love cheese), the selection of burgers is amusing and tasty, and the fried mushrooms are out of this world.

And then there is pie. The chocolate meringue, I can quite honestly say, is solid and dependable. But it's just one of many pies in the case. I've grown attached to the

banana split pie, partially because it's the first of its sort I'd ever come across and partly because it tastes EXACTLY like a banana split. The pie's banana-vanilla custard is evocative of the ice cream and the long banana from the dish it represents. There's a layer of crushed pineapple, a fine line of chocolate syrup and a floofy top of whipped cream with maraschino cherries. So good.

166 South Broadview Street
Greenbrier, Arkansas 72058
(501) 679-5009

WOODGROVE ANTIQUE MALL AND TEA ROOM

One of the most complex, extraordinary heritage pies I have encountered in my search for Arkansas's best pies came at the back of an antique mall that doubles as a rock shop. That's where I encountered the Stromans and the Tea Room pie.

The Stromans reopened the tea room at the back of the Woodgrove Antique Mall in July 2015. Nick runs the store up front, Sheila manages the tearoom, and their son Matthew creates delectable entrées, sandwiches and desserts that pull people in.

The space is beautifully crowded in the most amazing of ways – with mismatched antique tables and chairs. Each setting is based around a particular type of rock, from rose quartz to smoky quartz, lapis lazuli to malachite, obsidian to amethyst. There are rocks on the table, trees made with each particular stone and color coordinated accessories. Each diner chooses a tea cup from a cupboard on the wall opposite the kitchen, and the tea of their choosing is prepared in one of dozens of classic tea pots by Faith Lawrence, who dresses appropriately and creatively for the marvelous space.

I was welcomed by all four of these generous and sweet people on that afternoon, introduced all around and given an opportunity to try some pie.

"I was told there was a tea room here years before," Sheila shared with me, "and that tea room had a particular pie. When we reopened, people came asking for the original Tea Room pie. We started digging through the hundreds of cookbooks the previous owners had left behind, and finally located it in an ancient cookbook."

The pie is worth every bit of effort – and that's saying something, since this isn't a quick pie. The crust of crisped rice, flaked coconut and melted chocolate chips, is set first. Then the filling of whipped cream and cream cheese with bits of toasted coconut, toasted pecan and caramel are brought together. The whole affair is topped with more coconut, then drizzled with more caramel and chocolate. This Tea Room pie is lovely, delectable, and quietly complicated, just like you would expect from the sort of person who you would meet in such a place.

Chef Matthew also creates other pies like buttermilk and lemon icebox, and his chicken salad is considered the best in the area. The menu changes daily but the focus is always on light, delectable tea room foods meant to comfort and calm. Take a couple of hours to enjoy a spot of tea and a slice of pie.

314 West Main Street
Heber Springs, Arkansas 72543
(501) 269-2284

CHUCK'S DINER AND STEAKHOUSE

Right alongside the Little Red River off Wilburn Road, there's a red roofed eatery where steak can be found. Chuck's Diner and Steakhouse serves lunch during the week, fine steaks and seafood on weekend evenings, and pie all the time.

Chuck Hocking opened the restaurant in 2011. The black lightboard next to the door always has a listing of pies to enjoy – which regularly include pies such as peanut butter, chocolate icebox, lemon icebox and the house favorite, buttermilk coconut.

35 Swinging Bridge Drive
Heber Springs, Arkansas 72543
(501) 362-2100

CAFÉ KLASER

It started in a little green house in downtown Heber Springs in 1998. Today, Chef Billy Klaser and his son, Chef LB Klaser, operate Café Klaser in a location overlooking the Little Red River. The family operation includes Billy's daughter Ellie, who's both a hostess and an artist in residence. The elder Klaser apprenticed at the Breakers Resort in Palm Beach, Florida before moving up to sous chef and then taking on executive chef duties at Country Club of Little Rock, Lake Village Country Club and Walnut Lake Country Club before opening the family named café. Today the restaurant is known for excellent stuffed steak and stuffed shrimp, pastas and sauces and osso bucco, as well as fried catfish and pizza sub sandwiches. The eclectic menu always includes pie – especially fluffy meringues.

1414 Wilburn Road
Heber Springs, Arkansas 72543
(501) 206-0688

MACK'S FISH HOUSE

Mack's Fish House on the east side of Heber Springs, a short distance from the Greers Ferry dam, is one of the largest family restaurants in the area. There's a tall case in the dining room packed with pies. It's the only place in the state where I have encountered a Boston cream, cream pie – a pie with the flavors of a Boston cream pie's vanilla custard, chocolate ganache and cake, all suspended within a creamy custard in a traditional pie pan. Chocolate mousse pie and a marvelous apple pie are also available, as are a dozen more.

559 Wilburn Road
Heber Springs, Arkansas 72543
(501) 362-6225
MacksFishHouse.net

PEGGY SUE'S PLACE

Peggy Sue's Place opened in 2015 just a couple blocks off Main Street. Coconut and chocolate meringue and peanut butter pies are usually available by the slice, as are a number of fried pies, some of which are sugar-free.

1901 West Quitman Street
Heber Springs, Arkansas 72543
(501) 270-4007

HANNAH'S LITTLE BAKERY SHOP

A few miles north of the dam on Greers Ferry Lake, Hannah's Little Bakery Shop sits at the end of a building that also hosts a convenience store. The tiny counterspace has no tables at which to dine, but it does have cases of fresh-made cookies and cinnamon rolls, a rack of fresh bread and a cooler packed with pumpkin rolls and creamy things. Of note are gorgeous baked handpies in apple, peach and coconut, flaky and delectable.

6729 Heber Springs Road North
Drasco, Arkansas 72530
(870) 668-9190

THE RED APPLE INN

A saltine cracker pie once brought me to a table at Local Lime in Little Rock for a conversation with Scott McGehee, a conversation about his grandmother, Ruby Thomas. Ruby was the chef at the famed Red Apple Inn in Heber Springs, which I need to tell you about. But before I tell you about that, I have to tell you why the Red Apple Inn is there. It's a dam's fault, which means I also need to tell you a bit about Carl Garner.

Let's start with Carl. I was blessed with the opportunity to enjoy Carl's conversations several times before he passed at the age of 99 in 2014. Carl lived in north central Arkansas just about all of his life. He was born in Sulphur Rock, went to college at Arkansas College (now Lyon College) in Batesville, worked his way through the surveying program and started teaching the course while he was still there, then signed on with the Army Corps of Engineers. By 1945 he was the chief of the engineering division for the Little Rock District, and he was in charge of the building of Greers Ferry Dam. He would go on to also lead the efforts to keep the lake clean, earning national recognition from the Keep America Beautiful campaign in 1970. Folks call him the "Father of Greers Ferry Lake," and the dam's visitor center is named for him.

If it wasn't for the dam, the Red Apple Inn might not have existed. That's where Herbert Thomas comes in. Herbert incorporated First Pyramid Life and helped form the First Arkansas Development Finance Corporation. He used a piece of legislation and a loophole to secure one of the best stretches of lakefront property in the state.

The Flood Control Act in 1938 had already paved the way for a dam on the Little Red River, but it took some time to determine where the dam would go and how much water it would hold. Prospectors bought up much of the land around the area in the 40s, but by the mid-50s they sold out, not knowing when or if anything was going to happen. Thomas came in, bought 500 acres of ridgetop and – to make sure he didn't lose access to any of it should it become an island (islands within Army Corps of Engineers lakes can't be owned by anyone), he ensured fill was brought in to shore up and connect all points on that ridge. When the lake filled, he had a stretch that tied together the shore and Eden Island.

Thomas sold some of that land for vacation homes. He also built a lodge and restaurant that opened in 1963 – and burned the following year. No matter – the next lodge and restaurant opened in 1965 and are still operating to this day as the Red Apple Inn.

And now, to his wife, Ruby. In the introduction to the illustrious tome *Feasts of Eden*, the cookbook she wrote encapsulating the flavors from the kitchen of the Red Apple Inn, Ruby talked about how the restaurant came to be.

"The inspiration for the Red Apple Inn took root long before that, however, during a forty-two day Mediterranean cruise in 1954 with Henrietta and Sam Peck, owners and managers of the lovely old Sam Peck Hotel in Little Rock. They had furnished the hotel with antiques and interesting objects they had collected in their travels and were always looking for ideas to make their hotel more personal and hospitable. Collecting antiques had always been a hobby of ours, and we were fascinated by their eye for the unusual in both furnishings and food."

Ruby went on to write about tours she and Herbert would take in Costa Brava, Spain and Barcelona's Old Town, the latter of which they shopped for furnishings, furniture and carpet that would define the look of Eden Isle and, by extension, the Red Apple Inn. She also wrote about her husband's particularities.

"Herbert Thomas had such strong views on the food he ate and how it should be served, you might have thought he spent most of his time at the dinner table. But he had strong views about everything," she wrote. On describing how the restaurant came about, she shared "After Eden Isle was named, it seemed natural that we call the inn 'The Red Apple Inn.' This is where we wanted to create tempting food in a quiet and beautifully natural setting. Food, and the enjoyment of leisurely meals together, had always been important in our relationship and in rearing our children. I have always enjoyed preparing a meal that satisfies all the senses. Now I had an opportunity to share with others the pleasures of relaxed dining.

"We thought of bringing in well trained chefs from the surrounding cities. But we ended up working with the talented local women who were eager to show that they could prepare the traditional southern dishes with the taste and elegance we were looking for."

Feasts of Eden is out of print, but if you can manage to find a copy, you should obtain and cherish it. The tome is a time capsule illustrated with the photography of Thomas S. Gordon, documenting a precious moment in Arkansas food history, not only capturing the food but the sense of place that was the Red Apple Inn during the tenure of Ruby Thomas in its kitchen, a style I hope I muster when I aim the lens at each pie, each dish I personally shoot in my continuing documentation of Arkansas food.

Which brings me to Scott and the piece of pie before me that day at Local Lime, the day he gifted me a copy of *Feasts of Eden*. We've talked for years about the original Red Apple Inn Paradise pie. It's important to this book effort.

Scott regaled me of stories of growing up in the kitchen, not just home kitchens but in those of his grandmother and his father, two paragons in Arkansas's food culture. Ruby's Red Apple Inn and Frank McGehee's Junanita's Café are both held in high esteem for their contributions to our restaurant lexicon here. Scott himself founded Boulevard Bread Company before starting Yellow Rocket Concepts with John Beachboard, Russ McDonough and Ben Brainard. Today, those Yellow Rocket restaurants – ZaZa Fine Salad+Wood Oven Pizza Company, Big Orange, Local Lime (which we'll talk about on page 287), Lost Forty Brewing and Heights Taco and Tamale Company – are the vanguard of a new era in Little Rock food culture. Scott tells me one day his last restaurant concept will bring back the golden days of mid-century Arkansas restaurants, with all the classic restaurant dishes we loved and many of those we once enjoyed in an earlier age.

Which brings me, finally to the Paradise pie. Scott and I talked about the pie's heritage as I sampled that first forkful. It's a Depression-era pie (like the Oark General Store's oatmeal pie, see page 58), made with cheap ingredients every kitchen might have on hand, meant to stretch and make do with what one has. Ruby Thomas introduced that pie at the Red Apple Inn, and every effort to take it off the menu was met with protest. The simple ingredients combine to make a marvelous, surprisingly light and rich pie, a flavor that holds that sense-of-places as well as any photograph in that marvelous cookbook.

Scott had made a couple of changes that day, toasting the nuts and coconut before adding them. He'd also slightly sweetened the cream, which we both agreed wasn't necessary. And he agreed I could share this recipe.

305 Club Road
Heber Springs, Arkansas 72543
(800) 733-2775
RedAppleInn.com

PARADISE PIE

3 egg whites
1 cup sugar
20 soda crackers (small squares – Scott says he uses 23)
1 cup pecans, chopped
½ pint heavy cream, whipped
1 teaspoon vanilla
7 ounces grated coconut

Beat egg whites until almost stiff. Add sugar gradually, continuing to beat. Fold in crumbled crackers and nuts. Scrape into 9 inch pie pan that has been well buttered. Bake 20 minutes at 325 degrees. Cool. Top with whipped cream flavored with vanilla, and sprinkle with grated coconut.

This recipe serves six.

Ruby's note to the recipe: "I first had this simple but delicious dessert 30 years ago in Booneville. It is still a favorite at the Red Apple. It is quickly made and freezes well.:

Paradise pie is still to this day on the menu at the Red Apple Inn.

ROUND ROCK DINER

The Round Rock Diner in Greers Ferry offers all sorts of options for breakfast, lunch and dinner, including a righteous plate of nachos and a selection of salads and sandwiches. The fried pies are made in-house and come packed with a different filling each day – sometimes apple, sometimes chocolate, always good.

8249 Edgemont Road Suite 3
Greers Ferry, Arkansas 72067
(501) 825-2060
Facebook.com/RoundRockDinerGreersFerry

JANSSEN'S LAKEFRONT RESTAURANT

On the north shore of Greers Ferry Lake a few miles from Greers Ferry, Janssen's Lakefront Restaurant offers magnificent views, especially of sunsets. Its pies are piled-on fluffy rounds, with chocolate mousse and coconut cream being amongst the favorites of diners who visit.

9999 Edgemont Road
Edgemont, Arkansas 72044
(501) 723-4480
Facebook.com/JanssensLakefront

LITTLE RED RESTAURANT AT INDIAN HILLS

Nick Ruhotina and his wife, Kelly Weeks Ruhotina, came to Fairfield Bay in July 2017 to take over at the Little Red Restaurant at Indian Hills. The couple moved here from Germany, where they had lived the past 25 years and where they had their own restaurant. At Little Red, they're creating a new European-inspired menu combined with classic Arkansas hospitality for the longstanding eatery.

Chef Nick has created a rather unusual yet gorgeous pie for the restaurant, a butter pecan icebox pie. The double-layered creation comes topped with a housemade praline sauce that matches perfectly. A must-try.

337 Snead Drive
Fairfield Bay, Arkansas 72088
(501) 884-3800
Facebook.com/LittleRedIndianHills

MONA LISA CAFÉ AND SANDWICH SHOPPE

Beans, greens and tasty things are the sort of food you'll find on the menu at the Mona Lisa Café in the hillside town of Shirley. Lisa Hackett runs the restaurant in her husband's hometown, sourcing ingredients for each day's breakfast and lunch from local farmers and producers. She makes perfect foldover omelets and lush biscuits with gravy made from scratch. There is always pie on the lunch buffet.

500 Arkansas Highway 9
Shirley, Arkansas 72153
(501) 723-4848

PJ'S RAINBOW CAFÉ

Mountain View's most popular pie shop is also one of its most eclectic dining destinations. From the moment you walk through the door, you realize there's something to look at in every direction, including the ceiling, where tiles have been replaced with placards advertising area businesses.

That's one of many ways you know you're within PJ's Rainbow Café. Between two walls packed with area memorabilia, you'll find booths and tables full of folks. During the warmer months, you'll meet people from other states and other continents. During the winter, locals fill in the gaps.

PJ's, owned by Pat and Chuck Mahaney, has long been known as a great place for an excellent breakfast or a good lunch a half-block off the square, the sort of place you start at when you're getting ready to head out to the Ozark Folk Center or preparing to sit and listen to bluegrass on the downtown square or in the park beyond it.

At the back right corner stands the entrance to Pie Narnia – a double-sided cooler always full of pie made by Ms. Reda. They come in so many flavors, including a strawberry rhubarb cream pie, peanut butter chocolate cream pie, and a baked Ozark mountain pie that includes chocolate walnuts and coconut. I tried the banana split pie, which was a very rich banana split pie top with slices of strawberry in their own syrup. So decadent.

Robbie Mahaney, Pat and Chuck's son, was in when I came to shoot the pies for this book. He shared with me a bite of a new project he's working on, a lemon curd pie created from a 100-year-old newspaper clipping recipe. PJ's means to save Ozark flavors as they are, and with pies like this, they'll do well.

216 West Main Street
Mountain View, Arkansas 72560
(870) 269-8633
Facebook.com/PJsRainbowCafe

JO JO'S CATFISH WHARF AT JACK'S FISHING RESORT

Right over the White River and almost under the Arkansas Highway Five bridge north of Mountain View, you'll find Jo Jo's Catfish Wharf, the on-site restaurant at Jack's Fishing Resort. This jumping-off point for those who want to spend a week or weekend hiking, motorcycling, fishing or visiting the nearby Ozark Folk Center State Park is also an excellent place to enjoy a meal at the end of your day.

Jack and Mary Hale Hinkle established the resort back in 1961 as a good place to enjoy the area's trout fishing. While hot fried pies and a peanut butter pie are on the menu, it's the house-made old fashioned chocolate possum pie that you'll want to put in your belly after a day of catching (or not catching).

151 Jacks Resort Road
Mountain View, Arkansas 72560
(870)585-2121
JacksResort.com

BETWEEN THE BUNS

Located inside a building that once housed the Estes One Stop at the corner of Arkansas Highways 5 and 56, Between the Buns offers slices of pie daily, including pecan, lemon meringue and coconut cream, alongside its burgers and barbecue.

100 Arkansas Highway 56
Calico Rock, Arkansas 72519
(870) 297-3400

THE SKILLET RESTAURANT
and the OZARK FOLK CENTER

The Skillet Restaurant at the Ozark Folk Center in Mountain View happens to have not only some of the best fried chicken in the state but great pies as well. The restaurant (which runs with the season at the Ozark Folk Center and closes in the winter months) serves both the park and the community seven days a week. The breakfast buffet includes egg casserole, sausage and bacon, big biscuits and grits and the like. On Sunday the buffet includes some of the best fried chicken in the Ozarks, alongside homestyle vegetables, rolls and cornbread. Menu service is also available.

Ms. Nina puts out a spread of pies every day in four flavors – lemon icebox, coconut cream, apple, and a chocolate peanut butter cream that's beloved amongst returning customers. The apple pie is served a la mode with cinnamon ice cream. As far as the Arkansas flavor in all of that – Yarnell's makes the ice cream, and the stone ground artisan chocolate comes from northwest Arkansas's KYYA.

More pies are available on park at The Smokehouse, which in addition to smoked meat sandwiches and pizza offers handmade fried pies in apple, peach or cherry. The biscuit-like crust is the perfect edible pouch for those fruit fillings as you walk the park and visit the resident craftsmen, artisans, performers and musicians who share their art on the premises.

1032 Park Avenue
Mountain View, Arkansas 72560
(870) 269-3851
OzarkFolkCenter.com

OZARK FOLK CENTER FRIED PIES

3 ounces evaporated milk
½ cup water
½ cup block shortening (a stick of Crisco), melted
1 ounce white vinegar
2 cups self-rising flour
½ cup plain flour
8 ounces of filling (this can be chocolate custard, a cooked fruit mélange, etc.)

Mix together evaporated milk, water, shortening and white vinegar. Blend flour into liquid. Using an electric mixer, mix until texture of dough is silky, not sticky or dry. Adjust with small amounts of liquid if too dry to roll or small amount of flour if sticky.

Pull an amount the size of a big walnut and roll into ball. Roll into a six-inch circle on floured board or parchment paper.

Place four ounces of any type of filling toward one side of the circle. Brush the edges of the circle with evaporated milk. Fold in half and seal edges with fork or fingers. Punch holes in the top using a fork two times. This prevents explosion.

Use vegetable oil to deep fry at temperature of 350 degrees for 5 minutes or until golden brown. If you pan fry, turn pies when first side browns.

Makes a dozen.

HEIDI'S UGLY CAKES

The White River and North Fork River join in a valley at the town of Norfork n north central Arkansas, a somewhat undiscovered area for many travelers. The fishing, as you can imagine, is excellent. Above the confluence sits the Jacob Wolf House, a two-story dogtrot structure constructed by the merchant blacksmith who was elected as a representative to the General Assembly of Arkansas Territory in 1826. The facility, built in 1829 as the first permanent courthouse for Izard County in Arkansas Territory, is one of the oldest structures in the state. Just down the hill on a high river bank, you'll find Heidi's Ugly Cakes.

Heidi Price may be my spirit animal. The eatery is her one-woman show. The Florida native who married an Arkansas man and moved to the area after Hurricane Ivan manages this place, cooks, runs the register and makes the most righteous Reuben sandwich I've ever encountered. The irregular space has a dining section up a couple of steps towards the back and a couple of tables right by the front door, with the kitchen and a beverage center in-between.

A window at counter-level into the kitchen offers a showcase for some of the more homely looking handpies I've seen – gorgeously homey, if that's a thing. They come in so many flavors – blackberry, blueberry, peach, apple, cherry – and they're big, too, the size of an extended hand. Anyone who doubts whether Heidi makes hers from scratch needs to just take one look at these and understand she does it all, including the glazing. She calls them "baked fried pies" because people don't understand what they are without the word "fried."

But she doesn't do just handpies. In the case, there are always slices and sometimes whole peanut butter pies, which she introduced to me as her award-winning pie.

Thing is, from the moment I walked through the door, Heidi talked with me as if we'd known each other for years, referring to me as "love" and offering me anything I might want. When I went out the door it wasn't a matter of "bye" or "have a good day." She told me "see you soon." I think I will.

71 Fishermans Street
Norfork, Arkansas 72658
(870) 499-7437
Facebook.com/HeidisUglyCakes

PJ's RIVER RUN RESTAURANT

PJ's River Run Restaurant overlooks the White River in Norfork. As part of PJ's White River Lodge, the eatery offers high-end steaks alongside West Coast and Southern cuisine. A classic prime rib dinner is a good candidate for completion with a slice of the housemade Key lime pie. Open seasonally.

384 Lodge Lane
Norfork, Arkansas 72658
(870) 499-7500
PJsLodge.com

THE GRILL AT WHISPERING WOODS

I know when I get a recommendation for good pie from another great piemaker, it has to be spot-on. I am certainly not disappointed by the restaurant suggested by several Mountain Home restaurateurs, who keyed me in to The Grill at Whispering Woods.

Kim and Richard Quiblier come from different backgrounds but managed to find their way to Arkansas and, like so many who discover the state, decided to stay.

Richard, who was born in Washington, DC to Swiss parents, trained in Lausanne, Switzerland and worked in that country for 20 years before coming back to the States to become the executive chef for the company that caters all the big PGA and LPGA golf events. Kim was born in Devon, England and traveled a good portion of her life before joining the same company to coordinate on-site corporate hospitality for those events. The two met, married and spent years together on the circuit.

A few years ago, Kim and Richard decided to settle down. So they Googled "small resort for sale," as you do... and found that the Whispering Woods Cabins and Grill over Norfork Lake was available. They didn't have any intentions on coming to Arkansas to stay, but one visit and they were ready to sign the paperwork. The Quibliers opened The Grill under Chef Richard over the Independence Day weekend in 2015.

Richard is a pie-making wizard, by the way. I was expecting to sample his version of vinegar pie, which I'd only found at one other Arkansas restaurant (Olde Tyme Restaurant on the Square in Mountain Home, for that matter, see page 104). Instead, I stood agog for several moments staring at the blackboard covered with the day's flavors, which included passion fruit pie with raspberry sauce, Dutch apple raisin pie with ice cream and tiramisu pie along less glamorous flavors such as peanut butter, chocolate chip almond coconut, coconut cream and Key lime (as well as the aforementioned vinegar pie). It was the Banofee pie that really caught my attention though – an English favorite that, though I have a recipe, I've never encountered in another Arkansas restaurant. It is absolutely as delicious as you would expect, with a thin layer of sliced fresh bananas and dark chocolate between the rich buttery toffee custard and a delightful whipped cream.

4245 Arkansas Highway 177
Jordan, Arkansas 72519
(870) 499-5531
WhisperingWoodsAR.com

HOLY SMOKES BBQ

The best peanut butter pie I have found in north central Arkansas has to be that offered at Holy Smokes BBQ. This remarkably light yet decadent slice of creamy pie has a salient balance of salt and sugar and a nutty sapor that tastes just like the peanut butter parfait at your favorite dairy bar. The housemade pie is the only pie offered by the relatively new barbecue joint, which has taken home a couple of People's Choice awards for its cuisine at the annual Mountain Home Taste of the Town event. A must-try.

400 Arkansas Highway 201
Mountain Home, Arkansas 72653
(870) 425-8080

SKIPPER'S RESTAURANT

Locally known for its catfish and waffles, Skipper's Restaurant offers a daily variety of pies. The eatery, opened in 2008, is in direct lineage from the famed Sandy's Restaurant, which served Mountain Home from the 1970s onward. In season, the strawberry pie is delightful.

711 Arkansas Highway 5
Mountain Home, Arkansas 72653
(870) 508-4574
SkippersGoodFood.com

ADITA'S SEAFOOD AND GRILL

Mountain Home may not seem like the sort of spot you'd expect to find a Belizian restaurant, but Adita's Seafood and Grill offers favorites from the coastal Central American country perched on the edge of the Caribbean. Delicacies such as chicken salbutes, carne guisada and a variety of empanadas are offered.

Amidst the Belizian desserts such as ChocoFlan and churros, you'll find pies. The lemon pie with its mountainous meringue top is quite popular, as is the coconut cream.

1310 US Highway 62 West, Suite 12
Mountain Home, Arkansas 72653
(870) 424-2961

LAKE COUNTRY COOKHOUSE

Housed in the River Rock Hotel, the Lake Country Cookhouse is a New American restaurant offering a splendid array of meat-heavy oversized salads, openfaced Manhattan sandwiches, and big breakfasts with homefries. A key dessert is a rich coconut cream pie, weighty with a deep golden custard.

1350 US Highway 62 West
Mountain Home, Arkansas 72653
(870) 425-5544
TheRiverRockInn.com

OLDE TYME RESTAURANT ON THE SQUARE

From June 11, 1890, to April 15, 1891, Nannie Stillwell Jackson wrote about the best and meanest moments of her life on a small farm in southeast Arkansas. The University of Arkansas Press published that journal in 1982, under the title *Vinegar Pie and Chicken Bread: A Woman's Diary of Life in the Rural South, 1890-1891.*

Vinegar pie has long been associated with Arkansas. The 19th century economy dessert was often utilized in the late days of winter, when the bounty of the farm was at its lowest and no fresh fruit or nuts were to be found. Its simplicity (similar to Chess Pie) was in how it created something unexpected from plain, ordinary ingredients.

While Arkansas has moved away from much of its rural past, vinegar pie is still served in a meager handful of restaurants. Nowhere is it celebrated more than at Olde Tyme Restaurant on the Square in downtown Mountain Home. A cavernous room full of noise and color across the street from the county courthouse, Olde Tyme proudly offers vinegar pie, not just on its menu but on posterboard pasted about the place. The simple dessert is its most popular order, and for ample reason – it's sweet yet a little tart, with a crispy top crust.

609 South Baker Street
Mountain Home, Arkansas 72653
(870) 425-1013

VINEGAR PIE

4 large eggs
2 Tablespoons apple cider vinegar
1 ½ cups sugar
1 stick unsalted butter, melted
½ teaspoon cinnamon
1 teaspoon vanilla
1 pinch salt
1 pie crust set into a 9-inch pie pan.

Preheat oven to 425°F.
Beat eggs, vinegar, sugar, melted butter, cinnamon, vanilla, and salt until well combined and slightly thickened. Pour batter into pie crust and bake for 25 minutes. Center should be set. Cool before serving.

HOUSE OF PIZZA

You probably wouldn't expect a pizza joint to have great pie, but in Mountain Home, one of the best Key lime pies you can find is at House of Pizza. This eatery in a strip mall on the east side of town is hip, green and lovely. The pie itself is a creamy, delectable and gorgeous delight.

40 Plaza Way, Suite 26
Mountain Home, Arkansas 72653
(870) 492-2351
HouseOfPizzaMH.com

KT'S SMOKEHOUSE

Originally opened in 2006, KT's is likely the best place to grab ribs in Gassville. There's even a competition to see who can eat the most (as of right now, the record is 34). The joint is known for a toothsome peanut butter pie, the only dessert on the menu.

KT's Smokehouse
406 East Main Street
Gassville, Arkansas 72635
(870) 435-5080

NIMA'S PIZZA AND BAKERY

Nima's Pizza opened in the 1990s and served its community well. In 2003, it was purchased from its original owners by a Las Vegas couple, and within a few years, it gained international notoriety. Rick and Jane Mines loved visiting the Mountain Home area and decided to retire there, as well as purchase Nima's with no restaurant experience. They learned, though, and utilized a collection of premium aged cheeses, specialty oils from the Devo Olive Oil Company in Branson and time-consuming doughs and ingredients to create pizza masterpieces.

They started entering, and winning, the competitions at the International Pizza Challenge in Las Vegas in 2008 - and they even won the title of second best pizza in the world in 2013 for their Flowering Pepperoni pizza.

But the Mines offer other things than pizza. In particular, this is the sole restaurant in the entire state where you can find an Italian grape pie. Unlike most of the pies in this book, this one has a yeast crust and comes out looking like a round loaf of bread, full of gorgeously rich red grapes.

The Mines recently added a bakery, which makes cakes and scones and more traditional pies. The chocolate cream pie is certainly worth a stop on its own.

109 South School Street
Gassville, Arkansas 72635
(870) 435-6828
NimasPizza.com

178 CLUB

Bob and Dee Fox moved to Bull Shoals in 1975, when they purchased the Coral Courts Resort. Seeing a need, they built - a bowling alley. That's right - the Foxes' son was an avid bowler in school and needed lanes, so the family built a bowling alley. In 1980, they added a full service restaurant, the 178 Club, a steakhouse where you can bring in your catch of the day and have it prepared for you, complete with soup, salad and all the fixings. Martin and Lisa Earhart bought the 178 from the Foxes in recent years but continue to offer the same menu and care as before.

The pies at the 178 Club include an apple slab pie, baked in its own cast iron skillet and meant to be split. There's also the bright green Grasshopper pie, a crème de menthe pie on a chocolate cookie crust, that's quite effervescent.

2109 Central Boulevard
Bull Shoals, Arkansas 72619
(870) 445-4949
178Club.com

GASTON'S WHITE RIVER RESORT RESTAURANT

Executive Chef Rick Gollinger heads the kitchen at Gaston's White River Resort, a nationally known location beloved by trout fishermen. The restaurant offers many trout and seafood selections, alongside pasta, steak and chicken. There's almost always a dessert featuring pie. The peanut butter and chocolate pie is not to be turned down.

1777 River Road
Lakeview, Arkansas 72642
(870) 431-5202
Gastons.com

HANK AND KATIE'S BAKERY AND CAFÉ

Hank Hudson and Kate Asher opened this spot along Highway 178 in Bull Shoals. Hank passed away in 2017, but Kate continues to run the bright little red-and-white shop, complete with a case that always includes pies. Cream pies such as fluffy coconut, lemon, peanut butter and chocolate are almost always available, tucked alongside cherry cream cheese, apple and pecan pies in the case under the daily supply of doughnuts, turnovers and muffins.

1417 Central Boulevard
Bull Shoals, Arkansas 72619
(870) 445-4433

BUFFALO POINT CABINS AND CONCESSIONS

The restaurant at Buffalo Point Cabins and Concessions is open Memorial Day weekend to Labor Day each year, offering several pies including pecan, lemon icebox, chocolate or coconut cream – but the best is the house specialty, a peanut butter icebox pie.

2261 Arkansas Highway 268
Yellville, Arkansas 72687
(870) 449-6206
BuffaloPoint.Net

TEETER'S SOUTH FORK CAFÉ

Between Mountain Home and Ash Flat on US Highway 62/412, the best place to stop for pie is Teeter's South Fork Café. There's barbecue, breakfast and probably the best taco salad in north central Arkansas. Check the cooler for slices of chocolate cream, strawberry cream and pecan pie.

652 Highway 62 West
Salem, Arkansas 72576
(870) 895-5880
Facebook.com/TeetersSFCafe

BAILEY'S COUNTRY COOKIN'

When in Melbourne, look for the red building behind the big rocking chair. That's where you can get yourself some vittles at Bailey's. The friendly staff is not above donning costumes to enhance the good times, and it's not uncommon to see one (or two, or even three) people running around in monkey suits. The restaurant, opened in 2014, is probably best known for a two pound patty burger and a double burger challenge that few have managed to complete. It's also known for its pies – chocolate and coconut meringue pies and a substantial peanut butter pie to boot.

811 Main Street
Melbourne, Arkansas 72556
(870) 368-5454
Facebook.com/BaileysCountryCookin

CALABAMA RESTAURANT

At the corner of Arkansas Highways 56 and 289 south of Horseshoe Bend, you'll find the Calabama Restaurant. This local favorite serves up Angus steaks, seafood, lobster, walleye, a famed Chicken Morney and other items. In a case by the register, look for plates of glazed handpies filled with fruit. The delectable almost-shortbread crust alone is worth the couple of bucks for one of these beauties, which you might be best planning to take home after a big meal. Or get one with your breakfast coffee.

20 South Bond Drive
Franklin, Arkansas 72536
(870) 322-7288

CINDY'S DINNER BELL

Cindy's Dinner Bell is tucked into a small mall in Horseshoe Bend – a unique location where you can enter one of three different doors to access the spacious L shaped dining room. The pies are traditional – apple, coconut meringue and chocolate meringue – and they go quick. Call a day in advance to get the flavor you want.

811 Second Street
Horseshoe Bend, Arkansas 72512
(870) 670-4232

CAROL'S LAKEVIEW RESTAURANT

Carol's Lakeview Restaurant in Cherokee Village is not easy to find if you don't know where to look. Its location overlooking Lake Thunderbird on a road crossing through the community is not the sort of thing you'd find if you stuck to the major highways.

The restaurant is named for Carol Johnson Steen. She and her husband Dennis moved to the area in 1991, purchasing and opening the restaurant. They had both worked together in restaurants they'd owned in Wisconsin, while Dennis had also spent time as a truck driver. The move to Hardy and the subsequent purchase of the Cherokee Village eatery was a retirement move.

Both Dennis and Carol have passed on, but their son Patrick and daughter-in-law Toni continue the tradition of big meals and over-the-top pies served each day in the

cedar-planked restaurant. There are a lot of pies to talk about and try, too – including the swirled fudge marble pie, the extremely tall peanut butter icebox and strawberry icebox pies, a gooey cherry pie, and even the light and tart cherry surprise pie.

200 Iroquois Drive
Cherokee Village,
Arkansas 72529
(870) 257-3595

BLUFF STEAKHOUSE

The Bluff Steakhouse at Biggers Bed and Breakfast in Hardy is a good place for a nice dinner over steak, potatoes and salad. The one pie to end the meal should be the excellent Key lime.

20 Bluff Road
Hardy, Arkansas 72542
870) 856-4718
BiggersBnB.com

GRANDMA'S COUNTRY COOK'N

Much as you would expect from any restaurant that names itself after your favorite cooking relative, Grandma's Country Cook'n in Hardy and Ravenden offers traditional meringue and fruit pies. Both locations close during January and February but are open the rest of the year.

412 US Highway 62
Hardy, Arkansas 72542
(870) 856-2342

71 US Highway 63
Ravenden, Arkansas 72459
(870) 869-0181

WOOD'S RIVER BEND RESTAURANT

At a mere 1300 feet from the border, Wood's Riverbend Restaurant is about as close as you can get to Missouri and still enjoy a slice of Arkansas pie. Opened in 2000 on a riverbank across the road from Mammoth Spring, the headwaters of the Spring River, Wood's serves steaks, catfish and burgers with one of the best views in the area.

There are always a variety of pies available, including meringues, double-crusted fruit, pecan and sugar-free creams.

80 Main Street
Mammoth Spring, Arkansas 72554
(870) 625-9357
Facebook.com/
WoodsRiverbendRestaurant

NOT YOUR MAMA'S BAKERY

Katie Ponder opened Not Your Mama's Bakery along US Highway 62 in Imboden in March 2017. The little white house is where you'll find breakfast pastries and lunch, alongside an ever-changing array of desserts, including triangular handpies. Look for yours under a glass dome on the counter.

917 West Third Street
Imboden, Arkansas 72434
(870) 378-9049
Facebook.com/NotYMBakery

7B COUNTRY CAFÉ

Strawberry, Arkansas is about halfway between Batesville, Ash Flat and Walnut Ridge, at the intersection of Arkansas Highways 25, 117 and 230. There aren't many places to catch a bite in the little town, but if you're wanting pie, you should head to the 7B Country Café, which opened in 2017 and which, often as not, has homemade pie on the menu. Pies tend to be of the meringue variety.

70-94 West River Drive
Strawberry, Arkansas 72469
(870) 232-1344

FOX CREEK BBQ

Fox Creek BBQ operates out of the old Batesville rail depot a couple of blocks from the main drag. It serves Black Angus steaks, salmon and barbecue alongside fried cherry and apple pies as well and slices of Key lime and chocolate peanut butter pies. Live country music is common on weekend evenings.

129 Lawrence Street
Batesville, Arkansas 72501
(870) 698-0034

NATALIE'S

Inside Natalie's in Batesville, Mardi Gras is the theme, with a host of mix-and-match tables and chairs, eclectic art and dividers, all covered in beads. The restaurant carries a constant scent of Creole spices and baking bread – a delicious combination to tempt anyone.

There are a number of darling desserts in Natalie's case on any particular day. These choices often include cloying little lemon tarts that you don't have to share with anyone else. There are also often hunks of lemon, coconut or chocolate meringue pie, as well as whole coconut cream, chocolate cream, cookies and cream and pecan pies in the case.

3050 Harrison Street
Batesville, Arkansas 72501
(870) 698-0200
WhoDatNats.com

E&B'S BIGGER BURGERS

Alongside the burgers and steaks at E&B's, you'll find slices of pie. The coconut cream gets big nods.

2170 North Central Avenue
Batesville, Arkansas 72501
(870) 698-9088

FRED'S FISH HOUSE

Fred's Fish House started out in Cord back in 1991. Fred Ward would have his sons fish for catfish out of the family pond and serve them up at a tiny café and grocery store. Word got out about that fish, and his sons ended up fishing that pond dry. He ended up moving the operation to Batesville and letting his son Randy run the shop. Fred's other sons Cameron and Brandon also jumped into the business, which is known for its hot catfish, spicy brown beans, homemade dressings and hush puppies.

The Batesville location is in an old church. A second sits on the main avenue through downtown Mammoth Spring, within peeking distance of Woods' Riverbend Restaurant and a Frisbee throw from the Missouri border. There's a third location in Mountain Home. All three offer Fred's five layer vanilla pie or five layer chocolate pie, caramel apple pie, peanut butter pie and coconut meringue pie, and sometimes fried pies are also available.

Fred's Fish House
3777 Harrison Street
Batesville, AR 72501
(870) 793-2022
FredsFish
Housebatesville.com

Fred's Fish House
215 Main Street
Mammoth Spring, AR
72554
(870) 625-7551

Fred's Fish House
44 Hwy 101 Cutoff
Mountain Home, AR
72653
(870) 492-5958
FredsFishHouse.com

BECKY'S SOUTHSIDE GRILL

On the south side of town, across from South Side School, you'll find Becky's Southside Grill. This family restaurant offers seafood buffets with crab legs, catfish and mudbugs on Friday nights and home cooking whenever you ask. The pie case is packed with meringue and cream pies. Of note – a peanut butter meringue pie with a lot of lift.

2121 Batesville Boulevard
Batesville, Arkansas 72501
(870) 251-2229

TADPOLE'S CATFISH BARN

Off US Highway 167 between Batesville and Bald Knob, there's a seafood buffet where shrimp, frog legs and catfish are the stars. You can also get ribs, barbecue and a host of sides at Tadpole's Catfish Barn (plus crab legs for an additional price) alongside country fixings like okra and pinto beans. The dessert bar includes a fine array of cakes, cobbler, banana pudding and both pecan and meringue pies.

6201 Batesville Boulevard
Pleasant Plains, Arkansas 72568
(501) 345-3474

RAMBLER GRILL

The Rambler Grill is really two restaurants in one – a pizza shop and take-and-make shop on the right, a steak and seafood house on the left. The restaurant's two sides pack out at lunch and dinner with hungry folks from around the area.

There are a number of pies in the case constantly at the former convenience store turned eatery. An entire section of floor to ceiling refrigeration unit is dedicated to the pies in all their variations – which range from the area's most popular possum pie to chocolate, peanut butter, and coconut creams; strawberry and cherry cream cheese; and a gracious number of revolving fruit double-crust and lattice pies, including a fat-lattice apple pie dusted with plenty of cinnamon and sugar.

442 Highway 5
Rose Bud, Arkansas 72137
(501) 556-4262

BAILEY'S BBQ, CATFISH AND MORE

Along US Highway 64B in downtown Vilonia, you'll find Bailey's BBQ, Catfish and More. The little red building is also where substantial, buttery-crusted fried pies are made in a range of flavors.

1073 Main Street
Vilonia, Arkansas 72173
(501) 796-3487

SAWBUCKS AUTHENTIC AMERICAN NEIGHBORHOOD GRILL

The very first Sawbucks Authentic American Neighborhood Grill wasn't really located in a neighborhood but at the corner of US Highway 64 and Arkansas Highway 5 in the El Paso Community. On the southeast corner of the intersection, an old woodclad building that once served as a truck stop now houses the original location of this small local franchise.

There are three pies to note – the peanut butter, the chocolate meringue and the lemon meringue. Each is a decent slice of pie, and each is offered at the different Sawbucks locations in Beebe, Conway, Maumelle and of course El Paso today.

Grav Weldon

1118 US Highway 64
El Paso, Arkansas 72045
(501) 796-0112

1800 Club Manor Drive
Maumelle, Arkansas 72113
(501) 734-8626

1515 Dave Ward Drive
Conway, Arkansas 72034
(501) 504-6065

1901 West Dewitt Henry Drive
Beebe, Arkansas 72012
(501) 882-6363

ZACK DIEMER'S CHERRY CREAM CHEESE PIE

My brother has the task each holiday season of creating a pie, and this is the usual suspect: the traditional cherry-pie-filling-topped favorite done large. He makes it up in a Tupperware Large White Round Storage Container (Tupperseal) that outdates both of us. The thing is thirteen inches in diameter and about three inches tall. You can substitute four eight-inch pie pans instead.

1 box graham crackers, pounded to crumbs
4 8-ounce packages cream cheese, room temperature
2 14-ounce cans sweetened condensed milk
1 tablespoon vanilla extract
1 cup lemon juice
2 21-ounce cans cherry pie filling

If you haven't done it already, beat the hell out of the graham crackers until they're big moist crumbs of graham cracker dirt. Press into the bottom of the Tupperware container. Set aside.

Beat the tar out of the cream cheese until it's sorta fluffy. Add in everything else but the cherries. Make sure the lumps are out. Slide into the fridge and let chill for four hours.

Top with the cherry pie filling and serve. If you feel really fancy, get a can of cherry pie filling and a can of blueberry pie filling and go nuts with it.

MARTHA JEAN'S DINER

One of the most splendid examples of peanut butter chocolate meringue pie I have ever seen, I found at Martha Jean's Diner in Beebe. The country-style restaurant on the north side of town on Arkansas Highway 367 always has several different pies on the whiteboard. From a sturdy and slightly sweet crown of meringue to separate layers of peanut butter cream and heavy chocolate custard, this pie is worth a detour.

5419 Highway 367 South
Beebe, Arkansas 72012
(501) 882-3100

SUTTLE'S ROAD HOG BBQ

The Suttle family opened Suttle's Road Hog BBQ as a food truck in 2004. The restaurant did so well, the family opened a permanent brick-and-mortar shop on the south side of Beebe in 2015. The case by the register is always full of pie, in particular cream cheese pies, including Butter-finger, blueberry and even pumpkin cream cheese, as well as possum pie. The cherry cream cheese pie in particular is a real winner, as is Mrs. Glenda's Mamaw pie, a blend of whipped cream and cream cheese, coconut, caramel and pecans. There are also fried pies available.

2008 West Dewitt Henry Drive
Beebe, Arkansas 72012
(501) 882-1034
Facebook.com/SuttlesRoadHogBBQ

DAISY'S LUNCHBOX

The cutest place to dine on the White County Courthouse square in Searcy is, hands down, Daisy's Lunchbox. The gorgeous blue and white room with its fireplace and chalkboard specials serves up equally cute fruit tarts and pies with character and flavor. Suzanne Raiford's operation offers grand flavors such as lemon meringue, coconut cream, chocolate, cherry, peach, apple and pumpkin throughout the year, both in slices and in personal rounds. But it's the gorgeous personal berry tarts on the counter by the register that garner my attention – shortbread dough tarts topped with gorgeous hearts filled with cherries or a blend of raspberries and blueberries. Daisy's Lunchbox offers light lunches from 11 a.m. to 2 p.m., but has pastries any time it's open.

311 North Spruce Street
Searcy, Arkansas 72143
(501) 281-0297

J&M MEAT AND SEAFOOD

A butcher shop may seem like a strange place to find fried pies, but not in Searcy, where J and M Meat and Seafood offers fresh fried Flywheel pies alongside beef, pork and an entire case of freshly delivered shrimp, fish and mudbugs. J and M also smokes meats and sells prepared sandwiches and lunches.

106 West Mulberry Avenue
Searcy, Arkansas 72143
(501) 268-6328

MAIN STREET CAFÉ

You can be forgiven if you thought the coconut meringue pie at the Main Street Café in Searcy came from a manufacturer – the perfect meringue in the perfectly prepared pie crust looks like the sort of thing you'd see in a fancy magazine. But make no mistake – this pie, with more coconut cream than coconut meringue, is a marvelous pie made right on-site and worthy of your attention.

Melissa Wallace runs the operation started by her mother, Marilyn Cooper in 1992 along with her sister Ginger. The family operation offers other pies, too, including chocolate meringue, strawberry cream cheese, and gorgeously cute apple lattice tarts baked right into whole apples. Chocolate gravy is also on the menu.

1511 West Pleasure Avenue Suite A
Searcy, Arkansas 72143
(501) 268-3887

THE MIXING BOWL

This take-and-make only operation on the south side of town, preparing entrées and desserts for folks to take home and warm up in their own ovens. There are also several cream pies on the menu, including lemon, coconut, Key lime and Butterfinger flavors.

1229 West Beebe Capps Expressway
Searcy, Arkansas 72143
(501) 305-4845
Facebook.com/TheMixingBowlOfSearcy

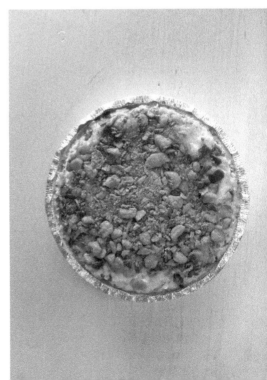

KIBO MIDNIGHT OIL COFFEEHOUSE

This shop gets its name from Africa's highest peak, the tip of Mount Kilimanjaro. The group that created this sprawling coffeeshop on the south side of Race Street made their way to that summit in 1998. They decided what they wanted to do was to fund projects in cooperation with East African natives. Today the group supports local artists and the community by offering space for meetings and local art displays.

The shop itself opened in 1997 but was purchased in 2009 by the Kibo group. The beverages are prepared with beans from the Rozark Hills Coffee Roasterie out of nearby Rose Bud. There are also teas, ciders and other seasonal drinks (including a Hot Apple Pie in a Mug) as well as a seasonally changing menu.

Kibo Midnight Oil Coffeehouse also has a bakery, and amongst its many offerings are fruit tarts and cream tarts, such as the excellent (and extraordinarily pink) raspberry tart.

801 East Race Avenue
Searcy, Arkansas 72143
(501) 268-9014
KiboMidnightOil.com

GLENN'S SMOKEHOUSE

This barbecue joint offers a daily dessert that sometimes includes sliced pie; its coconut fried pies are a pretty good bet for a nice finish to a dinner of Pig Pie (like a Frito chili pie but with barbecue pork) or fried ribs.

1016 South Main Street
Searcy, Arkansas 72143
(501) 279-1211

TRAIL'S END DINER

Though this eatery is actually located out at Georgetown, a bit of a stretch from Searcy, it's worth the trek to check out the restaurant's fresh river catfish and coconut pie.

2012 Highway 36 East
Searcy, Arkansas 72143
(501) 742-1151

KJ'S RESTAURANT

Stan and Karen (KJ) Robinson opened KJ's Restaurant in the White County burg of Judsonia in 2006. The Robinsons' sons Craig and Ben innovate ideas into menu items, much of it based on the countless hours the boys spent watching Food Network growing up. The restaurant is known for hand-cut steaks, crab legs, the bacon-wrapped KJ's Choice Chicken and excellent breakfasts. The restaurant also offers pies, in particular an almost always available coconut meringue pie low on the fluff rise but high on the toasted coconut flavor. Chocolate meringue is also popular.

616 Arkansas Highway 367
Judsonia, Arkansas 72081
(501) 729-4200

SHORTY'S RESTAURANT

In nearby Providence, north of Judsonia on Arkansas Highway 157, there sits an old style dairy diner that makes an excellent bowl of chili and a grand plate of fried catfish with all the fixings. Terry Treece runs Shorty's Restaurant, the only game in town.

The eatery brings in folks from several towns over for its excellent hamburger steaks and a gracious plate of chocolate biscuits and gravy. The triumvirate of pies are all meringue – chocolate, coconut and the rare peanut butter – the third of which has a marvelous butter-nut tone to its flavor.

3393 Arkansas Highway 157
Judsonia, Arkansas 72081
(501) 729-4777

MARKET CAFÉ

Not much has changed at the Market Café in Bald Knob since it first opened in 1945. Sure, the bar has been re-topped, the plaid tile has been replaced with triangular mosaic and the walls have been painted, but much remains the same about this classic Arkansas restaurant that sits along US Highway 367 south of town.

That includes the coconut cream pie, which is still made with the same coconut chiffon recipe that was used here when the eatery first opened. The nice firm whipped peaks come from cream of tartar, not meringue, and the entire pie is like a cloud. A great nostalgic stop.

2312 Arkansas Highway 367 North
Bald Knob, Arkansas 72010
(501) 724-3996

My friend Melinda LaFevers is an author, re-enactor and general good egg. She's collected a lot of recipes over the years, including a handy cheese chiffon pie that can be augmented in so many ways.

MELINDA'S NO-BAKE CHEESE CHIFFON PIE

One eight-ounce package cream cheese, softened
½ pint heavy whipping cream
Sugar to taste, ½ to 1 cup (powdered or granulated is fine)
½ teaspoon vanilla flavoring
Graham cracker crust or your favorite pie crust
Optional: canned pie filling, fresh or canned fruit (blueberries, cherries, strawberries)

Prepare pie crust. Cream together cream cheese, sugar and vanilla. Whip cream and fold into cheese mixture. Refrigerate until set. If desired, top with pie filling or fresh or canned fruit before serving.

For a heavier pie and more of a cheese taste, use two packages of cream cheese. For a lighter fluffier pie, use a full pint of whipping cream. For a caramel cheese chiffon, boil an unopened can of sweetened condensed milk for three hours (make sure it stays covered with water or it could explode) let cool, and use in place of sugar.

THE BULLDOG DRIVE IN

The Bulldog Drive In was opened in 1978 by Bob Miller, who raised the money for his fledgling enterprise by working summers during high school and college on a pipeline. Other restaurants had operated in the building where he constructed his dream; they'd all failed, but Miller was determined to succeed. The Bulldog (the Bald Knob high school mascot) was also where Miller's wife, Lece, worked in high school.

The restaurant developed a following of local folks who were thrilled with a reasonably priced drive-in that offered pit barbecue, burgers and cheap plate-lunch specials.

Out-of-towners make the special stop in through the late spring and summer months because of a very special item—the restaurant's famed strawberry shortcake. But any time of year, there is pie – usually thick and creamy coconut and chocolate meringue pies as well as pecan and lemon icebox. Order your slice and have a seat.

3614 Highway 367
Bald Knob, Arkansas 72010
(501) 724-5195

FARMHOUSE CAFÉ

From time to time, at the bottom of the ever-changing specials board featuring such things as pot roast with potatoes and carrots, fried chicken with corn on the cob and PurpleHull peas, or chicken and dumplings with green beans, you'll see offered a nice, delightful lemon icebox pie.

133 US Highway 167 North
Bald Knob, Arkansas 72010
(501) 724-2393

BALD KNOB PHILLIPS 66 TRAVEL CENTER

You, yes you, can pocket one or more of the two-handed delights behind the counter at the travel center on US Highway 165 north of where it splits from US Highway 67 in the northeast Arkansas town of Bald Knob. The 24-hour a day convenience store and truck stop is a good place to grab a handpie any time, day or night.

The pies come in traditional flavors such as apple, chocolate, peach, peanut butter, sweet potato, coconut, and pecan, and more unusual varieties such as cherry cheesecake as well as fried S'mores pies filled with chocolate cream, marshmallow fluff and graham cracker bits.

142 US Highway 167
Bald Knob, Arkansas 72010
(501) 724-1385

TONYA'S FAMILY RESTAURANT

Tonya's Family Restaurant is the best game in town for fried pies, offered in so many flavors - peach, apple, cherry, pineapple, cocoa, coconut, chocolate, vanilla and banana. They're a good wrap-up to a meal of chicken and dressing or baby back ribs. Coconut cream pie is also sporadically available.

5162 Arkansas Highway 367 North
Bradford, Arkansas 72020
(501) 344-1234
Facebook.com/TonyasFamilyRestaurant

LACKEY'S SMOKEHOUSE BARBECUE

The purveyor of the north Delta's best-known chicken-filled tamales also offers fried pies. Scott Whitmire's barbecue and Clint Lackey's tamales are the perfect pair to bring people to Newport for lunch or dinner – and the savvy eater knows to bring a cooler to take some Lackey's tamales home for later. Check the counter to see if coconut cream pie is available as well.

601 Malcolm Avenue
Newport, Arkansas 72112
(870) 217-0228
Facebook.com/LackeysSmokeHouse

IMAD VILLAGE GRILL

This unusual eatery raises funding to help operate Newport's IMAD Village Community Center for youth. IMAD stands for "I'm Making A Difference." The grill started out as a food truck before moving into Newport's Village Mall in November 2017. It's a constantly evolving idea which runs a soul food buffet on Sundays as a donations-accepted operation where all the proceeds go towards the IMAD Summer Village Program. Selections include meatloaf, country fried steak, beans, greens, potatoes and more. The grill's regular menu of burgers, barbecue sandwiches, fried catfish and taco salads sometimes includes sweet potato pie.

2101 Malcolm Avenue inside Village Mall
Newport, Arkansas 72112
(870) 523-8814
Facebook.com/IMADVillageGrill

DAIRY KING

Get your fried pies hot or cold at Dairy King in Portia. The main dining spot in town offers hot strawberry cream cheese pies made to order. You'll also find cold fried pies in a basket by the register straight out of Ozark Kitchen in Cave City in flavors such as raisin, blueberry, chocolate and apple.

201 West Front Street
Walnut Ridge, Arkansas 72476
(870) 886-6301

RENEE'S CAFÉ

The old house atop the hill by the Black Rock bridge overlooks the edge of the Arkansas Delta. Inside, its wood paneled dinette and den are both packed with reclaimed booths and dining room tables. There's always a board full of specials, including three entrées items and a whole spread of vegetables.

There are always pies available by the slice in so many flavors: chocolate, coconut, pecan, lemon icebox, French silk, and if you're really lucky egg custard too.

3430 US Highway 63
Black Rock, Arkansas 72415
(870) 878-9283
Facebook.com/
MadJourneyCam

DORA'S SALE BARN CAFÉ

Listed in different places at Dora's Sale Barn Café and the Lavada Sale Barn Café, this restaurant tucked into the east end of an actual cattle sale barn offers breakfasts and lunches of substance to hungry diners. Purveyors of such delicacies as stuffed bell peppers and chocolate gravy on biscuits, the Sale Barn offers lunch and sometimes even breakfast buffets as well as menu service. Of note are the pies – apple, pumpkin, strawberry cream cheese, peanut butter, blueberry cream cheese and the like, that appear on the bar in individual bowls and saucers for easy enjoyment. Go back and have another.

706 Townsend Drive
Pocahontas, Arkansas 72455
(870) 248-0232
Facebook.com/DorasSaleBarnCafe

JUNCTION 166 CAFÉ

Vada Swann has been making pies for decades. She started out in the restaurant business in Poplar Bluff 65 years ago. "I waited the tables, I done the cooking and the serving," she cackled. I'd walked in one Friday morning on my search for pies and asked who was responsible for the pies. Mrs. Swann was asked to come out. She

brought with her Gabrielle Patterson, who admitted to being taught the art of making pies by Vada over the past ten years. The pie that had caught my eye was a lemon meringue with a gorgeously topped magazine-quality image I was all too happy to shoot.

Vada says the Junction 166 Café started out small, but over the decades it's been expanded repeatedly. The pie selection has always been hefty, and on any day there will be slices of coconut meringue, pecan and chocolate meringue in the case.

3071 US Highway 62
Pocahontas, Arkansas 72455
(870) 892-8756

HILLBILLY JUNCTION

Opened in the summer of 2017 by Janet and Ronald Barnett, this restaurant is becoming known for its seafood buffet and salad bar. If you're lucky fruit lattice pies will be on the counter. Get a slice of cherry. Pecan and fried pies are also available.

12859 Arkansas Highway 115
Maynard, Arkansas 72444
(870) 647-1324
Facebook.com/HillbillyJunction

PARKVIEW RESTAURANT

Corning is one of two county seats for Clay County (the other being Piggott to the east). It benefits from being the first town with any sort of facilities on the south side of the Missouri border. For many years, several hotels operated there for travelers coming into the state.

Of them, the Parkview has kept a strong clientele through the years. The restaurant was originally called the PanAm since it sat next to the Woods' family's PanAm service station and consisted of just the portion of the restaurant with the kitchen and lunch counter. The Parkview Tourist Court (later Rusty's Parkview Motel and Restaurant) was built in the 1950s.

The facility is commemorated in a series of postcards issued over the decades. One reads: Offering all conveniences to the traveling public. Twenty-eight rooms, tile baths, air-conditioning, telephone in every room, controlled heat, free television, Simmons Beauty Rest mattresses, free swimming pool. Beautiful city park adjoining for your pleasure. Restaurant and auto services next to motel. A really delightful place to stop.

The restaurant still offers the same country diner fare that kept it on the map all these years – including a special of a whole chicken that's dismembered, battered, fried and served in about 20 minutes. That in itself is a singular reason to visit. Then there's the pie – coconut cream pie that's tremendously rich and yellow and packed with shredded coconut on the bottom, with a toasted coconut sprinkling on its top cream.

1615 West Main Street
Corning, Arkansas 72422
(870) 857-6884

HEN HOUSE CAFÉ

Piggott is about as far north and east you can get in Arkansas. Parallel to the Missouri Bootheel, the town's biggest claim to fame is for its connection with Ernest Hemingway, who married native Pauline Pfeiffer in 1927, moved in with her parents in a two-story house in the town and wrote goodly portions of *A Farewell To Arms* in their barn out back. Today, visitors from all over the world visit the Hemingway-Pfeiffer Museum and Educational Center run by Arkansas State University.

The town square is mostly one small park, but across from that park there's an adorable restaurant decked out like a farmhouse on the inside. The Hen House Café opened in 2016 with a suitable farmhouse style menu, with a Hen House grilled chicken plate, farmhouse hamburger steak and some nice hefty burgers and salads.

The pies are whole or by the slice, and there's usually a meringue pie sitting on an old scale by the register. While there are usually a range of slices from Reece's peanut butter to lemon to chocolate, the coconut meringue appears to be the local favorite, and on my most recent visit I was startled when I asked about the sort of pies and my waitress offered to have a pie made for me while I waited. I'm interested to see how this adorable restaurant manages to fare over the years to come.

260 West Court Street
Piggott, Arkansas 72454
(870) 634-6578
Facebook.com/HenHouseCafe13

BATTEN'S BAKERY

Batten's Bakery may have the strangest culinary lineage of the Arkansas Delta. The Paragould mainstay has been around since 1954, which makes it the oldest bakery still operating in the Upper Delta. Albert Batten started making doughnuts and selling them on Saturday and Sunday mornings. Mr. Batten would get up early in the morning and make doughnuts and sell them until they were gone. Customers say he didn't believe in day-olds, so if a regular came into the kitchen garage late in the day, he was apt to throw in a few extra. Over the years, the offerings expanded to cakes, pastries and such. A few individuals even claim that Elvis Presley was once spotted there downing a bearclaw — though the veracity of such a statement is questionable. Mr. Batten also made doughnuts for local grocery stores to sell, and his golden rings became the Greene County standard.

When Mr. Batten's health waned, he passed it on to an employee. Bonnie Abbott had worked there since she was a young woman and never worked at another establishment. She bought it in 1980 and ran it another 20 years. In the 2000s, Leon Johnson bought the place and kept it going another four before putting the place up for sale.

Enter Mike and Bridgette Batten. The couple worked in the corporate world; he was a design engineer, she was a director of systems management. While in the area in 2004 they learned the bakery, which just happened to bear their last name, was available. It seemed like Providence, so soon the younger Battens had themselves a shop. They've managed to collect many of the recipes used by both Albert Batten and by Bonnie Abbott, and they turn out a goodly number of baked goods six days a week for the citizens of Paragould.

Batten's Bakery offers a singular traditional pies I've never found at another Arkansas retail establishment – a chocolate old fashioned handpie filled with cocoa, butter and sugar rather than custard or pudding. The flavor of this pie, its flaky consistency and its density all remind me of the good things about growing up in Arkansas. Bridgette says the recipe comes from her grandmother.

Batten's offers several other varieties of fried pies, and in the morning you can have one warmed up with your coffee. Doughnuts are, understandably, the hot item at breakfast, but the restaurant has also become known for huge danishes, fried cinnamon rolls and apple fritters are large enough to fit a half-dozen box by themselves.

The Battens may not be the original Battens who made Batten's the bakery for Paragould, but they continue a tradition that dates back nearly 60 years.

1735 Paragould Plaza
Paragould, Arkansas 72450
(870) 236-7810
Facebook.com/BattensBakery

KISS THE COOK

When I mentioned I'd be writing another book on pie in Arkansas to the Battens, they both told me to go check out Kiss the Cook. I'm glad I did.

Libby Glasco began the operation on US Highway 49 south of town in 2001. It's a combination café and take-and-make place with excellent pimento cheese and a really nice brisket sandwich. Classic pies such as coconut cream, peanut butter and pecan often appear in the cases, but it's the singular lemon lime icebox pie that caught my attention – a perfectly tart and bright pie to extinguish the heat of three-digit temperature days in the heart of summer.

5301 US Highway 49 South Suite A (in the Carriage Hill Plaza)
Paragould, Arkansas 72450
(870) 335-2665
KissTheCookYum.com

NANCY'S BAKING COMPANY

You don't expect to find pie in most coffee shops, much less a frozen yogurt joint. But that's exactly where you can find slices of freshly made pies in Paragould. Nancy's Baking Company is represented with a case full of slices at Swirlz Frozen Yogurt and Caribou Coffee Company on the west side of town. The slices come in a range

from chocolate meringue to strawberry delight, coconut cream, lemon meringue, pecan and even raisin. Nancy's also makes small raisin, apple, cherry and chocolate handpies by the dozen. Whole pies available on order.

Nancy's Baking Company
2709 West Kingshighway
(at Swirlz of Paragould)
Paragould, Arkansas 72450
(870) 236-6866
SwirlzOfParagould.com

GINA'S PLACE

Tucked into the far side of Fountain Square off Highland, you'll discover a great lunchroom for plated lunches and nifty sandwiches.

Ann Maynard and Glen McKay started Ann's Restaurant in 1983. Their daughter Gina worked there through high school but left to go to business school and start her career. When her mom decided to retire in September 1997, Gina and her brother Vernon suggested they buy the place and take it over – but Ann said no. She didn't want them to go through the strife of running the restaurant.

Another person purchased the place, but went back to Ann a month later and said it wasn't going to work, so Gina and Vernon McKay bought it and took it over immediately.

Today, Gina is the sole proprietor. She decided after Vernon left to rename it Gina's Place, but her eatery still serves much of the same menu, along with a fine selection of pies. Every day five pies – peanut butter, Key lime, lemon icebox, pecan and Turtle – are offered, and daily pie choices sometimes include coconut, apple, cherry or whatever the cooks decide to whip up that day.

2005 East Highland Suite 109
Jonesboro, Arkansas 72401
(870) 910-3900
EatAtGinas.com

BISTRO ON THE RIDGE

Bistro on the Ridge offers a variety of catering favorites, sandwiches and a case full of pie, including several meringue pies in the flavors of chocolate, chocolate peanut butter, coconut, peanut butter and lemon.

914 Southwest Drive
Jonesboro, Arkansas 72401
(870) 268-6780

CHEF'S IN

This breakfast and lunch shop operates Sunday through Thursday. Pie is almost always part of the lunch buffet, usually in chocolate or coconut cream varieties but also in seasonal varieties such as strawberry. If the raisin cream pie is available, get it.

105 Burke Avenue
Jonesboro, Arkansas 72401
(870) 934-8962

GODSEY'S GRILL

Around the corner Main Street you'll find Godsey's Grill, a happening bar and grill that spreads across two storefronts. On the weekend, Godsey's offers a number of housemade pies, including the popular peanut butter in its chocolate crust. There are also off-site made pies offered daily, including a caramel apple pie, Snicker bar pie and a bourbon pecan pie.

226 South Main Street
Jonesboro, Arkansas 72401
(870) 336-1988
MyGodseys.com

Godsey's Grill Songbird
3800 East Johnson Avenue
Jonesboro, Arkansas 72401
(870) 336-0280

FANCY FLOUR BAKERY

Out on East Nettleton, between Caraway and Stadium, there's a bakery on the north side of the road that, when you enter, will knock you off your feet with the scent of sugar. Fancy Flour Bakery specializes in cupcakes and cake balls but also offers a fine variety of fruit pies to order.

2606 East Nettleton Avenue
Jonesboro, Arkansas 72401
(870) 336-9869
FancyFlourBakery.com

DEMO'S SMOKEHOUSE

There are two locations for Demo's Smokehouse – one on US Highway 49 on the northeast side of town, the other on Church Street just north of Highland. The barn-like barbecue joint serves St. Louis style ribs, smoked chicken and fried pies in a variety of flavors, golden and dusted with sugar. Pecan pie slices are also available.

1851 South Church Street
Jonesboro, Arkansas 72401
(870) 935-6633
DemosSmokehouse.com

4115 East Johnson Avenue
Jonesboro, Arkansas 72401
(870) 203-9944

SUE'S KITCHEN

The peanut butter pies from Sue's Kitchen has such a lovely flavor of honey to it. It's just like whenever I used to mix up peanut butter and honey to put on sandwiches when I was a kid. I know for certain why Vincent Price love that pie.

Sue Robinson Williams was a local caterer who'd been covering the Jonesboro area since 1967. She decided to open her restaurant in 1985, but in 1994 she decided to turn back to catering and went with serving up her good eats alongside her son John for several years. In 2010, John decided to revive the restaurant in his mother's name in the old Church Street Station building, which has served as a post office, a courthouse annex and a jail over its lifespan. Today, the restaurant sprawls across the cavernous main floor of the building, with large windows from the dining room on the south side and a long lunch counter on the north side. The area that once served as the downtown post office is now the counter area for the register.

In addition to Vincent Price's favorite peanut butter pie, there's also a magnificent pink lemonade pie that's become pretty well known for both its beauty and flavor, a popular pick-up for bridal and baby showers in Jonesboro.

524 South Church Street
Jonesboro, Arkansas 72401
(870) 972-6000
SuesKitchenJonesboro.com

PENNY'S PLACE

Down US Highway 49 south of Jonesboro, a few miles before you get to the cross-over of Arkansas Highway 14 at Waldenburg, you'll find the village of Weiner. Penny's Place, the residential diner that serves these parts, is a place where you'll find farmers, grain elevator workers and fishermen converge for breakfast and lunch.

The restaurant started off as J & D's Dairy Bar, which was built by Jackie and Darrel Bryant across from the rice gin back in 1972. The Bryants ran the place until 2004, when it was purchased by Penny Sitzer. Penny is known for smoking meat out back and for large cinnamon rolls – but from time to time you can also find a lemon icebox pie on the whiteboard. Unlike other versions of this delicacy, this one's almost the consistency of cheesecake, thick and blonde and substantial. Penny has also been known to turn out raisin, coconut meringue and strawberry pies as well.

210 South Van Buren (US Highway 49)
Weiner, Arkansas 72479
(870) 684-2260
Facebook.com/Penny10101

GAVIN'S DOWNTOWN

About the only thing open on the downtown square in Harrisburg save the Poinsett County Courthouse is Gavin's. The restaurant has become popular with Jonesboro natives looking for a fantastic steak.

The homemade strawberry pie is on my short list of favorite pies anywhere – a shortbread crust with a cream cheese layer, fresh sugared strawberries and dairy whipped cream. It's all that you want and get in the Bulldog Restaurant's famed strawberry shortcake, but unlike that delight, this one is always available. Absolutely perfect.

117 North Main Street
Harrisburg, Arkansas 72432
(870)578-0385
GavinsDowntown.com

RICKI'S DINER

Ricki's Diner is a burger and country food restaurant on Arkansas Highway 1 just south of Harrisburg with several pies on the menu. The sweet potato pie is earthy and old-fashioned, as if it were straight from the garden.

403 South Illinois Street
Harrisburg, Arkansas 72432
(870) 271-5001

LITTLE PIGGY BBQ

Cream pies are available as choices for catering from Little Piggy BBQ in Harrisburg, where chocolate and coconut cream are favorites.

500 Normal Avenue
Harrisburg, Arkansas 72432
(870) 680-7923

PARKER PIONEER HOMESTEAD

Just south of Harrisburg every October, a recreated 19th century town is brought to life. Parker Pioneer Homestead is a collection of buildings covering the time period, with houses, businesses and farm facilities operated by four generations of the Parker family. During the annual festival on this farm, visitors can experience harvest on the farm, including processing corn for cornmeal, sorghum plants for molasses, and more.

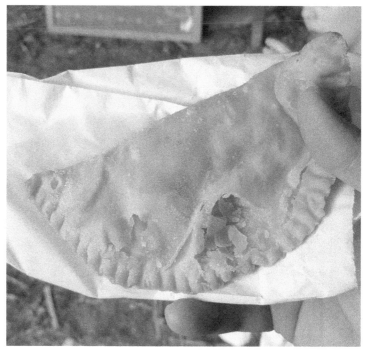

Along with the traveling magician's show, printing office and general store, there are edible delights, including kettle corn, homemade cakes, pork rinds, soup beans, and fried pies. The pies in particular are fried throughout the festival and served hot.

16944 Homestead Road
Harrisburg, Arkansas 72432
(870) 578-2699
ParkerHomestead.com

Shalom Dunn

I've participated since 1991 in the world's largest medieval re-enactment group, the Society for Creative Anachronism. Through the organization, I've met a lot of very talented individuals and incredible cooks, including a gentleman by the name of Shalom Dunn, who shares this unusual but appropriate-for-Arkansas pie recipe that local members of the SCA absolutely adore.

BACON DATE PIE

1 cup dark corn syrup
3 eggs
1 cup sugar
2 tablespoons butter, melted
2 teaspoon pure vanilla extract
1 cup chopped extra crispy bacom
1 cup chopped dates
1 (9-inch) unbaked OR frozen**
deep-dish pie crust

Preheat oven to 350°F. Mix corn syrup, eggs, sugar, butter and vanilla using a spoon. Stir in bacon and dates. Pour filling into pie crust. Bake on center rack of oven for 60 to 70 minutes. Pie is done when center heat reaches 200 degrees. Tap center of pie lightly – it will spring back when done. Cool for two hours on wire rack before serving. Garnish with fresh whipped cream and crispy strips of bacon.

**To use prepared frozen pie crust: Place cookie sheet in oven and preheat oven as directed. Pour filling into frozen crust and bake on pre-heated cookie sheet.

KIMBERLY'S

Kimberly's only serves lunch (and the occasional Tuesday night dinner), but the little place on Lockard Street offers a lovely array of desserts, including a delectable cherry cream pie.

200 North Lockard Street
Blytheville, Arkansas 72315
(870) 824-6630

BENNY BOB'S BBQ

The city of Blytheville has become pretty well known in Arkansas food circles for its dedication to the pig meat sandwich. Several legendary purveyors are keen on pork barbecue, sometimes served on a bun and sometimes served on white bread. Of these joints, just one offers pie. Benny Bob's BBQ sells its pies fried and suggests a scoop of ice cream to go along with the piping hot pockets in flavors of apple, peach or chocolate.

847 East Main Street
Blytheville, Arkansas 72315
(870) 763-0505

SANDBAR GRILLE

Harry and Janet Keatts opened the Sandbar Grille in Osceola in 2007 in the former Ford's BBQ location along Arkansas Highway 140. The Sandbar's lagniappe is a small cornbread muffin served with butter. The Angus beef steaks are hand cut, the white beans with cornbread is a coveted comfort dish, and everything from the chicken salad to the sweet poppyseed dressing is homemade.

The Keatts also have a magnificent collection of pies, including chocolate and co-conut and a wispy light lemon icebox pie that's just darling.

1100 West Keiser Avenue
Osceola, Arkansas 72370
(870) 563-5700

WILSON CAFÉ

Locals will tell you that there's always been a tavern in the heart of Wilson. It's had many names and many proprietors, but the little dining spot right on the town square has been going on and off for more than 100 years. The Wilson Café operating in that building today carries the tradition on -- and yes, it's still referred to by locals as The Tavern.

The little Mississippi River town along the Great River Road is named after R. E. Lee Wilson, a county resident who traded his late father's cleared farmland for timberland, then held onto the property and started what would eventually become a company town. He built a sawmill, and by 1886 there was also a company store and residences. The Wilson Tavern was opened sometime around the turn of the century.

In 1925, R. E. Lee Wilson's similarly named son returned from his honeymoon to England with a vision of what the town of Wilson should look like. The new buildings that went up during this time were of Tudor influence, and older buildings were retrofitted to match this new brown-and-cream wood-and-brick style. Every building took on this veneer, including the local department store, post office, bank, gas station and grocery store. Today, these buildings still stand.

In what was once Wilson Tavern (and many other things), a restaurant now operates as the Wilson Café. What's beyond the doors of this cottage is a surprisingly updated menu with a locavore commitment, thanks to Chef Joe Cartwright. The Memphis-born culinarian was raised in West Memphis, who attended school at Arkansas State University as a music major and began his cooking career at Lazzari Italian Oven in Jonesboro. Cartwright worked his way up through the Memphis food scene with stints at the Mesquite Chop House and Spindini before landing the newly reopened Wilson Café.

As always, locals pack the place out -- but now they're joined by others who come from Memphis, Jonesboro and even further away.

The pies are the same sort of pies you'd expect from a family cook, but with the touches of a well-trained chef. The sweet potato pie is perfectly spiced, and the chocolate chess pie has a gorgeously dark flavor strong on cocoa and butter notes. Both are served with hand-whipped cream. .

2 North Jefferson Street
Wilson, Arkansas 72395
(870) 655-0222
EatAtWilson.com

CLARA'S MIDWAY CAFÉ

The Midway Café dates back generations in downtown Tyronza. Today, the restaurant bears the name Clara's Midway Café after owner Clara Green. The restaurant still bears its original wood paneling and is festooned with photos of Tyronza's past.

Clara and her staff offer pies every day, ranging from Pineapple Dream to lemon icebox, chocolate, strawberry and pumpkin. The café's Millionaire pie is dotted with bits of peaches and pineapple with a touch of cherry in its firm yet not-too-sweet cream layer.

153 North Main Street
Tyronza, Arkansas 72386
(870) 487-2090

NO-BAKE LEMON ICEBOX COOKIE PIE

This is a recipe I came up with as I improvised a new way to make lemon icebox pie.

6 ounces cookies (lemon, lemon sandwich, ginger snaps, graham cracker, oatmeal, your choice), crushed
1 stick butter, melted
1-14 ounce can sweetened condensed milk
1-8 ounce block cream cheese, room temperature
1/3 cup lemon juice

Beat the cookies into crumbs, then fold in melted butter. Press into pie pan. Blend all other ingredients together and pour into crust. Chill two hours, slice and serve.

BOURBON STREET STEAKHOUSE

A greyhound track may seem an odd place to find pie, but once you ride the escala-tors to the Bourbon Street Steakhouse within Southland Gaming and Racing in West Memphis, you'll agree it's worth the stop. The restaurant has excellent prime rib and crab cakes The coup de resistance comes in the wedges of pie available at the end of the meal – a Key lime firm as cheesecake, and a bourbon pecan pie that should come with an alcohol content warning.

1550 Ingram Boulevard inside Southland Gaming and Racing
West Memphis, Arkansas 72301
(800) 467-6182

RON'S FAMILY AFFAIR RESTAURANT

This downtown joint serves up classic soul food in West Memphis, like chitlins, turnip greens, smothered pork chops and gumbo. The restaurant is one of the few places left in Arkansas where you can get butter roll – a pan-baked dough saturated in sugar and butter . A variety of cakes and pies are offered, including sweet potato.

526 East Broadway Street
West Memphis, Arkansas 72301
(870) 735-3368

BIG JOHN'S/TACKER'S SHAKE SHACK

Loretta and John Tacker started a Tastee Freeze in Marion in 1977. Big John, whose nickname came from his size, stature and heart, was a personality to be reckoned with in the town, and soon folks started referring to the place by his name. The Tastee Freeze became Big John's Pizza, then it became the Shake Shack (John's sister Sherry had a Shake Shack in Tyronza). Eventually it came to be known as Big John's Shake Shack, and sometimes Tacker's Shake Shack. John died in 2005, but Loretta Tacker keeps it going. She works alongside her children and even one of her grandsons in this three-generation eatery.

John had a one-half pound burger he came up with called the Big John. It's still on the menu right next to country ham sandwiches, catfish, chicken, barbecue and milkshakes. Frankly, Big John's Shake Shack serves just about everything.

If there's a type of pie you like, this Shake Shack probably has it. When you enter you'll see fried peach, cherry, chocolate, apple and caramel apple fried pies in wedges sitting in a case by the register. There's a standing case full of whole pies, and slices in a case under that. Those choices don't include the icebox pies in the back, or the hot fudge pie cooked to order.

Loretta makes pecan pies from the nuts that fall from the trees in her own yard, and she's been making lattice-topped pies since her grandmother showed her how when she was a kid. That hot fudge pie recipe comes from Loretta's friend Jeannie Oher and has been on the menu since the 1980s. Loretta's friend Butch convinced her to start making fried pies back in the 1990s.

Out of the hundreds of restaurants and thousands of pies I've shot and tasted, I can honestly say I have never come across another Tang pie. The tongue-sparking icebox creation, flavored with the powdered beverage mix reportedly consumed by astronauts, is the craziest version of flavor you can get in an orange dreamsicle-style pie.

409 East Military Road
Marion, Arkansas 72364
(870) 739-3943

MIKE'S FAMILY RESTAURANT

At the corner of Arkansas Highways 1 and 306, there's a green roofed building with its row of rocking chairs out front. Mike's Family Restaurant was originally opened in 1993 by Mike Linam, who just thought having a store to stop at along the highway was a good idea. The restaurant began as a little grocery with a snack bar inside, but business grew and it became a lot for Mike, his wife and daughter to handle. Eventually he closed the store and concentrated on the restaurant.

Mike's is known for great steaks and catfish (all U.S. pond raised), for sandwiches and for great desserts – including t homemade pies in chocolate, coconut, pecan, apple, cherry, lemon icebox, strawberry and whatever else is requested.

49 Old Military Road West
Colt, Arkansas 72326
(870) 633-8916
Facebook.com/MikesFamilyRestaurant

THE NEST

In the Cherry Valley community, there's a new restaurant called The Nest that's serving rectangular fried pies in such flavor as lemon, chocolate and pecan. Slices of sweet potato and apple pies often appear on the menu as well. Look for the little gray building right next to the Dollar General

3790 Arkansas Highway 1
Cherry Valley, Arkansas 72324
(870) 318-1341

ANN'S COUNTRY KITCHEN

The buffet at Ann's Country Kitchen in Patterson has a rotating set of features that include country greens, beans and everything in-between, you'll often find meringue and pecan pies on the menu.

102 South Main
Patterson, Arkansas 72123
(870) 731-0004

WHITE RIVER CAFÉ

The White River Café in Augusta showcases ribeye steak six nights a week. The lunch specials vary from beef stroganoff to poppy seed chicken to lemon pepper pork chops, and peanut butter pie is a common dessert in the rotation. Fried pies are also available.

109 South 2nd Street
Augusta, Arkansas 72006
(870) 347-1101

GENE'S BARBECUE

Gene's Barbecue lies at the center of that crossroads, not just by highway miles but by services rendered and goods offered. From the pickles on the counter to the catfish on the table to the celebrated offerings in the back room, you just can't get more Delta than this.

Gene's started out as a place called Sweet Pea's Pit Barbecue, opened in 1971 by Lewis DePriest. He sold the business to his brother Gene in 1994 and it's been Gene's ever since. In the fall and winter months the restaurant serves as a jumping off point for dozens of duck hunters. And in 2005, it became the go-to place for people who arrived in Brinkley before setting off into the Big Woods to find the elusive Ivory-Billed Woodpecker. Today, Gene's offers a burger named for the legendary bird, as well as delectable catfish and hearty breakfasts. The pies on the menu are Flywheel Pies, served up at the end of the meal.

1107 Arkansas Highway 17
Brinkley, Arkansas 72021
(870) 734-9965

MS. LENA'S PIES

Mrs. Lena Rice was well known for her pies, both whole and fried, which she made in her little house beside Arkansas Highway 33 in DeValls Bluff. After she passed, her daughter Viv took up the mantle to keep the pie tradition going. She and her brother Carl would get up early every Saturday morning and make up to eight hundred fried pies. They'd make up the filling, and then Viv would make up the dough and Carl would roll it out. They'd bake through the shop's opening at 9:00 a.m. Twelve hours out of every Saturday they made the little pies, turning out six flavors that would be picked up singly, in dozens and in big boxes by people who came from up to a couple hours' drive in every direction to pick them up.

The regular flavors were apricot, apple, chocolate, coconut and peach, with other flavors such as chocolate cherry (woodpecker), cherry rotating for that sixth choice. Each came wrapped in a paper napkin, and if you ordered a half dozen or more, they came in a clamshell box with the lid carefully and barely closed with just a piece of masking tape. The pies were almost always still hot and fresh because so many people came through that Viv and Carl could barely keep up with the orders.

Viv also made whole pies, and her half-and-half chocolate coconut pie became a thing of legend, one side a fantastic coconut meringue with creamy filling and flaky bits of coconut throughout, the other a smooth sweet chocolate with a traditional meringue.

Making eight hundred fried pies is hard, and though Viv's daughter Kim joined her in the kitchen, it got to be too much. Fried pie days are rare, and if they're offered, get a box. But still go when they're not out, because all those whole pies are magnificent, too.

2885 Highway 33 South
DeValls Bluff, Arkansas 72041
(870) 998-1385

FAMILY PIE SHOP and CRAIG BROTHERS BAR-B-Q CAFÉ

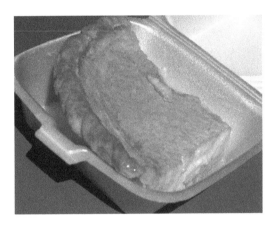

Mary Thomas went to be with the Lord on April 16th of 2016. For decades before, she had been cooking up pies several days a week in a shed by her house across the street from the famed Craig Bros. Café. Diners would enjoy their sandwich or ribs and then scoot across the street to buy a slice or whole pie of meringue or egg custard from Ms. Mary.

Today, the folks at Craig Bros. are still selling pies, and I've been told they're still coming from across the street. You see, family's still making pie in the shed marked with spray paint, keeping Ms. Mary's tradition going. Get those slices at Craig's when you pick up a sandwich.

15 Walnut Street
DeValls Bluff,
Arkansas 72041
(870) 998-2616

CR SMALLS AND COMPANY

Palestine has long needed a good restaurant, and for the past couple of years it has found one in CR Smalls and Company. The metal framed building is decked out within in country girl chic, with a burger of the week every week. The pies range from peanut butter chocolate to pecan and even Boston cream pie.

105 Saint Francis Country Road 815
Palestine, Arkansas 72372
(870) 630-8222
Facebook.com/CRSmallsCo

HURLEY HOUSE CAFÉ

Joe and Shirley Hurley purchased the old Carol's Kitchen at the corner of US Highways 63 and 70 in Hazen back in 2003 and put the family name on it. Today the Hurley House Café is a popular local spot for catfish, big breakfasts and tasty burgers. The Hurleys offer Flywheel pies for dessert in a variety of flavors, from blackberry to apple and even chocolate, as the only dessert.

92 South Maple Street
Hazen, Arkansas 72064
(870) 255-4679

NICK'S BAR-B-Q AND CATFISH

E.C. Ferguson opened Nick's in 1972. Though he passed away two decades ago, his family continues to operate the popular restaurant. His widow, Dorothy, is in her nineties and still making the rib rub and sauce. His grandson Clay Waliski and Ferguson's sons Todd and Craig run the business today. The shop serves fried catfish fillets, chopped and sliced pork and beef, ribs, and smoked chicken as well as yellow cheese dip, fried green tomatoes and phenomenal onion rings. The joint sells hot Flywheel peach, chocolate, coconut apricot and apple fried pies. Nick's also sells a peanut butter pie and what it lovingly refers to as Grandma's Homemade Pecan pie, which is wrapped in plastic and sold at the register to take home.

1012 Bobby L. Glover Highway
Carlisle, Arkansas 72024
(870) 552-3887
NicksBQ.com

PRUETT'S BAR-B-QUE AND CATFISH

Just off Arkansas Highway 31 in Lonoke, Pruett's offers catfish and one of the best fried bologna sandwiches for miles around. The chocolate and coconut meringue pies are excellent

108 East 8th Street
Lonoke, Arkansas 72086
(501) 676-2622

Ray's Dairy Maid once stood alongside US Highway 49 in the Barton community, to the west of Helena-West Helena. It was the provenance of Nana Deane Cavette, who ran the place and whose coconut-pecan pie earned her some renown, especially when Alton Brown shared this very recipe for the delight in his book *Feasting on Asphalt: River Road Run*.

NANA DEANE'S COCONUT PECAN PIE

10 1/2 ounces granulated sugar
3 large whole eggs
2 ounces unsalted butter, melted
4 ounces buttermilk
3 ounces pecans, chopped (approximately 3/4 cup)
1 tablespoon all-purpose flour
3 ounces sweetened coconut flakes
1 teaspoon vanilla extract
Pinch salt
1 pie crust (pre-baked)

Preheat oven to 350 degrees.

In a large mixing bowl, combine the sugar, eggs, melted butter, buttermilk, coconut, pecans, flour, vanilla and salt. Pour into a 9-inch pre-baked pie crust.

Bake for 45 minutes or until the pie is golden brown and the center is barely set.

Cool for 40-45 minutes before serving.

FIRST LADY'S APPLE PIE

Arkansas First Lady Susan Hutchinson's glorious apple pie is a delight enjoyed on special occasions. This beautiful golden pie was served on the announcement of the initial Arkansas Food Hall of Fame announcement at the Governor's Mansion.

Crust

2 cups flour

2/3 cup + 2 tablespoons Crisco

3-4 tablespoons ice water

Sift two cups of flour into a mixing bowl. Add shortening and criss cross with two table knifes until blended. Add ice water slowly until the mixture has the consistency of Play Doh. Using your hands, form a ball with the dough. Lay on a flat surface and roll out with rolling pin to flatten. Carefully lift dough and place in bottom of baking pie pan. Repeat this process for the top layer of crust for the pie and set aside.

Filling

1 stick butter

3 tablespoons flour

½ cup brown sugar

½ cup sugar

2 tablespoons vanilla

A dash of cinnamon

8 Granny Smith® Apples

Preheat oven to 350 degrees F. Add butter to a skillet on medium heat and melt. Add flour, brown sugar, sugar, vanilla and cinnamon to the skillet and blend together. Remove from heat and allow to cool slightly.

Slice apples and place in a bowl. Pour mixture over apples, coating each slice thoroughly. Pour into pie pan.

Carefully lay top crust over the top of apples, making sure to pinch the bottom and top crusts together with your fingers. Pinch off any excess crust. Bake at 350 degrees for about one hour or until crust is golden brown.

ROSIE'S DINER

Soul food is always on the menu at Rosie's Diner in Helena-West Helena, where neckbones and candied yams are the star. The relatively new eatery run by Rosie Moss and Kat Carter offers a daily lunch special that could be anything from fried pork chops to ribs, oysters on the half shell to liver and onions. When pie is available, it is sweet potato, and it's the perfect way to wrap up a good hearty stick-to-your-ribs lunch. Butter roll also makes the rounds at Rosie's and is worth your time.

303 Valley Drive
Helena, Arkansas 72342
(870) 228-5115
Facebook.com/RosiesDiner16

BENDI'S DINER

In the heart of the Arkansas Delta, not far south of Interstate 40, Bendi's Diner serves breakfast and plate lunches to crowds. The eatery, located on the east side of the small town, also offers doughnuts and deli meats. Its contributions for this book are in the area of fried pies, which it sells in a variety of Flywheel flavors.

101 North 6th Street
Clarendon, Arkansas 72029
(870) 747-1447

THE WILLOWS

The Willows has been DeWitt's go-to for family gatherings since 1988. In 2016, several members of the Carter family purchased the restaurant and are now making a go of it as a combination country/soul/Cajun style restaurant.

Roy and Patsy Carter, along with daughter Tammy Pisani and her husband Chris, and with daughter Regina Scarbrough and her husband Russell, are reviving the longstanding restaurant with a refreshed menu packed with both classics and new interpretations.

One thing that's close to the original Willows tradition are the pies. Strawberry and blueberry cream pies are common at the restaurant, as are glazed apple handpies.

1306 South Whitehead Drive
DeWitt, Arkansas 72042
(870) 946-1055
Facebook.com/Willows72042

DELTA GRILL

There are out-of-the-way places we sometimes find by taking a side route or turning off the interstate. But Elaine's position between the Mississippi and Arkansas Rivers south of Barton makes it one place you can't just end up at, not without intent.

It is worth the drive down from Helena or Marianna. Elaine is a primary location on the Delta Heritage Trail State Park route, and it's recently started to garner attention as the Birdhouse Capital of the World.

On the main downtown drive, you'll find the Delta Grill. Opened in 1957, it has served generations of Elaine residents and duck hunters who come through each fall and winter. It does a plate lunch special, offers burgers and fries and every night does a fish fry. Pie slices are almost always available in chocolate, lemon or coconut meringue, or in pecan.

The fried pies at Elaine Grill are made off-site but fried as you order. My particular choice on my first visit of strawberry was excellent – sugar-packed fresh berries wrapped in ample crust. Other flavors are also available.

219 Main Street
Elaine, Arkansas 72333
(870) 827-6325

Stuttgart, Arkansas carries the dual moniker of Duck and Rice Capital of the World. While I don't have a recipe for duck pie, I do have this rice cream pie recipe from *Talk About Good Cooks*, an old cookbook published in the late 1970s by the Southland Women's Club.

RICE CREAM PIE
Submitted by Mrs. J. R. Haynes of Hazen

1 package vanilla pudding and pie filling
2 ¼ cups milk
3 egg whites
1/3 cup sugar
3 egg yolks
1 baked 9-inch pie shell
1 cup cooked rice

Prepare pudding mix as directed on package, only instead of 2 cups milk use 2 ¼ cups, add 1/3 cup sugar and the three beaten egg yolks, when pudding has boiled and thickened add 1 cup cooked rice. Mix and turn into pie shell, make meringue from the egg whites. Top pie and bake well until lightly brown.

COUNTRY STYLE EATERY

Nadine Bryant runs the Country Style Eatery on Michigan Avenue on the north side of Stuttgart. It's exactly what it says on the tin – a place to get good country vittles. That includes pie, in the form of a buttery buttermilk custard. If it's on the menu, get it. Also the best place to get chicken and waffles in the Grand Prairie.

111 East Michigan Street
Stuttgart, Arkansas 72160
(870) 456-1836

LOS LOCOS

While in Stuttgart, be on the lookout for an orange food truck. This place specializes in great tacos and Mexican fare but also goes full-American with desserts. Look for fried apricot pies, individual lime cream pies and even non-pie pumpkin pie shaved ice on the rotating specials. Delivery available.

106 East 17th Street (location may vary)
Stuttgart, Arkansas 72160
(870) 659-8285

KIBB'S BBQ

Going to go get some Kibb's BBQ sandwiches or ribs? When you step up to the window, whether it's outside at the window surrounded by hand-painted signs or within in the tight dining area, be sure to ask for them to fry you a couple of pies. Peach and apple go well with the spicy sauce.

1102 East Harrison Street
Stuttgart, Arkansas 72160
(870) 673-2072

NO BAKE PUMPKIN PIE
Mona Dixon

1 16 oz. can pure pumpkin(not the pie mix)
1 can sweetened condensed milk
1 large box or 2 small boxes instant French vanilla or cheesecake pudding
1/2 carton non-dairy whipped topping
3/4 tsp pumpkin pie spice (I usually add a bit of extra cinnamon)

Mix all ingredients together and pour into prepared graham cracker crust. Top with more whipped topping and/or with chopped nuts. Refrigerate til set. This can be made with gluten-free pudding and gluten-free graham cracker crust.

CHARLOTTE'S EATS AND SWEETS

On the edge of the Arkansas Delta, not far from Little Rock, you'll find the farming community of Keo. There's not much in the town, but in a 1920s building a block off Highway 165, you'll find Charlotte's Eats and Sweets.

Its proprietor, Charlotte Bowls, has gained a reputation for creating some of the most beloved pies in the South. She, her daughters and her extended family of employees, begin baking before sunrise.

Charlotte's regularly offers caramel, chocolate and coconut cream pies. Other pies, such as egg custard and lemon meringue, are baked on particular days. The shop only opens for lunch, and by eleven each morning, customers are waiting. Some are locals. Others come from further afield, drawn in by tales of great pie.

But Charlotte's Eats and Sweets wasn't supposed to be about pie. It was a short-term situation Charlotte Bowls got herself into back in 1993. The building, which used to house a pharmacy, was still full of the furniture and stuff the previous owner had left behind more than a decade before. There wasn't much room, and she had to do a lot of clearing out before getting enough space for a tiny kitchen and counter together.

The folks in Keo were grateful for a good spot to grab a bite to eat, and they encouraged Charlotte to expand her menu. She worked too on clearing out the pharmacy front to back and utilizing every bit of room in the building… and as she cleared it out, the crowd just continued to fill every seat, day after day.

Today, Charlotte's Eats and Sweets still packs a crowd most days. Some folks have asked Charlotte why she doesn't just make more pie. She'll tell you, she'll only make enough pie to fill as many crusts as will fit on her tables and in her oven each day. Every day, every slice is gone before the doors open.

If you know you want to go and have a feeling you can't make it in time for the doors to open, I suggest placing your pie order to go, like the locals do. Don't forget to ask for your pie.

290 Main Street
Keo, Arkansas 72046
(501) 842-2123

On many a November day, along tree lined roadsides and across orchard-clothed flatlands, you may see people of all ages engaging in a particular rite of autumn. Each man, each woman, each grandparent or child gazes at the grounds, bends over and picks up a handful of brown ovoid nuts and places them in whatever they manage to utilize to carry such a bounty.

Pecans are native to Arkansas. They were highly valued by Native Americans, who traded and consumed them. Spanish explorers thought they were another sort of walnut and called them nueces, or "fruit of the walnut." They're a great source of protein, and somewhat easier to crack than walnuts.

Pecan trees are common across the state, and you'll see them here and there. I even have one in my backyard, though the squirrels seem to reap the bounty the tree offers before the nuts hit the ground.

BROWN SUGAR PECAN PIE

2 eggs, beaten
2 sticks (1/2 pound) butter, melted
1 cup light brown sugar
1/4 cup sugar (the white stuff)
1 teaspoon vanilla
1 tablespoon all-purpose flour
1 cup chopped pecans
1/2 cup pecan halves
1 blind baked flour pastry pie shell (store-bought is acceptable, too)

Heat oven to 350 degrees.

Beat the heck out of the eggs. Pour in the melted butter, both sugars and the vanilla and incorporate thoroughly. Shake chopped pecans with all-purpose flour and add to the mix.

Pour into pie shell. Top with pecan halves. Bake for 45 minutes or until inserted toothpick comes out clean.

EAST END CAFÉ

The East End community lies just south of the Pulaski County Line off Arch Street Pike. This Saline County area is home to many people who commute to work in Little Rock.

The East End Café lies somewhere between home cookin' and a community hangout, with a library at the end of the restaurant. No, really – customers kept bringing their books and lining the shelves at the eatery's west wall and it just stuck. Now you can bring one or take one or just pull one to read on while you're enjoying your meal, whether it's breakfast, lunch or dinner.

Sherry Wilcox makes the whole pies that are sliced each day for sharing, from coconut and pumpkin to Millionaire and egg custard, and they're always pretty good. It's the platter-sized fried pies, though, that will grab your attention – ten-inch-long half-moons full of apples or chocolate or whatever, served with ice cream. Get yours to share – they'll serve halves on separate plates for you.

20622 Arch Street Pike
Hensley, Arkansas 72065
(501) 888-4444

THE HIVE BAKERY AND CAFÉ

It started with honey – in particular, Hartz Honey Hole, a cute little yellow cottage along the Dollarway Road in White Hall where one could find anything that involved the bee-autiful sweet... er, sorry, terrible pun. It really stings.

Janet and Michael Hartz started with the Honey Hole in 2013, but in 2015 took a big step, moved half a block down the street and took over a much larger building with Dogwood Village, a shop with plenty of unusual merchandise, clothing and gifts with the heart of the Hartz Honey Hole within. In 2016, the Hertzes opened a bakery café, The Hive, which today offers bread from Country Village Bakery in Star City, sandwiches with meat from Petit Jean Meats, and three pies sold by-the-slice or whole at the café – French silk, peanut butter and pecan, the last of which has beautiful honeyed notes amidst local pecans. Be sure to allot yourself time to explore the store.

7106 Dollarway Road (at Dogwood Village)
White Hall, Arkansas 71602
(870) 247-2404
VisitTheHive.com

THE FAMILY DINER

This lunch and dinner spot on Arkansas Highway 365 specializes in rib-filling lunches like chicken spaghetti and hamburger steak. A case of pies – double crusted fruit, meringue-topped, pecan and chess – should be checked out on entry.

116 South Arkansas Highway 365
Redfield, Arkansas 72132
(501) 397-5008

COLONIAL STEAKHOUSE

Colonial Steakhouse actually started out in an antebellum home at the corner of 5th and Beech, the creation of Mildred Compton, who opened it on August 10, 1973. She sold it to Scott Mouser, a 22-year old local resident whose mom had once worked at the school housed in the current location. After a fire destroyed the old house on Beech in 1987, Mouser purchased the demolition rights for the 8th and Pine property and set about renovating. He moved the restaurant into the first floor and leased out the second level for mortgage offices and such, and he still owns the building today.

Mouser sold the restaurant to Joe and Donna Coker in 1993. Coker took on a restaurant that had long established itself as a hub for the community, a place where families came for every important life event. On June 3, 2014, he sold the restaurant to Dana and Wayne Gateley. Dana had been a waitress at Colonial Steakhouse for more than a quarter century.

Colonial Steakhouse is only open for dinner Tuesday through Saturday nights, and it never advertises for hires, since family members of staff come in when extra bodies are needed. Many members of the staff have other jobs as well. Some employees have been there 40 years, and there have even been three generations of the same family working there at the same time.

Colonial Steakhouse's menu was created from the recommendations of its patrons and the suggestions of its staff. Veronica Scarver, who started working there when

she was just 14 years old, is responsible for the famed black bottom pie. This very rich, deeply boozy pie is a heavy end to the night. It's the only black bottom pie that has a regular place on any Arkansas restaurant menu.

111 West 8th Street
Pine Bluff, Arkansas
71601
(870) 536-3488
TheColonialSteak-
house.com

COUNTRY KITCHEN

The Country Kitchen originally opened in 1953 on the north side of Pine Bluff, a country diner complete with bar and barstools, booths and tables clothed in red, chrome and wood. The original owners retired in 1987 and sold the restaurant to Mark McCool who, along with his wife and sons Jayson and Jeremy, still runs the restaurant today.

Of the desserts offered at the restaurant, the one to choose is the lemon icebox pie, with its very loose and not too thick graham cracker crust, a rich flavorful custard, a well-beaten layer of cream and more graham cracker crumbs on top. It's not a sturdy pie - you won't be able to pick it up whole for a bite - but it's soft and oh so sweet and a cloud to consume.

4322 Dollarway Road
White Hall, Arkansas 71602
(870) 535-4767

GRIDER FIELD RESTAURANT

As far as I can tell, the only place to get a good pie at an airport in Arkansas is at Grider Field. Since 2008, the Grider Field Restaurant has offered a phenomenal soul food buffet with fried fish, fried chicken, smothered pork chops, and more. The desserts are provided by Jimmie Lee's Pound Cake, a local sweets caterer who specializes in pound cake and remarkable down-home pecan and sweet potato pies.

709 Hangar Row
Pine Bluff, Arkansas 71601
(870) 536-4293

To order direct from Jimmie Lee Pound Cake, call (479) 445-8374.
20% of all proceeds from pie sales go to fund the New Hope Scholarship.

LYBRAND'S BAKERY

Lybrand's Bakery is the oldest bakery in Pine Bluff. Dairy company employee Curtis Lybrand married his wife, Emma Jean in 1940, and the pair decided to go into the bakery business. They opened the original Lybrand's Bakery with three hundred dollars in seed money and a ton of enthusiasm along the 100 block of Main Street in 1946. That place didn't take, so six months later they went to a spot in East Harding. They moved to another Main Street location another six months later. It's at 1308 Main Street that Lybrand's Bakery really began to take hold.

The Lybrands originally made cakes and doughnuts. It didn't take long for Danish pastries, coffee cakes, yeast rolls bread and pie to be added. Eventually they started making wedding cakes, and a Lybrand's wedding cake became the cake for high-class nuptials in town. In 1965, a second location was opened. Today, Lybrand's Bakery is operated by Joey and Marcia Lybrand, with two locations—one at 2900 Hazel Street and one on Dollarway Road in White Hall. It's much more than a bakery now, with full breakfast in the mornings and sandwiches and lunch specials in the afternoons.

Lybrand's makes a number of traditional pies. It's common to see coconut and chocolate meringue as well as pecan pies in the case on any given day, with other varieties depending upon the season and the holiday..

2900 South Hazel Street
Pine Bluff, Arkansas 71603
(870) 534-4607
Facebook.com/LybrandsBakery

6201 Dollarway Road
White Hall, Arkansas 71602
(870) 247-5498

R. A. PICKENS AND SON STORE

One of the biggest treasures amongst Arkansas's Delta eateries sits on what had once been a very important plantation. The R. A. Pickens and Son Company started out in 1881 as the Pickens Plantation at Walnut Lake, south of Dumas. At one point, some 500 people were employed in the various enterprises on the land – which included everything from cotton farming and ginning to a saw mill. Today it's still a busy hub and home to a great southeast Arkansas restaurant... in the middle of an honest to goodness country store.

Reuben Adolphus Pickens was one of a family of pioneers that first settled the community of Walnut Lake in 1881. He became a progressive farmer who held hundreds of acres of plantation lands in the area -- as well as a cotton gin, a Hereford cattle business and a commissary that served the dozens of workers and families that lived in the area. Walnut Lake would eventually be renamed Pickens for his family.

Before 1948, farmers and their families would come to the commissary to purchase staples, trade, sell crops and gather to share news and enjoy a bite. Though not a restaurant back the, there was always something to eat at the counter, such as jerky or colas or fried pies.

After the original store burned in 1948, the business was rebuilt as a Quonset-style structure. Today, it serves as Pickens' grocery store, apparel shop, post office, community center and eatery. Food is served every Monday through Friday at breakfast and lunch - the latter of which lays claim to a famed squash casserole, deviled eggs and rice and brown gravy. Then there are the pies - coconut and chocolate meringue, peanut butter, peach and strawberry in season topped with whipped cream - whichever is available is worth your fork.

122 Pickens Road
Pickens, Arkansas
71662
(870) 382-5266

HOOTS BBQ

David and Suzie Powell spent a couple of years after retirement traveling from place to place by RV. When they grew tired of that, they decided to head back to their hometown of McGehee and open up a barbecue joint. The Powells bought the old cattle sale barn out on US Highway 65 and fixed it up. They opened Hoots BBQ in 2012. David passed away in 2015 but Suzie still runs the place.

They found a lot of excellent items while traveling around in their RV. Hoots gave them a place to put it all. Inside, the walls are covered with old tin and chalkboards. The interior is full of eclectic items, from pipe fitting light fixtures to reclaimed restaurant tables. There's a bar to the right when you enter, and a bakery to the left, with the heart of the restaurant at the back. At the bakery, you'll find a number of cakes offered. Don't overlook the lemon icebox pie, a thick wedge of creamy citrus delight.

2008 US Highway 65
McGehee, Arkansas 71654
(870) 222-1234

AMISH AND COUNTRY STORE

Just north of Lake Village, there's a small brown store beside the road with an old black horse buggy out front. This is the Amish and Country Store, and it's packed with jams, jellies, pickles, cheese and honey along with soaps, household items and furniture produced by local and regional Amish and Mennonite communities.

Within the case under the register, you'll also find pies – whole and sliced pecan and sweet potato pies, and fried handpies from a dough-

Gray Weldon

nut-style dough filled with apple, cherry, peach or blueberry filling.

3040 US Highway 65
Dermott, Arkansas 71638
(870) 538-9990
AmishAndCountryStore.com

RHODA'S FAMOUS HOT TAMALES AND PIES

Rhoda Adams will tell you, when you come to her shop, that God gave her the ability to make pie. She thanks Him every day. "God knows nobody ever told me nothin'. People come ask me how to do this and how to do that. I go about tellin' em' how I make 'em sometime but I don't tell 'em my recipe!" she laughs one October morning as she fills the tiny pies she'll sell a dollar each from the counter.

Rhoda started selling pies out of her home for her church. All the proceeds from her pies, cakes and tamales went back to that church. Word got out about her cooking gift, and people started showing up at her house. She decided to open a restaurant. This eatery started out as a trailer in 1973, where Rhoda would offer her soul food every day. One of her sons helped build onto it repeatedly to how it looks today.

When I first came to this place, the sign proudly declared this the home of Rhoda's Famous Hot Tamales. After *Arkansas Pie: A Delicious Slice of the Natural State* in 2012, I noticed she'd changed the name to Rhoda's Famous Hot Tamales... and Pies. Also soul food and burgers. Rhoda has never missed an opportunity for promotion.

Rhoda's pies come in several varieties – chocolate and coconut meringue, fried pies, pecan pies and sweet potato pies and these great pies that are half pecan and half sweet potato. The sweet potato pie is firm, not-too-sweet made-from-the-real-deal pie with just a bit of fibrous potato left in the mix. The pecan pie—a rich, deep-colored custard with a hint of butter and bourbon overtones. It's meaty and a little cloying, but there's a depth to each bite, a little Lower Arkansas that sticks with you.

Rhoda and James had 15 children and more than 70 grandchildren and great grand-children – some of whom she's never met. The family is spread from Florida to Las Vegas, and peppered across Arkansas.

In Spring 2017, Rhoda Adams, along with James and their daughter Dorothy, came to Little Rock to accept a special commendation, as Rhoda's Famous Hot Tamales and Pies was inducted into the inaugural class of the Arkansas Food Hall of Fame. Even after more than 45 years of operating her restaurant, Rhoda is still grateful.

"Everywhere I've been, people have been good to me," she says. "And how I came up famous, I don't know. People come in here and they say to me 'hey, Rhoda, how ya' doin'?' I say 'pretty good, how you doin'?' I've been doing this many, many a year, and I thank God for it."

714 Saint Mary Street
Lake Village, Arkansas 71653
(870) 265-3108

RAY'S DRIVE IN

Ray's Drive In isn't just a dairy bar. It's a landmark by which travelers navigate. Located at the corner of US Highways 278 and 425, the Ray family's longstanding eat-

ery has been offering the area's largest menu since 1964. The fried pies are available by the register, marked by the type offered each day. They're great to dunk in a milkshake, which Ray's also offers.

203 US Highway 425
Monticello, Arkansas
71655
(870) 367-3292
RaysHamburgers.com

PIGGY SUE'S BBQ

The best steak in town may come from a barbecue joint. Piggy Sue's BBQ is all about the sandwich, with great pork and brisket, but the ribeye is rather excellent. Get a slice of lemon icebox or pecan pie to go when you're done.

521 US Highway 425 South
Monticello, Arkansas 71655
(870) 367-8466

Grav Weldon

COUNTRY VILLAGE BAKERY

There are too many items to confuse the mind at the bakery at Country Village near Star City. Between cakes, pies, doughnuts, loaves of bread and cookies and jams and jellies and canned goods and such, there is much to make the mouth water. Yet it's a very good idea to keep your sense of purpose, to walk in and order a blueberry or peach fried pie or three. Made from preserves created on-site, wrapped in doughnut dough and deep-fried, this is a pie with heft and moxie, and it deserves your attention.

158 Knight Haven Circle
Star City, Arkansas 71667
(870) 628-3333

RISON COUNTRY STORE

If you're looking for a good fried pie on your wanderings into Lower Arkansas, stop at the Rison Country Store. The oversized convenience shop has a lunch counter at the back and a stack of fried pies in wax paper in a box up front. Sugar-dusted and tasty.

1890 US Highway 63
Rison, Arkansas 71665
(870) 357-8262

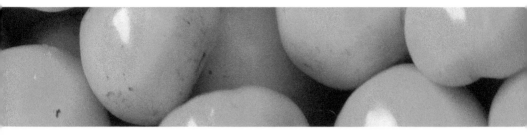

Every June, the city of Warren turns out in red to celebrate the annual Bradley County Pink Tomato Festival. This recipe notes the important Arkansas state fruit and vegetable in its own piecase.

BRADLEY COUNTY PINK TOMATO PIE
by Angela Norton

1 9-inch deep dish pie shell
3-5 lg. tomatoes, peeled, sliced to about ½" thick (remove the seeds)
1/2 tsp. salt
1/2 tsp. pepper
additional herbs if wanted: basil, parsley, garlic salt, etc.
3/4 C. grated cheddar cheese
3/4 C. grated mozzarella cheese
1/4 C. scallions or chives
6 strips cooked bacon (optional)
1 C. mayonnaise

Bake pie shell for 10 minutes at 375 degrees. Layer tomatoes in shell and sprinkle with salt, pepper, and additional herbs & spices if wanted.

Mix together mayonnaise, cheese and scallions/chives. Spread mixture over tomatoes in pie shell. Bake at 350 degrees for 30 minutes until brown and bubbly. Crumble bacon on top. Allow to stand 5 minutes before serving.

GOLDEN GIRLS FISH AND BURGERS

A couple of blocks off the Bradley County courthouse square in Warren, you'll find a lunchroom called Golden Girls Fish and Burgers. Cathy Rice's restaurant offers sandwiches, burgers, catfish and homemade fried pies.

209 Myrtle Street
Warren, Arkansas 71671
(870) 226-8666

MOLLY'S DINER

Back in the 1960s, 1970s and 1980s, there was a certain kitsch that cropped up in restaurants all over the United States -- places where every sort of memorabilia was placed helter-skelter on walls, posts, sometimes even ceilings. Molly's Diner in Warren takes that aesthetic up to eleven. The establishment is well worn, irregular floor to its ancient rusty barstools, from wood-backed and seated booths to mismatched tables and chairs. Every space on Molly's Diner's walls comes packed with aging, curling signage ranging from the historic ("Snooker 50 cents") to amusing (Arkansas State Bird, a Razorback with wings).

Molly's Diner has gorgeous slices worthy of your time. The famed pies greatly represent our state's love for the pastry-clad filling-packed vessels we love so much. Once you have a seat at one of the many tables inside the not-perfectly-leveled dining room, your waitress will take your pie request and soon receive your choice from a window to the kitchen, over which a sign clearly stated Thru These Windows Pass The Greatest Food In The World. Half a dozen grace the pegboard each day, the name of each on a double-holed slat that's removed or replaced as pies are made and eaten. Apple, coconut, chocolate peach, pecan, lemon icebox, caramel apple, sugar-free chocolate, even fried pies may appear on that dessert board.

If you select the caramel apple one day, as I did, give it a few moments. Accept the offering of a cup of coffee. Wait. Even with five minutes of sitting, I found my gorgeous slice to be a bubbling crust-borne slip of napalm on sampling. About 15 minutes late I enjoyed the gratifying remainder.

201 South Myrtle
Warren, Arkansas 71671
(870) 226-9913

GRANNY'S GRILL

Granny's Grill in Hampton offers burgers, sandwiches, home cooking, coconut cake and a variety of fried pies.

313 South Lee Street
Hampton, Arkansas 71744
(870) 798-4824

COUNTRY VITTLES

Housed in an old Rexall Drug store a few blocks from the dead center of town, Country Vittles offers its meals cafeteria-style, with homestyle casseroles (tater tot casserole, really!), ham, yams, beans and other things. The pies are individually plates, usually coconut or chocolate meringue.

301 Main Street
Crossett, Arkansas 71635
(870) 304-3504

TRIPLE CROSS BBQ

Located in the old Chuck Wagon BBQ trailer within eyeshot of the old Fordyce depot, this food truck is a stepping stone to a future brick and mortar location. For now, Triple Cross offers barbecue and barbecue stuffed potatoes, along with a full array of fried-on-demand Flywheel pies.

100 South Main Street
Fordyce, Arkansas 71742
(870) 352-2605

TRACKS BBQ

The best ribs to be found in the vicinity of Bearden come from Tracks BBQ, an unpretentious stop along the old US Highway 79 Business route, where pies are your only choice for dessert.

360 1st Street Northeast
Bearden, Arkansas 71720
(870) 687-2277

TJ'S PLACE

Housed in a former Minute Man restaurant, TJ's Places is one of the few spots in Camden where you can get a fried Flywheel pie through the drive-thru. Pull up, place your order and be prepared to move when the next person gets behind you. The cook will wave out the window at you when your piping hot is ready.

1385 California Avenue SW
Camden, Arkansas 71701
(870) 837-1707

LENNY B'S BBQ

Lenny B's BBQ operates out of a food trailer alongside US Highway 78 on the southwest side of Camden. The place has become well known for excellently smoked turkey, beef fries and for its excellent fried pies that come in several flavors.

2040 California Avenue SW (US Highway 79)
Camden, Arkansas 71701
(870) 837-2725

WOODS PLACE

Over the generations, there's been much soda made in Arkansas. Coca-Cola, Dr. Pepper and Pepsi have bottling plants in Little Rock, Fort Smith and Paragould. But two Arkansas-created sodas are still made here today. Grapette and Orangette came out of Camden in the 1920s, one of the "Fooks Flavors" sold out of the trunk of Benjamin Tyndle Fooks' car. The soda brands died off in the 1970s after being sold a couple times over, only to be brought back by the Wal-Mart folks in 2000.

Woods Place in Camden is the place where Grapette is celebrated.

James Woods purchased the former Kreg's Catfish location in 1984 and gave it the new name. It didn't take long for the restaurant to garner attention of folks from the area and visitors to nearby White Oak Lake.

Woods Place does a mighty fine plate of catfish fillets and hush puppies. Everywhere you look, there are nods to Grapette – on the walls, on the ceiling, and of course in the glass right in front of you. In fact, Woods may be one of the very few places around that has Grapette on tap.

The pies at Woods are fried pies from Flywheel in Prescott, cooked to order when you ask, in apple, peach or chocolate, the only dessert on the menu.

1173 West Washington Street
Camden, Arkansas 71701
(870) 836-0474
EatAtWoodsPlace.com

My partner, Grav Weldon, loves a good buttermilk pie. This recipe includes coconut, which he also adores.

DAVID FRANKS'S BUTTERMILK COCONUT PIE

1/2 cup (1 stick) butter, softened
1 cup sugar
3 large eggs
3 Tablespoons flour
1/4 teaspoon salt
1 cup buttermilk
1 1/2 teaspoon vanilla extract
(1/2 teaspoon almond extract)

Preheat oven to 425° F. Prepare 9" pie crust and chill.

In large bowl, gradually beat sugar into butter until light and fluffy. Add eggs one at a time, beating well after each. Whisk flour and salt together, then gradually beat into egg mixture. Beat in buttermilk and extract(s). Add coconut and blend well.

Pour filling into (unbaked) chilled crust. Bake for 10 minutes at 425°, then reduce heat to 350° and bake for an additional 35 minutes. Center should be firm. Pie will puff up as it bakes and collapse as it cools. Serve at room temperature.

TOWN HOUSE RESTAURANT

There was, at one point during the middle of the 20th century, a number of lodging/ dining establishments around the state called the Town House Motel and Restaurant. Vestiges are preserved in postcards, showing locations in Conway, Arkadelphia, Camden, Pine Bluff and El Dorado. The last remaining Town House Restaurant in Arkansas recently moved from its original building to a new place, but the pies are still made from the same recipe at the new facility. The pies are of the cream variety – chocolate, coconut and lemon.

615 Griffith Street
El Dorado, Arkansas 71730-5937
(870) 863-4519

OLDE TOWNE STORE

The exterior may say general store, but inside El Dorado's Olde Towne Store are things you should consume to stay healthy – tea, supplements and an array of edibles. And then there's pie - whole pies to take with you or a slice to enjoy while you're there.

The pies come from heritage recipes and include the likes of buttermilk, Toll House (chocolate chip), egg custard, pecan and buttermilk pecan, the last of which combines the delectable custard of a good buttermilk pie with a top crust of Arkansas pecans.

113 North Jefferson Avenue
El Dorado, Arkansas 71730
(870) 862-1060
Facebook.com/TheOldeTowneStore

FAYRAY'S

Try as I might, I cannot sneak into Fayray's without Chef Michael Rice's notice. He never really takes a break, just divvies his time between the kitchen and the dining area, where he gets to know each and every one of his customers that come through the door of this eatery that anchors the downtown entertainment district.

That's okay, though, because there's also this great slice of pie that comes from his kitchen that you should enjoy when you go, a send-you-to-bed nightcap that combines sweet and aperitif in one setting. That's the bourbon pecan pie, emphasis on the bourbon and the pecan and, well, the pie. The substantial and slightly fiery (did I mention bourbon?) slice is paired with a snowball of vanilla ice cream, the whole affair drizzled with dark chocolate.

110 East Elm Street
El Dorado, Arkansas 71730
(870) 863-4000
FayRays.com

URBANA SNACK SHACK

If you're around the Felsenthal Wildlife Refuge or in the area east of El Dorado, pick up a bite and a fried pie at the little tan building, a tiny made-to-order lunch counter.

1173 Urbana Road
El Dorado, Arkansas 71730
(870) 962-9900

MAGNOLIA BAKE SHOP

A couple of years ago, I had a chance to speak with Stephen Stroope, who owns Magnolia Bake Shop with his wife Betsy. First thing I asked him was how long the bakery had been around. "Since water," he chuckled.

The bakery was started in 1928 by Carmie Schobel Stroope, who'd been a dairy worker for several years. Stroope ran it for four years before selling it in 1932 to his wife's two sisters, May and Hassie Beaty. They had the bakery for decades, never marrying, just turning out great baked goods.

Stroope's son Joe Franklin Stroope, who studied at the Wilton Cake Decorating School before marrying his high school sweetheart, Martha, heading to California and starting a family and two bakeries. Joe came back in 1961 and bought the bakery from the two sisters. His three sons also worked there, the youngest of them being Stephen, who was 10 at the time. "I'm very lucky, and old enough to realize it," Stephen told me. "It's lucky to be born into a business like that."

Joe kept the bakery open seven days a week, every day of the year. He finally sold the bakery to his three sons in 1984. Stephen's two older brothers have retired, but he keeps the store the same. Anything on the shelves is what you would have found decades ago. Stephen credits his father. "Everything, I mean everything, is made from scratch. Everything's still made like he did. He loved baking. I can see him when I do something, just plain as day. He's the whole reason for it."

Magnolia Bake Shop is best known for its cakes, but it also puts out traditional double crusted pies – apple, peach and cherry. There's usually a pecan pie around somewhere, and during the holidays sweet potato and pumpkin pies also make an appearance.

103 North Jefferson
Magnolia, Arkansas 71753
(870) 234-1304
Facebook.com/1MagnoliaBakery

THE BACKYARD BARBEQUE COMPANY

There's a case behind the counter at The Backyard Barbeque Company in Magnolia that's always full of pie. Since the restaurant opened in 1989, the case has become legendary, a trove of delicious pie creations that stretch the imagination (and the waistline). My first visit there I encountered the mountainous, eclectic combination that was the joint's banana pudding pie – layers of vanilla custard, bananas and vanilla wafers under a rich, eggy meringue. It's one of many - from the cool and tart Key lime pie to the cherry cream cheese, from the coconut to the magnificently creamy coconut meringue, cookies and cream meringue, pecan, cherry, chocolate silk and coconut meringue. Plus, each summer, a strawberry cream pie with the tallest whipped cream cap you'll find around Lower Arkansas, is made available. Every pie is available by the slice or whole pie. Oh, and the brisket sandwich is good, too.

1407 East Main Street
Magnolia, Arkansas 71753
(870) 234-7890

MARLAR'S CAFETERIA

Ever heard of a funeral pie? The humble dessert with the heart of dried fruit was once a common culinary element in Arkansas. The dessert – usually a double crusted pie with re-hydrated raisins – was something that could be whipped up quickly should the need arise and would keep for a few days. Hence the funeral pie, a dish that could be created from what was in the cabinet and which could set out and be sliced from for sustenance in times when thoughts are not on food.

There are few of these served at Arkansas restaurants. For instance, Chef's In's raisin cream pie (page 136) would not qualify, for it couldn't be set out. Marshall Restaurant (page 77) produces a thin one.

The best one I have encountered by far is served at Marlar's Cafeteria in Magnolia. The eatery, originally opened in 1958, is owned by Ray and Traci Lindsey but retains its original mid-century south Arkansas aesthetic. The low concrete block building sits along North Vine on the northwest side of Magnolia.

Marlar's Cafeteria's slices are set on the top shelf at the end of the cafeteria line: egg custard, coconut custard, sweet potato, raisin. That raisin pie came together as swollen, buttery raisins between crusts, so luscious, so rich. It's a good pie to have with a big glass of milk.

The dining hall also offers whole pies to take home, alongside an entire wall-sized freezer full of take-and-make entrées and sides such as chicken enchiladas, spaghetti, smothered steak, tuna casserole, squash casserole, dumplings, chili, gumbo and at least a half dozen different cakes.

2116 North Vine Street
Magnolia, Arkansas 71753
(870) 234-6900

THE SMOKIN' BULL

Emerson, which lies just a few miles north of the Louisiana border, is best known for an intriguing display of bravado that takes place each year during its classic PurpleHull Pea Festival – a series of races that combines old fashioned engineering knowhow with sheer bravado. Of course, I am speaking of the World Championship Rotary Tiller Races. The combined festival and event takes place the third weekend of June each year.

Emerson has one restaurant of note, but it's a doozy – The Smokin' Bull. Omaha steaks and massive handpatted burgers are the stars on the menu at this oversized restaurant alongside US Highway 79. The pies are getting their own notice, too –

homestyle sweet potato and pumpkin in the winter and Kirbi Waller's dandy meringue pies whenever she whips them up.

306 South Elm Street (US Highway 79)
Emerson, Arkansas 71740
(870) 547-2020
Facebook.com/SmokinBullEmersonAR

BARR'S JUNCTION

The term possum pie and four-layer delight are interchangeable across the state – and both share a unique pie format, sometimes being served in a crust in a traditional round pie pan while other times being assembled in a 13x9" casserole. The latter version can be found at Barr's Junction, a spot on the road at a Y intersection in the little community of Rosston. This four-layer delight can be found several times during the week, but rarely on Saturday, when the

Grav Weldon

restaurant lets all the pies sell out before closing for the Sabbath. Other pies are also available on an as-made basis.

6683 US Highway 278
Rosston, Arkansas 71858
(870) 871-2426

BURGE'S HICKORY SMOKED TURKEYS AND HAMS

Burge's operates in an old dairy bar at the crook in the road on Arkansas Highway 29 just north of downtown. The restaurant offers the famed smoked turkey and ham, which is cured and smoked in a facility across the street, alongside traditional dairy bar favorites such as burgers, fries and soft-serve. The pies are fried pies from Flywheel Pies of Prescott. Learn more about this longstanding Lower Arkansas favorite and its Little Rock counterpart on page 284.

526 Spruce Street
Lewisville, Arkansas 71845
(870) 921-4292
SmokedTurkeys.com

TJ's BACK WOODS BISTRO

TJ's Back Woods Bistro started out as a food truck, but today serves scratch made entrées, sides and pastries in a respectable building on the south side of Lewisville.. Best known for its crawfish, TJ's also offers steak and sides and a satisfying strawberry pie. Apple and cherry double-crust also available.

2024 Arkansas Highway 29
Lewisville, Arkansas 71845
(870) 921-4900
Facebook.com/tjsbbco

DOC'S PLACE

Garland City lies to the east of Texarkana along US Highway 82. There on a Friday or Saturday night, you can kick up your heels over a plate of fish at Doc's Place, where the décor includes, I kid you not, the twin heads of a two-headed calf. The fried pies come in apple, chocolate or peach at the end of a dinner of catfish and hush puppies.

301 Arkansas Highway 134
Garland City, Arkansas 71839
(870) 683-2226

OLD TYME BURGER SHOPPE

There was a moment I realized my contributions with *Arkansas Pie: A Delicious Slice of the Natural State*, had made a difference. That moment came in June 2013, when a fellow journalist and my friend Debbie Haak and I stopped in at the Old Tyme Burger Shoppe in Texarkana and had a bite with the folks who run the place, and heard how proud they were to be listed in the book as one of the state's best restaurants for pie.

Well, it is. Opened in 1991 by Randy Thomas, this spot is packed with the sort of memorabilia that conjures roadfood memories of the 1960s. It does a great burger, sure, but its milk chocolate meringue pie is one heck of an experience, as is its creamy coconut meringue. Fried Flywheel pies are also on the menu in a variety of flavors.

1205 Arkansas Boulevard
Texarkana, Arkansas 71854
(870) 772-5775
Facebook.com/OTBS1991

SUE AND CAROL'S KITCHEN

The little brick building that houses Sue and Carol's Kitchen literally faces right into Texas. Its previous location, which opened in 1979, was downtown in the old Hotel Grim. This spot along State Line Avenue has been its home since the move. Its red booths and wooden tabletops tend to draw as many locals as travelers wanting a substantial bite. They find it here, along with delicious chocolate and coconut meringue pies and, during some summer months, strawberry pie as well.

938 North State Line Avenue
Texarkana, Arkansas 71854
(870) 774-0859

FLYWHEEL PIES

Gary and Nell Ray Allen started Fly Wheel Pies in 1984. At the time, Gary was a meat salesman with a route. Nell Ray would make up these fried pies for family gatherings. One night over the kitchen table, Gary looked at Nell Ray and said "I bet I could sell these." The unusual name was Gary's nickname for Nell Ray, a reference I'm told was due to her driving skills. As Gary was reported to say, the flywheel is the part of the engine that spins around but never goes anywhere.

The pies took off. After Nell Ray passed away in 1999, Gary remarried, and second wife Rosemary came into the business. The pies spread. Eventually, the Allens were ready to retire. That's where Independent Case Management comes in.

"ICM had offices in Prescott. Our job is to provide services and supports to adults with developmental disabilities," says Steven Hitt, Independent Case Management's general manager. "Employment is one of those issues. We decided to buy it and hire people with disabilities." The business changed hands in 2015.

The operation needed to expand, and with the help of the City of Prescott, the slightly renamed Flywheel Pies moved into the old McRae Middle School cafetorium. Today, twelve employees work to make pies that are sold and served in 32 Arkansas counties.

"It's handmade from start to finish," adds Paula Ledbetter, ICM's administrative assistant. "The filling, dough, everything , that's pretty awesome to me. We have 16 different flavors. We just started pecan, which is amazing."

Watching the assembly process is fascinating. Eight women work the H shaped assembly table at any particular time. The two on the end pull balls of dough out of bins and roll them out, slapping them onto ceramic saucers. The next pair spoon in the filling and fold them over. Another couple trim the pies and make sure the air is out. The two ladies on the end crimp the edges with regular four-tined dinner forks, then set each on a tray. From there, the pies are frozen, then Steven takes them out. Most go to the distribution point at ICM's Little Rock office. Steven personally delivers others.

"The money goes back into supporting our programs," Steven says. "Our profits go back into the non-profit. We are probably the world's only non-profit fried pie plant." The pies appear on restaurant menus all over the state. Each eatery chooses the

flavors they want to utilize. When they advertise handmade pies, they aren't kidding. Steven says he's offered to have crimping machines and dough rollers brought in, but the ladies that work the pies today will have none of it.

On the average day, 2400 pies are made in that cafetorium. And there's reason to expand. Soon, Flywheel Pies will be on the internet, ready to order and ship. When that happens, more employees will be brought in at Prescott, more jobs for folks who could really use one.

Flywheel Pies are available for purchase by the public even now, available for pickup in Prescott or Little Rock. Expect to see growth into new markets, soon.

P.O. Box 849   (870) 887-5367
Prescott, Arkansas 71857   ICM-inc.org/Flywheels-Pies

RED RIVER CAFÉ

Truck stop restaurants seem to be a good place for pie in Arkansas. That's certainly the case at the Red River Café, which sits beside a truck stop off Exit 18 of Interstate 30 not far from the Red River. The café's main claim to fame comes in epic-sized burgers, but the dark chocolate custard meringue pie is an ambrosial enjoyment one should consider, especially on a rainy day with good strong coffee.

5279 Highway 67 West (I-30 Exit 18)
Fulton, Arkansas 71838
(870) 896-2590

BIG JAKE's BBQ

For the sake of this book, all the pies listed within are served at Arkansas restaurants. That being said, you can find the same sort of Original Fried Pie shop fried pies at Big Jake's BBQ locations on both the Texarkana and Arkansas sides of the state line. The dough is bready, and the fillings come in apple, apricot, chocolate, peach, pineapple, coconut, pecan and sugar-free apple, apricot and cherry flavors. There are also locations in Ashdown and Hope.

1521 Arkansas Boulevard
Texarkana, Arkansas 71854
(870) 774-0099
BigJakesBBQ.com

170 North Constitution Avenue
Ashdown, Arkansas 71822
(870) 898-2227

603 West Commerce Boulevard
Hope, Arkansas71801
(870) 777-1000

WOODEN SPOON RESTAURANT

Nestled into a house at the corner of Arkansas Highways 32, 41 and 108, The Wooden Spoon is about as close as you can get to where Arkansas meets two other states. It's just five miles from the Oklahoma border and eleven miles from where the Red River separates Arkansas and Texas, on a stretch named for the famed country music singer Tracy Lawrence (who was born in this town).

The light green building is a warren of rooms within, all painted different dark colors. A pie case separates what would be the living and dining areas of the original house, and it's usually loaded with meringue and pecan pies – except at the end of the day, when customers have eaten their fill.

724 Tracy Lawrence Avenue
Foreman, Arkansas 71836
(870) 542-7088

HERB'S CREAMLAND

Herb McCandless opened Herb's Creamland in Ashdown in 1954 and ran it until his death in 2013. The family still operates the red shop with white shutters along Dutch Webster Road, within sight of US Highway 71. The Route 66 décor is still sharp and the original Herb Burger and hand-battered onion rings remain on the menu, and if you're seeking pie you can order yours in the fried Flywheel variety – just be prepared for a bit of a wait.

116 Dutch Webster Drive
Ashdown, Arkansas 71822
(870) 898-2200

COUNTRY GIRLS CAFÉ

I've had a lot of fried pies over the years, but I don't think I've ever had one that was a butter-soaked as the one I picked up on my research trip to De Queen than this strawberry pie devoured at Country Girls Café on north US Highway 71. It took about 10 minutes from the time of order to the time the pie was delivered to me, too hot to handle, sprinkled with confectioner's sugar that had already melted into the buttered surface of this Flywheel pie. But that buttered pie was too good not to dive into. I approve.

122 Highway 71 North
De Queen, Arkansas 71832
(870) 642-2260

RANCH HOUSE CAFÉ

Walking into the Ranch House Café in De Queen is like walking into a restaurant's impression of a chuckwagon dinner, with 1970s style heavy wood furniture and red and white checkered tablecloths. Daily Bible verses come along with the daily specials, and the variety of nachos, especially Granny's Nachos, are not to be missed.

The pies come in creamy varieties such as coconut, chocolate and four-layer delight (possum) guaranteed to give a sweet end to a good country meal.

208 West Collin Raye Drive (US Highway 70)
De Queen, Arkansas 71832
(870) 642-6040

STILLWELL'S RESTAURANT

Stillwell's opened on the downtown square in 2009. The interior of exposed bricks covered with clocks is a good place for a sandwich and a cup of gourmet coffee. The views of the Sevier County Courthouse from seats in the front window are marvelous. The pies are in a case to the side; chocolate, coconut, peanut butter, pecan, pumpkin, buttermilk and apple are the usual choices.

301 West Stillwell Avenue
De Queen, Arkansas 71832
(870) 642-2872

BRANDING IRON BAR-B-Q AND STEAKHOUSE

Across from the historic downtown depot and museum in the heart of Mena, you'll find the Branding Iron Bar-B-Q and Steakhouse. Enter through the double doors, and right by the register you'll discover a fine selection of cream pies along the likes of Opossum (the only place in Arkansas where I've seen this spelling for the specialty), Key lime cream, cookies-and-cream and German chocolate cream pie.

It's the latter I'd draw attention to. Unlike most German chocolate pies I've encountered in my journeys, this isn't a pecan pie with coconut and chocolate thrown in. Instead, it's a creamy celebration, a chocolate cream pie laced with caramel and toasted coconut and tiny bits of pecan throughout.

The pies are already boxed, as the folks who run the Branding Iron suspect you will be full after your meal.

623 Sherwood Avenue, Suite B
Mena, Arkansas 71953
(479) 437-3240
BrandingIronMena.com

MAMA NELL'S CAFÉ

Serendipity allowed me to catch Mena's newest pie place during my swing through southern and western Arkansas on the Great Arkansas Pie Hunt. That's how I ended up on the doorstep of Mama Nell's. I had just dropped in at the Branding Iron and had noticed balloons on the other side of US Highway 71, so I decided to see what they were heralding. Turns out, the day before, Mama Nell's Café had celebrated its official grand opening. The interior, festooned with a maddening array of Valentine's Day and Mardi Gras celebration over a country cupboard décor crossed with a cowboy chuckwagon party, was inviting.

The Cajun/Creole restaurant was inspired by a real-life Louisiana woman who took Westley Cloud in and taught him how to cool when he was young. Today, Westley co-owns the café with Rusty O'Bryan, the gentleman you see here in the hat. Rusty and I hit it off immediately, as you might figure.

The pies, at least for now, are of the Flywheel variety, though there are sometimes peanut butter, pumpkin or sweet potato pies lurking around. Rusty will fry you up a pie and make you all the happier for dropping in.

800 US Highway 71 South
Mena, Arkansas 71953
(479) 216-6459

WILLIAMS TAVERN RESTAURANT

Here in Arkansas, finding a restaurant still standing from the 19th century presents a bit of a challenge – especially one still in operation. The oldest such structure still in existence stands in Little Rock – the 1827 Hinderliter Grog Shop, part of the fine collection of territorial buildings at the Historic Arkansas Museum.

The oldest restaurant building that houses an eatery today is Williams Tavern Restaurant. The structure was first raised not in Washington but in Marlbrook, some seven miles to the northeast, in 1832 by a man named John Williams. His place wasn't just his home – it served as a stopping-in point for the community and for travelers. It served as post office, stagecoach shop, and tavern and it became one of the best-known stops on the Southwest Trail between Memphis and the Red River. Wayfarers would arrive, purchase corn and hay to feed their horses and then have a bite to eat themselves. Many would camp around the inn before heading out the next morning.

Old Washington State Park, now Historic Washington State Park, was created in 1973. Structures from the 19th and early 20th century from around the area were moved in over the years, and thanks to a donation in 1985 by the Pioneer Washington Restoration Foundation, Williams Tavern found a home. It was restored and opened in 1986 for breakfast.

Today Williams Tavern is open 11 a.m. to 3 p.m. for lunch. There's often a buffet, or you can order off the menu things such as ham steak, hamburger steak, chicken fried steak and such – served up with so many possibilities of sides ranging from green beans and corn and fried okra to squash, zucchini and black-eyed pea salad. You can

get a burger there… which harkens back to tavern food tradition if not to the periodicity of the restaurant. And in the Yuletide season, the restaurant still presents a traditional holiday dinner of turkey, ham and all the fixings – on a buffet, all month long.

The desserts at the Williams Tavern Restaurant have become famous. They include a marvelous strawberry cake and a well-known and beloved Earthquake cake. Then there's this dish, a south Arkansas delicacy called Cushaw Pie. It's made from a goose-necked squash that's green with white or yellow stripes.

CUSHAW PIE

2 cups prepared cushaw squash puree
2/3 cup brown sugar
1 teaspoon ground cinnamon
1/2 teaspoon ground ginger
1/2 teaspoon salt

3 large eggs
1 teaspoon vanilla
12 ounces evaporated milk
Single pie crust

Combine cushaw squash puree, brown sugar, cinnamon, ginger, and salt in a medium-size mixing bowl. Add eggs and vanilla then beat lightly with a whisk. Stir in evaporated milk. Mix well. Pour into a pastry-lined pie plate. Bake on the lowest oven rack at 375-degrees for 50-60 minutes (until a toothpick inserted in the center comes out clean). Chill before serving.

105 Carroll Street (at Historic Washington State Park)
Washington, Arkansas 71862
(870) 983-2890
HistoricWashingtonStatePark.com

AUNT FERN'S FRIED PIES

Fern Snowden-Dixon shows up at the Howard County Farmers Market in Nashville every Friday. On Saturdays she's at Historic Washington State Park. She also attends farmers markets in Hope and Texarkana. But she's only been doing this for two years.

Fern started Aunt Fern's Fried Pies in 2015. She used to make whole sweet potato pies as her "side hustle" when her kids were young.. She also made pies for all sorts of fundraisers over the years.

A friend in nearby Wilton was trying to raise money to pay off the construction of their church. Fern donated six or eight pies. One of the ladies who tried one told Fern she needed to try a fried sweet potato pie, which that friend's mother made. She gave Fern four fried pies to try. On the way home, Fern decided she needed to try a bite of one. She ended up eating all four pies before she made it home – they were that good.

She had to make her own version of the treat (though she admits it's not as good as the ones she tried), then added other flavors, such as a chocolate pie made like a baked chocolate filling. She does walnut in a fried pie – which I haven't found anywhere else, and piña colada with both coconut and pineapple with a touch of rum flavoring in the mix. In all, she has eleven flavors, which she sells at farmers markets. Look for the fried pie shaped board advertising her pies, made by the market manager at Historic Washington State Park.

Fern has secured a restaurant in nearby Saratoga, which will open in late spring or summer 2018. She plans to sell cooked-to-order burgers alongside those marvelous fried pies.

1967 Main Street
Saratoga, Arkansas 71859
(870) 200-0046

PINKEY'S DRIVE IN

Delight is best known as being the home of musician Glen Campbell. It's also the home of Pinkey's Drive In, where you can grab a substantial lunch or a Club sandwich and a Flywheel fried pie to finish it off.

404 East Antioch Street
Delight, Arkansas 71940
(870) 379-2611

SMOKIN' RICK'S HICKORY HOUSE BARBECUE

A barbecue breakfast place? Yes, in Nashville you can have fried bologna and grits for breakfast and ribs and brisket for lunch. Take-out in the front and dining in the back' pies vary according to whim but fried pies are also always available.

815 North Main Street
Nashville, Arkansas 71852
(870) 845-1541

EM'S CAFÉ

Arkansas has the only publicly accessible diamond mine in the world. Folks come from all over the world to dig in the large plot behind the visitors center, and several times a year you'll hear about the latest diamond find.

If you're seeking pies rather than diamonds or want a place to grab a good breakfast

before or dinner after, try Em's Café. The red-and-tin interior is a comfortable place with omelets, burgers and the like on the menu. There are boards around the restaurant listing the day's pies, which come in several varieties including buttermilk, coconut, chocolate, apple and whatever ends up coming to the minds of the girls who work the kitchen.

319 North Washington Avenue
Murfreesboro, Arkansas 71958
(870) 285-4097

SWEETPEA'S BREAKFAST, BURGERS AND BBQ

Sweetpea's opened in 2014 in a wood-sided shack. You can smell the smoke from Sweetpea's from the intersection of Arkansas Highways 27 and 84 and US Highway 70. The restaurant isn't large, just five or six tables and two small counters – one for ordering, one for pickup – and a bin for policing your own table once you've dined.

Every day there's a different pie at Sweetpea's, and whatever it is will be lovely as you relax at your table, watching hummingbirds at the feeder. The flavors are all over the place, from caramel pecan cream to mixed berry to, I kid you not, a white chocolate "bug" pie for Halloween. Housemade fried pies in seasonal flavors also appear.

2897 Highway 70 West
Kirby, Arkansas 71950
(870) 398-4004
Facebook.com/Sweetpeas.fastfoodstyle

KIRBY RESTAURANT

The flat yellow brick building at the intersection of US Highways 70 and 84 in Kirby is home to the Kirby Restaurant, a country diner decked out in black and white serving burgers, chicken spaghetti and the like. Kirby Restaurant offers fried pies, and on occasion does serve up a respectable peanut butter pie as well.

2860 Highway 70 West
Kirby, Arkansas 71950
(870) 398-4441

GLENWOOD CITY CAFÉ

About half a block from Billy's House of Guitars, the Glenwood City Café sits in an old storefront. The wood-lined restaurant with its 60s motif tables offers breakfast and lunch each day. The most recent owner, Susie Cantrell, first took over in 2004. The restaurant closed in 2012 for lack of business, but Cantrell reopened it in the summer of 2017 when Caddo River Forest Products bought the shuttered Curtis Bean Lumber Company facility and began operation again.

At the Glenwood City Café, the peanut butter pie is a cream cheese icebox pie, a much lighter pie than the average. The pumpkin pie dolloped with fresh dairy whipped cream is redolent of cinnamon, nutmeg and a touch of clove, a substantial pie.

Glenwood City Café claims to have the best coffee in town… it also lists kid menu items under "curtain climbers," which I find hilarious. I've been asked to come back and order the chicken fried steak, purportedly better than you can find in Texas.

121 East Broadway Street
Glenwood, Arkansas 71943
(870) 356-3333

CADDO CAFÉ

The Caddo Café melds American favorites with Mexican selections, making it one of the few places you may be served chips and salsa alongside your pie. The fried pies range from coconut to chocolate.

53 US Highway 70 East, Suite C
Glenwood, Arkansas 71943
(870) 356-2397

SHANGRI-LA RESORT CAFÉ

Mrs. Varine Carr told me herself that the Shangri-La opened in 1956, and that she was there that day. When I joked that she must have been about three, she laughed, stopped and said "no." Coulda fooled me.

Daniel Maurice and Louise Mowbray Hunter opened the Shangri-La Resort just after Blakely Dam was completed to hold in Lake Ouachita. They started out with six motel rooms and two cabins and expanded over the years. From what I've been told, Austin and Varine Carr came on about a month before the resort was opened - Austin, as the carpenter, built many of the buildings at the resort. The Carrs became part owners of the resort in 1979 or 1980, and full owners in 2006.

Varine Carr assisted in the kitchen, eventually taking over the café. Though Ida Todd and Rosemary Johnson started the legacy of making delectable pies at the Shangri-La, it's Mrs. Carr who's perfected them and become so well known for them.

The resort is located on a peninsula that's about 20 miles from Hot Springs and almost as far from Mount Ida (though it has a Mount Ida address). It's hard to miss the classic sign along US Highway 270 that shows you the way. Another mile of undulating roadbed takes you to the edge of the lake and a spot barely touched by time.

Indeed, if it wasn't for the modern vehicles parked here and there, it'd be hard to discern it from photos from long ago. Postcards from years past show the same idyllic scene - a series of small cabins and a long single story motorcourt hotel spread along a peninsula into Lake Ouachita; a series of boat docks; lush vegetation of the forest separated from the deep blue waters of the lake by a tan strip of shoreline.

Mrs. Carr still gets up every morning and bakes those pies, 30 each morning, 30 pies that almost every day are gone before lunch is finished. Her son Phillip works alongside her, and Ila Green joins in to assemble them, make meringue and get the pies baking. Every single morning, when the first customers come in for breakfast, the pie cases are full – yes, I said cases. Your waitress, when you ask, will list all the pies available that particular day - apple, cherry, peach, blueberry, Dutch apple, coconut, chocolate, caramel, peanut butter, whatever has come from the kitchen that day.

987 Shangri La Drive
Mount Ida, Arkansas 71957
(870) 867-2011
ShangriLaResortAR.net

HARBOR RESTAURANT
and JENN'S MOUNTAIN HARBOR SPECIALTY FOODS

Not far from the Shangri-La Resort, you'll find the massive complex of Mountain Harbor Resort, an experiential family getaway with accommodations ranging from humble motel rooms to multi-bedroom cabins and houses, along with a full-service marina, world-class spa and excellent long-running restaurant.

The Harbor Restaurant has been in operation since 1959, offering three meals a day to those who stay on property and locals as well. Of note is Chris's peanut butter pie, both crusted and covered with dark chocolate, a richly decadent pie with the filling the consistency of cookie dough, the perfect heir and successor to the homemade cream pies baked on-site and sold for 30 cents a slice when the resort first opened.

Then there's Jenn's Mountain Harbor Specialty Foods. Jennifer Brewer does both fine dining meals such as prime rib and take and make dishes like lasagna and crawfish Étouffée for pick-up at her shop by the Mount Ida airstrip. She also offers a number of pies, including a lemon chess, white chocolate coconut and one she calls Better Than Sex that combines chocolate, cream, caramel and coconut. Jenn's is also the place to turn to for provisioning – that is, a place you can call and order up the food you will need for your stay at Mountain Harbor. Remember you'll need pie, too..

Harbor Restaurant	Jenn's Mountain Harbor Specialty Foods
994 Mountain Harbor Road	3489 Highway 270 East
Mount Ida, Arkansas 71957	Mount Ida, Arkansas 71957
(870) 867-2191	(870) 867-0113
MountainHarborResort.com	

PATTY'S DOWN THE ROAD

The original Patty's opened near Cajun Boilers along US Highway 270 West in Hot Springs years ago, and moved to this location closer to Lake Ouachita later. It's decked in old album covers and carries a Jimmy Buffett-style aesthetic.

Patty's serves up fried pies from Flywheel, adding a dousing of powdered sugar to the lush fruit varieties. But it's in the whole and sliced pies that the restaurant soars, varying between double-crust fruit, cream and meringue pies. The Better Than Sex pie – a caramel and toasted coconut cream pie with chocolate – is the sort of pie you should drive another few miles to experience.

6920 Albert Pike Road
Royal, Arkansas 71968
(501) 760-1007
Facebook.com/PattysDownTheRoad

MOUNT IDA CAFÉ

The Mount Ida Café has served the area since 1939, longer by far than Lake Ouachita has been around. The current location along US Highway East is packed with area nostalgia and serves a mighty fine chicken fried steak. Pies are sliced in advance and set out on a table by the reg-

ister on plastic-covered Styro-foam plates, because the wait staff knows you'll be too full to eat a slice once you're done with your meal. Blueberry and apple are amongst the daily choices in the rotation.

132 Highway 270 East
Mount Ida, Arkansas 71957
(870) 867-2283

MR. AND MRS. CHEF

Paul and Donna Uher sell pies at the Historic Downtown Hot Springs Farmers Market. The couple bake these pies in the wee hours every Friday morning at a local restaurant, before that eatery opens for the day.

It's a match made in the kitchen. Paul is well known for his restaurants around Arkansas. He had his own operation, Chef Paul's, on the south side of Hot Springs for more than a decade. During that time, Donna came to work for him.

"There was no romance at first. She was my sous chef. She was always a step ahead of me. It didn't irk me. It was great. Her tastebuds were as close to mine as I'd ever met. We ended up getting married. Best decision in my life was to hire her."

In the years since, both the Uhers have been involved in various culinary efforts.

"We worked at a Christian school here in town, and one of the boys used to call us Mr. and Mrs. Chef, and it stuck," he tells me. It seemed natural when the Uhers decided to go out on their own with this pie business, what they'd go by.

Once a week throughout the farmers market season, they're up the day before, starting their pie baking at four in the morning. The Uhers use recipes that date back decades and even centuries – which means what you get never saw the inside of a can.

"I don't want to take something out of a can," Paul tells me. "and put canned filling in my fresh pie dough. And depending on the tartness of the fruit, is how much sugar I use. I like the wild Maine blueberries. Flavorwise they're much better than the cultivated, they're small, they pop, but there are also a lot of blueberries here in Arkansas I buy from friends that are almost the same thing. They're small, they're not cultivated, and they pop."

That's right. Mr. and Mrs. Chef offers two different sorts of baked blueberry pie. Whatever they choose to tackle, it goes quick. They arrive at the market every Saturday morning at seven when the farmers market is open, and it's a rare day when they haven't already sold out by ten.

The Historic Downtown Farmers Market in Hot Springs is located at 121 Orange Street. The Uhers usually set up on the north end of the building. You can also order pies directly from Mr. and Mrs. Chef by calling (479) 259-4780 or by visiting and sending a message to Facebook.com/MrMrsChef.

Grav Weldon

CAFÉ 1217 and TACO MAMA

Chef Diana Bratton opened Café 1217 in 1997 as a combination gourmet-to-to and café operation. Diana, who received a culinary degree from El Centro College in Dallas and studied at the Culinary Institute of America in St. Helena, California and who also cut her teeth at the famed City Grocery in Dallas, opened the shop with the intent of bringing bright and fresh flavors to the Spa City. Café 1217's selections are inspired by California cuisine crossed with Diana's deep southern Texas roots.

The menu at Café 1217 is not static. Instead, there are a selection of different items offered each month, with even shorter-term daily and weekly specials showcased on blackboards above the counter. The pies share a similar rotation Within the case, you may find pecan, Turtle Delight, banana caramel, Dutch apple, lemon blueberry cream, salted caramel crunch, even butterscotch with marshmallow meringue.

Across the lot sits Diana's second restaurant, Taco Mama, which she opened after her mother told her it's what she needed to do. There's only one pie on the menu at Taco Mama, and there only needs to be one – the Tequila lime pie. The fresh-squeezed limes are strongly evident in the slightly boozy cream of this excellent meal-ender, a palate cleanser with bite.

Café 1217
1217 Malvern Avenue
Hot Springs, Arkansas 71901
(501) 318-1094
Cafe1217.net

Taco Mama
1209 Malvern Avenue
Hot Springs, Arkansas 71901
(501) 624-6262
TacoMama.net

AMBROSIA BAKERY

Open since 1975, Ambrosia Bakery offers specialty cakes and pastries in Hot Springs. Millie Baron and Mick Stoyanov purchased the bakery in 1996, and continue to share many of the original recipe desserts, including the popular Kentucky Derby pie.

307 Broadway Street
Hot Springs, Arkansas 71901
(501) 525-4500
AmbrosiaBakeryCo.com

THE ORIGINAL BURGERS & MORE

The Burgers & More Restaurants were founded by Richard and Norma English back in 1986. There were at one point four of the restaurants around Central Arkansas – but today, the only one left sits at the Mountain Pine Junction in Hot Springs. Mary K. Bass, the daughter of the Englishes, runs the place.

Over the years, license plates have accumulated on the walls, along with commemorative cola bottles and family photos. The restaurant, consequently, gets noticed for its excellent chicken fried steak and gravy and moist, flaky biscuits made from scratch. Strawberry, peach, apple and chocolate fried pies are offered for dessert, with ice cream if you wish.

145 Mountain Pine Road
Hot Springs, Arkansas 71913
(501) 767-4601

MUELLER'S BISTRO AND BAKERY

The best chocolate walnut pie in the Ouachitas can be found at Mueller's Bistro and Bakery, which sits at the north end of a strip mall just down the road from Oaklawn Park. Mueller's offers a number of pies, including lemon meringue and chocolate cream, alongside gorgeously decorated cakes and made-to-order sandwiches and breakfasts. Order ahead and hit the drive-thru for convenience.

111 Crawford Street
Hot Springs, Arkansas 71913
(501) 623-7005
BestBakeryHotSprings.com

MEL'S DINER

Cricket Graves is in charge of the kitchen and the smiles at Mel's, out past the Hot Springs Municipal Airport. The chocolate and coconut meringue pies are delectable.

1603 Airport Road
Hot Springs, Arkansas 71913
(501) 767-0595

MEL'S SOUTHERN DINER

On the other side of Hot Springs out on US Highway 270, there's Mel's Southern Diner, a completely different establishment. Opened in 2013, it offers an excellent burger, breakfast and a selection of fried pies in apple, peach, cherry and apricot.

4889 Malvern Road (US Highway 270)
Hot Springs, Arkansas 71901
(501) 262-9200
MelsSouthernDiner.com

J AND S ITALIAN VILLA

The Key lime pie at J and S Italian Villa is almost as thick as cheesecake. The two-layered varietal with its heavy graham cracker crust is almost too much at the end of a hearty meal of pasta or seafood at the longstanding Hot Springs favorite. Almost.

4332 Central Avenue
Hot Springs, Arkansas 71913
(501) 525-1121
JandSItalianVilla.com

Grav Weldon

JAVAPRIMO COFFEE HOUSE

One of the best chocolate cream pies I've had in Arkansas has a baked cream. I found it at JavaPrimo Coffee House in Hot Springs, and I've been thinking about it ever since. It's a perfectly sweet and slightly salted chocolate custard that's almost flaky, under a hood of hand-whipped dairy cream that's hand dolloped when you order.

It's more than evenly matched with the brews and teas from Java Primo's fine collection. Ask for a pie and beverage pairing.

4429 Central Avenue Suite A
Hot Springs, Arkansas 71913
(501) 318-9789
JavaPrimo.com

614 Main Street
Arkadelphia, Arkansas 71923
(870) 230-1337

FISHERMAN'S WHARF

You can walk, drive or even pull your boat up for pie at Fisherman's Wharf on Lake Hamilton. The recently renovated wood-clad building along Scenic Arkansas Highway Seven offers all manners of seafood and fixings, as well as homestyle Key lime pie.

5101 Central Avenue
Hot Springs, Arkansas 71913
(501) 525-7437

ROLANDO'S RESTAURANTE

A completely different Key lime pie exists at Rolando's Restaurante on Central Avenue downtown. This particular location features a patio out back in a hidden grotto. Learn more about Rolando's on page 237.

210 Central Avenue
Hot Springs National Park, Arkansas 71901
(501) 318-6054
RolandosRestaurante.com

MORRISON'S FRIED PIES

One of the best fried pie fruit trucks you will ever visit currently stands in the parking lot at the corner of Albert Pike and Airport Road. Morrison's Fried Pies opened in January 2017. It's a fully family-run business, with Edgar and Teresa Morrison in charge and their daughter Amber and son Timothy working alongside. Edgar spent 30 years in the bakery business before starting up this operation; he began his career in Texas. The food truck has caught on quickly, and any time you see the flags flying over the blue and white trailer it's worth a stop.

Edgar says the recipe for the dough goes back to the 19th century. Some of the fillings, such as blueberry and apple, are pretty traditional. Morrison's also has one of the best lemon cream fried pies I've ever tried, along with cheesecake, pumpkin and pecan. Even better? Morrison's has a full run of savory handpies as well, from beef and chicken empanadas to Natchitoches meat pies and even crawfish and Greek versions.

1333 Albert Pike Road
Hot Springs, Arkansas 71913
(501) 609-5864
Facebook.com/MorrisonsFriedPies17

ONE OF A KIND CAFÉ

Trish Phillips opened the One of a Kind Café a short jaunt off Scenic Arkansas Highway Seven on the south side of Hot Springs Village in 2015. She's a true believer in the organic farm-to-fork movement, and she sticks to her guns with the selection of fried pies offered at her food truck outside the One of a Kind Antiques and Obsoletes mall.

The fried pies Trish offers are made with dough that's just flour, eggs, milk, baking powder, salt and coconut oil, in which they are fried. They come in peach, cherry, apricot and apple and sometimes other flavors when local fresh produce is available.

The apple in particular was filled with some of the softest apples I've had in a pie. As in disintegrating on the tongue apple. Lightly spiced, barely sweetened, these apples were, honestly, apples - fresh, recently picked apples that tasted like apples. What I mean to say is, this was no pie filling out of a can, but a home-stewed filling. The apples were mild, not tart, and the effect with the soft crust was almost like homemade apple butter on biscuits. These are fried pies to be experienced.

372 East Glazypeau Road
Hot Springs Village, Arkansas 71909
Facebook.com/OneOfAKindCafe

HOME PLATE CAFÉ

Ever like a restaurant so much you decide to buy it? That's what happened to Jim and Aundrea Sparks after they stopped in at Home Plate Café in Hot Springs Village in January 2008. The Sparks had both worked in the restaurant business before, and deciding to take on this operation was a home run.

The oversized restaurant is festooned with baseball memorabilia, with a soundtrack on overhead audio to match. It's become a beloved stop for retirees who live at Hot Springs Village and for folks who fish the nearby eastern end of Lake Ouachita.

While the menus includes everything from burgers and sandwiches to chicken and steak, evening items vary based on the night. Some Tuesday nights it's German fare, others it's Cajun, still others French selections may be offered. Weekend nights look for the prime rib, one of the best in the Ouachita region.

Home Plate Café's desserts rotate, with a number of pies available. The sugar-free apple is definitely worth your time if you're counting calories. If you're not, dive into the possum pie the restaurant has to offer.

5110 North Arkansas Scenic Highway Seven
Hot Springs Village, Arkansas 71909
(501) 984-6969
HomePlateCafeHSV.com

THE SHACK

The catfish is famous at The Shack, Jessieville's hot spot for dining and dishing. The burgers are also pretty good, and there's always a basket of fresh-made Flywheel pies on the counter.

7901 North Arkansas Highway 7
Jessieville, Arkansas 71949
(501) 984-5619

SHORELINE RESTAURANT
at DeGRAY LAKE RESORT STATE PARK

DeGray Lake Resort State Park offers lodging of several varieties on the shore – including hotel rooms, camping slots and yurts already set up and ready for you to enjoy for a weekend. The Shoreline Restaurant, within the park lodge, offers a buffet breakfast as well as plated lunches and dinners. The pie of the park is Key lime, but a pretty nifty pecan pie is also available.

2027 State Park Maintenance Road
Bismarck, Arkansas 71929
(501) 865-5850
DeGray.com

DONALDSON COUNTRY STORE

Out south of Malvern off US Highway 67, over on the old road that served as highway before the railroad bypass was built, you'll find a feed-and-seed called the Donaldson Country Store. The long yellow building offers grocery items, farm implements and a half-dozen red and white topped tables for folks who want to grab breakfast or lunch, be it a fried bologna sandwich or BBQ loaf or one of the hearty stews that come in the wintertime. Burgers are braggable, and the store is a rare places where you can pick up deer corn for your property or a side order of cream cheese corn with your lunch. Dessert varies but often includes such wonders as candy crunch pie and peaches and cream pie. Fried pies are also available.

201 North Front Street
Donaldson, Arkansas 71941
(501) 384-2219

FRONT PORCH BAKERY and VIOLET FIELDS GIFTS

In Caddo Valley, just north of Interstate 40, there's a two story house with wind-chimes on the front porch. This is the home of Front Porch Bakery. Sara Huneycutt, an OBU graduate, teamed up with her grandmother to start the tiny bakery within Buck's establishment, Nana's Front Porch. The edifice, packed from end-to-end with consignment antiques, collectibles and T-shirts, is an unusual place for the bakery, but its kitchen is where Huneycutt prepares loads of eclectic cupcakes, moist cinnamon rolls and an array of cookies each week.

Huneycutt's coconut pie has received some renown, but it is the flaky baked handpies that got my attention. Available in apple, apricot and peach, the buttery pies are usually on the counter up front, and are only made up a couple of times a week. If you're lucky, there will be one waiting for you when you go.

190 Valley Road (across from Cracker Barrel)
Arkadelphia, Arkansas 71923
(870) 245-6998

FAT BOYS FINE FOOD

On the other side of the interstate, you'll find Fat Boys Fine Food, a barbecue joint that also serves plate lunches and burgers in a double-sided lunchroom. Fat Boys always has fried Flywheel Pies available to cook to order, and from time to time will also offer slices of meringue pies.

130 Valley Street
Caddo Valley, Arkansas 71923
(870) 246-6552

JIMMY'S FAMILY RESTAURANT

Doughnuts and fried chicken? Well, why not. In Malvern, Jimmy's Family Restaurant is in the same building and utilizes the same crew as Jimmy's Donut Hole. So yes, in theory, there's your chicken-and-doughnut breakfast right there. But when you're talking pie at Jimmy's, you should try the excellent chicken pot pie and also go to the cooler for a slice of doubly creamy housemade coconut cream pie.

938 South Main Street
Malvern, Arkansas 72104
(501) 467-3994

THE COTTON BOLL CAFÉ

There have been plenty of chefs to come out of the kitchens at The Capital Hotel in Little Rock (see page 276) who have gone on to other ventures. In Malvern, a couple from Mississippi who spent time at the esteemed hotel have opened their own place. James and Liz Shirey moved to Malvern about 20 years back. Both tenured at The Capital Hotel – James as culinary butcher and Liz as sous chef. A few years ago, they decided to open their own operation. The Cotton Boll Café is located in the old Pizza Hut building in the recessed area below US Highway 67 off the old highway heading to Perla, not too far from ACME Brick. Each day, the couple creates traditional dishes with locally sourced meats and produce, including a stand-up meatloaf, andouille chili, jambalaya and more, with an emphasis on Cajun influences. There are usually four to six pies available in everything including buttermilk, coconut, pecan, sweet potato, lemon, Key lime, apple, chocolate and pumpkin.

1606 East Page Avenue
Malvern, Arkansas 72104
(501) 229-1516

KEENEY'S FOOD MARKET

Back in the 1980s, I was a pre-teen spending time with relations in the Malvern area. I rode my bike a lot on the weekends. I loved to roll over to the junior high and ride up and down the slight ramps in the courtyard, then head up Cherry Street, rolling down the sidewalk into a dip and back out of it. I'd get a peach Nehi out of an old machine at the corner of Cherry and Highland, then turn down Mill Street and keep going to Main Street. A block beyond, I'd arrive at Keeney's Food Market. Back then, there were drinks inside the door to the left, produce further back and a deli counter where, if I asked nicely, I could get either a pickle loaf or bologna sandwich on white bread. It was always cool and a little dark going in, but it was a welcome spot and no one ever ran me out. I'd catch my breath, eat my sandwich and maybe some Cheetoes, drink my peach Nehi and get back out on the bike.

By that point, Charles and Maureen Keeney had ran that store for decades. When it opened in 1956, it was a community grocery like a dozen other such stores across Malvern and Perla. But by 2000, Keeney's was one of a few left and the couple were about to lose it. They could have retired at that point, but CK, as folks call him, decided to do something different. He and Maureen had about $45,000 set back for retirement. Instead, they reinvested into the store and stuck a restaurant inside.

Today, there are around 70 seats for diners tucked in the back of the old grocery store. CK and Maureen still run the place - he cooks, she runs the register. The Keeney's granddaughters wait tables. One of their daughters comes in to cook and wait, too.

Both of the Keeneys are in their 80s but they still get up at four every morning to work the store, which is open 6 a.m. to 6 p.m. six days a week. They do not plan to retire. There is usually a meringue or sweet potato or egg custard pie on the specials board, and it's worth a bite if you happen to make it through your lunch. If not, take it to go with you.

Keeney's Food Market
101 West Mill Street
Malvern, Arkansas
72104
(501) 332-3371

RANDY'S CITY CAFÉ

The entrées at Randy's City Café are not pretty. But those ugly biscuits and sloppy footlongs and such taste delightful. The only thing that comes out pretty at Randy's is pie, and there's always a variety available, whether it's strawberry cream cheese, banana split, chocolate meringue, apple or pecan – and each slice tastes as swell as it looks.

1216 East Page Avenue
Malvern, Arkansas 72104
(501) 332-0038

JJ'S TRUCK STOP AND RESTAURANT

What ever happened to the old greasy spoons, roadside eateries where you could get breakfast or a burger any hour of the day? There's still one in operation between Malvern and Benton on Interstate 30. Unlike many truck stop diners, JJ's isn't part of the same building that houses the gas station. It's part of a complex off Exit 106, complete with acres of parking for both passenger vehicles and tractor-trailer rigs. The restaurant's menu is packed with all the things you'd expect from a classic diner – ribeye steaks, hamburger steaks, ham steaks, beef liver, chicken fried steak, biscuits, corned beef, pancakes and eggs. There's also a daily lunch buffet offered.

The inside of the restaurant is clad in that sort of polished pine and mauve that was popular in the 1980s. Travelers can peruse a small selection of wares, and there's a game room and a telephone room along the back side of the main dining area. After all, the major customers for the establishment are truckers hauling cross-country, and it's nice to have a place where you can call home in comfort.

At the back of the room, right by the kitchen window, there are three letters on the wall – P I E. They're tacked to the wall above a case that always has at least some sort of pie in it. The pies are made in-house as needed and rotate between meringue, cream and fruit varieties. The double-crusted cherry pie's dough is almost of sugar cookie consistency, with a rich blend of cherries between top and bottom.

6106 Military Road
Malvern, Arkansas 72104
(501) 778-2295

OLDE CROW GENERAL STORE

Damon and Jana Helton have a farm where they raise beef, pork and poultry a couple of miles off the old highway that connects Benton and Hot Springs. They also own the Olde Crow General Store, a spot in the road where they sell the sundries you'd expect of a 20th century feed and seed, except with the marvelous and literally home-grown meats raised themselves. They also serve Petit Jean Meats deli meats and often have coconut and chocolate meringue pies to offer for lunch each day.

17202 Arkansas Highway 5
Benton, Arkansas 72019
(501) 794-2393

DAN'S I-30 DINER

Dan's I-30 Diner offers breakfast and lunch along the Interstate 30 west access road. Alongside such favorites as chicken and dressing and great omelets, daily pies are offered, such as egg custard or chocolate cream. Open since 2009, Dan's is one of the great Benton restaurants where chocolate gravy is offered on the weekends.

17018 Interstate 30
Benton, Arkansas 72019
(501) 778-4116
DansI30Diner.com

JIMMMY'S DINER

The sign outside Jimmy's Diner includes the line "It's All Good Too." While Jimmy's looks like it's always been on Edison Avenue on the southeast side of Benton, it's less than a decade old. James Gailey's is packed with memorabilia and photographs from Benton's past. The eatery is proud of its chocolate gravy, oversized omelets and a selection of pies. Any weekday there's usually a cream or meringue pie to be sliced from the cooler, and if you miss out on them you can order a fried pie that will come to the table covered in powdered sugar. Jimmy's also offers an all-you-can-eat Saturday morning buffet. Yes, the chocolate gravy's on that line, too.

821 Edison Avenue
Benton, Arkansas 72015
(501) 776-8400

BROWN'S COUNTRY STORE AND RESTAURANT

If you've driven Interstate 30 between Little Rock and Texarkana, chances are you've noticed the two story brown porch-wrapped building on the west side of the interstate in Benton. If somehow you've missed it, you might have seen a billboard advertising the 100 foot buffet, fried green tomatoes and an old fashioned country store..

That's exactly what you get when you walk through the doors at Brown's Country Store and Restaurant, the creation of Phillip and Cissy Brown. Phillip graduated in 1971 from Castle Heights Military Academy in Lebanon, Tennessee – in an area that had a plethora of country stores and restaurants. On returning to Arkansas, Brown pursued an accounting degree at UALR, where he met Cissy Carttar. Soon they began working to open a country store and restaurant, much like Phillip had seen out in mid-Tennessee. Phillip Brown's dad, Calvin, owned the building that once was home to Bud Schmand's Candyland. The couple renovated the facility while planning their wedding and, just a week after they married on June 8th, 1973, Brown's was opened.

At the time, Brown's was primarily a made-to-order breakfast place with sandwiches at lunch. It was a quaint and comfortable place where the waitresses wore long dresses and pinafores.

It wasn't long before the Browns were offering plate lunches, dipped sundaes and root beer floats. Soon they had their first buffet… a 10-foot-long start for what would eventually be the restaurant's claim to fame. Over time the buffet has grown, and today you can find fried chicken, catfish, Trace Creek potatoes and so much more along its length. At the end of the buffet, there's a fine selection of desserts, including fried pies and a rather nifty apple pie of some note. You can make it a la mode to your heart's content with the soft serve machine located on the side.

18718 Interstate 30 (west access road)
Benton, Arkansas 72019
(501) 778-5033
BrownsCountryRestaurant.com

Grav Weldon

Until 2014, the most popular place in Benton for pie was, hands-down, Ed and Kay's Restaurant. The eatery on the southwest side of town had been a stop for locals and hungry travelers for generations. Originally Ed and Alma's, the restaurant was purchased by the Diemers in 1982 and changed to Ed and Kay's – but many of the recipes remained. Of those, the pie recipes were the most coveted.

Miss Alma, the original pie goddess of Benton, offered PCP to her customers – pecan, coconut and pineapple pie, that is. The recipe lived on through the restaurant's end. This is that recipe.

PCP PIE

(pecan, coconut and pine-apple pie)

2 cups sugar
1 tablespoon corn meal
1 tablespoon flour
pinch of salt
5 eggs
1 cup pecans, coarsely chopped
1 cup drained crushed pineapple
1 cup flaked coconut
1 stick butter, melted
1 unbaked pie shell

Heat oven to 300 degrees.

Fold together sugar, corn-meal, flour and salt. Beat eggs, then add dry ingredients and mix thoroughly. Stir in pecans, pineapple and coconut. Fold in melted butter. Pour into an unbaked pastry crust in a pie pan. Cover edges of crust with aluminum foil.

Bake at 300 degrees for 45-60 minutes or until pie is set. Cool before serving.

SALEM DAIRY BAR

For folks heading out towards the Salem community in Saline County, the Salem Dairy Bar is a landmark. The longstanding burger and ice cream spot makes its own fried pies from scratch in apple and chocolate, fried to order while you wait.

6406 Congo Road
Benton, Arkansas 72019
(501) 794-3929

PAULA LYNN'S REALLY HOMEMADE SANDWICH AND SWEET SHOPPE

Paula Jordan learned to cook from her mother and grandmother. She and her husband originally opened Paula Lynn's Really Homemade Sandwich and Sweet Shoppe in a strip mall on Reynold's Road in 2010; the shop eventually found new digs a bit further east in an old dairy bar. The case by the door is always full of pie. In particular, there's a Chocolate Dream pie which is a layer of chocolate mousse over another layer of whipped cream cheese, almost a possum pie but without the nuts. The chocolate cream pie, with its chocolate custard on the bottom and fluffy whipped cream on top, is also a winner.

304 North Reynolds Road
Bryant, Arkansas 72022
(501) 847-2066

LUIGI'S PIZZA AND PASTA

Arkansas's flattest pie comes, not that surprisingly, from a pizza joint. Luigi's Pizzas and Pasta started out in the 1960s in southwest Little Rock before later relocating to its present station alongside Interstate 30 in Bryant, northeast of Alcoa Road. After a meal of hand-rolled tortellini or a large thin-crust pie, consider a pizza slice sized portion of blueberry pie, served a la mode.

22000 Interstate 30
Bryant, Arkansas, 72022
(501) 847-1110
LuigisPizzaAndPastaBryant.com

MAMA K'S

Mama K's is out of the way, south of Prattsville and Malvern but not too far out. The chicken fried steak is an area favorite. The pecan pie is a Karo-nut delight. Fried pies are also offered frequently on the rotating dessert special.

4593 Arkansas Highway 9
Leola, Arkansas 72084
(501) 332-7200

THE WHIPPET DAIRY BAR AND FAMILY RESTAURANT

Prattsville's one classic Arkansas restaurant is a haven for pie. The Whippet started off as a little dairy bar in 1966, and over the years has been expanded with one dining area after another. Today there's a huge seating area perfect for families, flanked on all sides with photos of each year's graduating class from the local high school.

Derek and Debbie Henderson purchased The Whippet in 1994 and own it today. It's well known for its fried catfish dinners, its burgers and several excellent homemade pies – in particular, coconut and chocolate meringue. The eatery also serves up more than a dozen flavors of Flywheel fried pies.

9011 US Highway 270 West
Prattsville, Arkansas 72129
(870) 699-4391
TheWhippet.com

UNCLE HENRY'S

Uncle Henry's opened in 1983 just southeast of downtown Sheridan as a farmer's stand where you could pick up fresh produce and nuts. Over the years, the barbecue operation within has won out, so while there are still smoked meats and nuts to find there throughout the year, the bigger operation is in the edibles you can consume on-site.

There's a big wooden cabinet by the register within that's full of pie slices. Of those, the turtle pie is of particular note, with its cream base swirled with caramel, pecans and chocolate. Uncle Henry's also offers whole what it calls "sampler pies," which are fruit pies filled quarterly with different fruits. These are coveted, especially by those who want one of those half-and-half slices of blueberry and cherry together.

202 South Rock Street
Sheridan, Arkansas 72150
(870) 942-3937

MOO MOO'S

This eatery on Sheridan's downtown square rotates pies amongst its sweets along with cookies and cakes, with different desserts offered daily. Meringue and fruit pies appear often.

120 West Center
Sheridan, Arkansas 72150
(870) 942-6666
Facebook.com/MooMoosCafe

TRUE SOUTH PECAN PIE
Kathie Dawn Johnson

1 9-inch pie crust
1-1/2 cups chopped pecans and/or pecan halves
3 eggs, beaten
1/2 cup white granulated sugar
3 Tbsp salted butter melted
1 cup dark corn syrup OR 1/2 cup light and 1/2 cup dark
1/4 tsp ground cinnamon
1 tsp vanilla extract

Preheat oven to 350F degrees. Place pan with pie crust on a baking sheet while preparing the filling.

In medium bowl, whisk together beaten eggs, sugar, melted butter, corn syrup, ground cinnamon and vanilla thoroughly. Put pecans evenly into the bottom of your pie crust. Pour filling slowly on top of the pecans. Bake about 45-50 minutes.
After 20 minutes, add a pie shield or aluminum foil over crust to keep it from getting too brown.

You know it is done when the middle of the pie is "set" and not jiggling like gelatin, and the center is a bit puffy. Allow to cool to room temperature before storing covered in refrigerator.

ROCK CAFÉ

Downtown in Waldron, on US 71B, you'll find The Rock Café, a clean red and white diner that's been around since 1936. Sit below ancient yellowed photographs of stars from Elvis Presley to John Wayne and order a meal that's served under wood paneled walls that have changed little with time.

The buffet differs from day to day – sometimes fried chicken, sometimes fried catfish, sometimes Mexican eats. The restaurant closes promptly at 2 p.m. during the week (except Friday), so don't expect a cooked meal if you show up at 1:55.

Homemade pies by the slice are usually available, and if not there are always the excellent fried pies. The hot piping pies come in peach, apple, cherry and blueberry. They're buttery, crispy on the outside and soft on the inside, and you'll probably order another after you eat that one.

355 South Main Street
Waldron, Arkansas 72958
(479) 637-2975

CHARBROILER RESTAURANT

The Charbroiler Restaurant offers burgers, steaks and a selection of homemade desserts each day, including a variety of cream pies and a respectable pecan pie.

58 US Highway 71 North (North Main Street)
Waldron, Arkansas 72958
(479) 637-3163

ED WALKER'S DRIVE IN
and MISS ANNA'S ON TOWSON

Fort Smith could be considered the state's most culinarily eclectic city – with a smattering of ethnic restaurants from around the globe. It's also home to so much pie – much of it you can sample for free on certain days of the week.

It's also home to one of the oldest eateries in western Arkansas. Ed Walker's Drive In opened in 1943 along Towson Avenue, mere blocks from the Oklahoma border. Though the ownership has changed throughout the years, there has always been an excellent French dip sandwich on the menu.

Miss Anna's on Towson started out as Goodson's on Towson, the second location for a family operation that had been providing home cooking and pies to Fort Smith for decades. Ed Walker's, though, is where good pies come from today - maybe not how you imagine. Let me explain.

Back in 2007, Ted Cserna bought Ed Walker's. It was, at the time, just being discovered for having the state's largest single-patty burger (five pounds of meat!) and rediscovered by folks outside the city for being the only place in Arkansas where you can pull up, flash your lights and order a beer you can drink in your car. The restaurant's endurance and location have grandfathered in that one little perk.

Cserna bought Goodson's on Towson, in 2012 and renamed it for his mother, who baked pies for the Goodsons over the years. Today, those pies are made down the street inside a tiny bakery at the back of Ed Walker's, which measures a mere 350 square feet, almost completely packed with ovens, warmers, sinks and counters. Only one or two people will fit at a time, making all the pies, cakes, pastries, breads and such served at both eateries.

That includes remarkable gluten-free coconut pies, where the crust is made by toasting coconut and butter in a pan before the custard and cream go in. It also covers the Chocolate Pie, the chocolate chip cookie crusted chocolate cream pie with more chips, shavings and even Hershey's Kisses in its makeup. There's also the Cherry Crisp, a cream cheese pie with a smart, tart bite, and a host of others.

Those same marvelous pies in the case at Miss Anna's are on the counters at Ed Walker's, ready to be sliced and served – a bond of pie uniting two longstanding Fort Smith favorites.

It gets better. Every Tuesday, all day long, you can get a free slice of pie with your purchase at Miss Anna's. A lot of people come and do just that at breakfast and get theirs to go for later. Every Tuesday, more than 100 pies are made, sliced and given away for free at the eatery. But any day, Miss Anna's has a case full of different pies. It's always worth a stop-in for a slice.

Ed Walker's Drive In
1500 Towson Avenue
Fort Smith, Arkansas 72901
(479) 783-3352
fortsmith.org/ed-walkers-drive-in

Miss Anna's on Towson
5001 Towson Avenue
Fort Smith, Arkansas 72901
(479) 649-6300
MissAnnasOnTowson.com

VILLAGE INN

The reason Free Pie Tuesdays began to happen at Miss Anna's? Tax Cserna told me straight out one day it was because it was working for another restaurant - which is the only reason why a non-Arkansas franchise is listed here. See, The Village Inn started up with Free Pie Wednesdays in 2012. I'm not certain if it was just the Fort Smith location or if others were involved, but the idea took off.

Village Inn actually began in Denver, Colorado in 1958, with franchises starting up around 1961. The restaurant chain has locations all through the Rockies and the Midwest, including a handful of locations in western and northern Arkansas. The restaurant's website makes the claim that it serves the "Best Pie in America." Well, the French silk is pretty good, as is its Caramel Pecan Silk Supreme, but many of the other Arkansas pies in this book could also qualify for that title. One way or another, Village Inn's Free Pie Wednesday continues. Get your slice with any purchase.

7620 Rogers Avenue
Fort Smith, Arkansas 72903
(479) 452-7007
VillageInn.com

LUCY'S DINER

Not to be outdone, the Fort Smith location for Lucy's Diner started its own free pie operation, offering pie TWO nights a week, on Monday and Wednesday. The eatery, which once operated 24 hours a day but which now closes each evening, bears its own dazzling array of housemade pies, including peach and cherry lattice pies, pumpkin, apple double crust and a host of cream pies in chocolate, chocolate peanut butter,

lemon, banana and coconut available on a rotating basis. The pies fit well in this an updated diner experience you can enjoy in either Fort Smith or at Lucy's other location in Rogers.

4605 Towson Avenue
Fort Smith, Arkansas 72901
(479) 646-1001

For free pie on Fridays in the area, check out Let's Eat in Alma on page 244.

LEWIS FAMILY RESTAURANT

Lewis' Family Restaurant has operated in the Fort Smith area for close to 40 years. The family moved into the current location in 1993. The restaurant's claim to fame comes from what may be the hottest dish in Arkansas – the Inferno Burger. Indeed, there's actually a club for people who have eaten the entire burger, which includes pepper jack cheese, jalapeños and chipotle mayo. Those who make it through gather from time to time and sit at a special table of honor in the center of the restaurant. The eatery is also known for great homestyle pies like its buttery coconut pie, a rather nice coconut meringue pie and a buttermilk chess pie that's one of Grav's favorites.

5901 US Highway 71 South
Fort Smith, Arkansas 72908
(479) 646-4309

RALPH'S PINK FLAMINGO

Ralph's Pink Flamingo is a wildly colored wonderland where every plate comes with a chunk of smoked sausage and every surface shines. Ralph Taylor and Tim McGuire jumped onto the barbecue competition circuit in 1998. From the day they first entered, they won again and again for their marvelous pork. They picked up the name Pink Flamingo because, as I've been told, "we're cheap, we're tacky and you don't want us in your yard." Ralph's wife and two sons joined the team and it wasn't long before they opened a restaurant at the corner of Old Greenwood and Country Club. When you enter, you pass through a hall decked with the dozens of trophies and ribbons the team managed to bring home.

The lovely lady that makes all the pies for Ralph's does an incredible job, not only with the well-known bourbon chocolate pecan pie but with other traditional favorites such as coconut cream and double-crusted cherry. Check the cabinet at the end of the food line to see what's in each day.

2801 Old Greenwood Road Suite 3
Fort Smith, Arkansas 72903
(479) 649-7427
PinkFlamingoBBQ.com

RIVER CITY BISTRO

Fort Smith's version of a New York deli is also where you'll find a good slice of Key lime pie. Get a Rachel while you're at it.

7320 Rogers Avenue #7
Fort Smith, Arkansas 72903
(479) 434-6474
RCBistro.com

PANADERIA MORENO

The best panaderia in Fort Smith for empanadas is likely Panaderia Moreno. The fat pineapple cream handpies that often appear on the racks are buttery and delicious.

507 North Greenwood Avenue Suite E
Fort Smith, Arkansas 72901
(479) 222-6259

BOB AND ELLIE'S DRIVE IN

You can get pie any hour of the day in Fort Smith at Bob and Ellie's Drive In on the south side of town. This longstanding diner offers anytime breakfast and burgers, and there are always pies in the case on the counter. You'll find peanut butter, cherry, apple, chocolate pudding, coconut and pecan pies rotated on a regular basis

6500 US Highway 271
Fort Smith, Arkansas 72908
 (479) 646-7559

PIG-N-PEPPER

Pig-N-Pepper is a longrunning barbecue joint that's popped up here and now and again in different locations around Fort Smith. Kirby Freeman's piquant sauce keeps folks coming in. A while back, I'd ventured in and noticed cream pies sold by the slice. On my most recent visit, the pies had been changed out – but no worries, their replacements are the excellent, buttery-crusted Letha's Fried Pies (see page 14), which come in a variety of flavor.

2700 South Zero Street
Fort Smith, Arkansas 72901
(479) 434-5900

EUNICE'S COUNTRY COOKIN'

Eunice's Country Cookin' has been around since 1976. It started in a tiny house on Jenny Lind Avenue by Ramsey Junior High (which once housed Catfish Cove, another Fort Smith mainstay). Eunice and Roy Waggoner ran the family shop along with their son and daughters until fire destroyed the house in 1997. Son Dennis Waggoner and his wife Cindy reopened the restaurant four months later in a storefront just off Rogers Avenue, where it has sat since.

Eunice's offers daily lunch specials and a handful of steady regular dishes, such as goulash and beef on rice. Dennis makes it all, including the fantastic meatloaf. There are always two types of pie, coconut cream and chocolate cream, with sometimes a fruit pie added for fun.

3325 South 74th Street Suite B
Fort Smith, Arkansas 72903
(479) 484-1465

GEORGE'S RESTAURANT

Since 1982, George's Restaurant has sat alongside Grand Avenue, a sturdy brown edifice that's consistently served up fare to the city's residents. Created by George and Alex Catsavis, the local joint offers dinner entrées, nachos, gyros and burgers — and for some reason, has a fondness for piling on big mounds of handcut homemade

French fries on anything within reason. The pies range from fruit to nut to a gorgeously decadent chocolate peanut butter. There are also several sugar-free varieties available.

2120 Grand Avenue
Fort Smith, Arkansas 72901
(479) 785-1199
GeorgesOnGrand.com

ROLANDO'S RESTAURANTE

The prettiest piece of Key lime pie in Fort Smith comes from one of its most eclectically decorated eateries. Rolando's Restaurante and its sibling spaces in Hot Springs and Fayetteville are the creations of Rolando and Sherri Cuzco. Rolando, who originally hails from Ecuador, brings his Latin American roots to the table. The eatery serves brightly colored platters full of entrées, rice, beans and sauces in so many varieties. The pie is a striking double-layer pie with a delectable creamy custard topped with a delectable top of whipped cream, counterpointed with a fine raspberry drizzle.

917 North A Street
Fort Smith, Arkansas 72901
(479) 573-0404
RolandosRestaurante.com

SANDY'S BAKE SHOPPE

Sandy's Bake Shoppe goes back to 1981. Mike Smith had spent 12 years working at Grand Bakery (now gone) and decided along with his wife Sandy to open their own place. Through multiple locations, the bakery has grown, and today it;s an open concept shop where you can watch every step of the baking process. In addition to

the cakes, doughnuts and bread on the menu, there's a complete selection of pies available, from pumpkin and pecan to several versions of cream and meringue.

5441 South 24th Street (Walmart parking lot)
Fort Smith, Arkansas 72901
(479) 242-4668
SandysBakeShoppe.com

MAMA'S COUNTRY CAFÉ

Mama's is the sort of place where you feel like you know everyone the moment you walk in. The Barling favorite offers home cooking and a fine selection of pies on weekdays, with Italian specials the groove on weekend evenings. Look for great chocolate, coconut, and lemon meringue pies on the counter.

203 Fort Street
Barling, Arkansas 72923
(479) 484-7773
Facebook.com/MamasCountryCafe

BOB AND WANDA'S WAGON WHEEL CAFÉ

Chef Lee's pies at Bob and Wanda's Wagon Wheel Café in Barling are a sure bet after a night of fried catfish or chicken and dumplings.

216 Fort Street
Barling, Arkansas 72923
(479) 478-8298
Facebook.com/BobAndWandasCafe

SHANE'S RESTAURANT

Shane's Restaurant has a goose on the sign and geese in the yard. The low wooden building sits next to a goose pond. It's not unusual to see birds wandering the property. Within, the atmosphere has not changed that much since the restaurant first opened its doors in 1973. There's a small case by the register, which manages somehow to house the second tallest meringue pie

in the state (behind only Sweet Treats, page 250). The coconut and chocolate wonders are complemented by pierced crust fruit pies, which are also available.

14962 North Arkansas Highway 23 (just north of Arkansas Highway 22)
Ratcliff, Arkansas 72951
(479) 635-2231

DINNER BUCKET

Experimentation isn't unusual for the Dinner Bucket. You never know what sort of pie you might find in the tall case by the door - seasonal strawberry or peach pies alongside blueberry cream, chocolate cream and possum; Hawaiian crème pie of banana and coconut custard together under a meringue; Butterfinger chocolate

cream with candy bar pieces on top; sugar-free lemon or apple slices or even fried pies. You'll have to drop in to see what's in the case next time you're by..

Dinner Bucket
19965 Arkansas
Highway 22
New Blaine, Arkansas
72851
(479) 938-7034

241

BOO'S BULLDOG DINER

Boo Polk bought The Bulldog Diner in 2013 and declared the need for a good, family food menu. Today, Boo's still serving up an absolutely amazing meatloaf, alongside big burgers and chili dogs and all-day breakfast to locals who come through.

The pies are stupendous. You must try the buttermilk pie, a buttery toasted coconut laden affair with the almost citrus note of cured buttermilk in its substance. Order it when you sit down.

3 South Main Street
Greenwood, Arkansas 72936
(479) 996-9097

REID'S HOMETOWN BARBECUE

This huge storefront along Arkansas Highway 10 in Booneville will probably make any crazy foodie's map because of The STUUUUUMP (I may not have added enough letter Us there, sorry) – a two pound barbecue sandwich that contains beef, pork, chicken and sausage layered with cheese sauce and jalapeno peppers, served between mounds of jalapeno cheese fries, all covered with what's called "hot slather" and served with three drinks. Well now. What draws my interest are the made-from-scratch fried pies, which can include such flavors as strawberry, blackberry, blueberry, chocolate, peach, pecan, lemon, or apricot. They're made when you order, so place yours when you get that crazy barbecue sandwich – or anything else, for that matter.

42 West Main Street
Booneville, Arkansas 72927
(479) 675-2159
Facebook.com/ReidsBarbecue

MEL'S HIGHWAY 10 CAFÉ

There's no sign in front of Mel's in Magazine, nor is there any sort of mark on the outside of the building that will show you what it is, just a flashing OPEN sign in a window under a red roof. That being said, if you do manage to find your way to the singular diner at the heart of this tiny community south of Mount Magazine, you will discover a chest-high case full of sliced pies – icebox pies, fruit pies and meringue

pies, too. These are good, but the handmade fried pies, which are baked a couple of times a week and usually come in fruit or chocolate varieties, are even better.

124 East Priddy Street
Magazine, Arkansas
72943
(479) 969-2233
Facebook.com/
Hwy10Cafe

FOWLER'S CAFÉ

In Danville, Fowler's Café welcomes all for good burgers and country cooking and some really marvelous pies, including a laden Millionaire, coconut meringue and chocolate cream . The original has done so well, the owners opened a second near the Dardanelle courthouse in 2017.

508 East 8th Street
Danville, Arkansas 72833
(479) 495-3344

512 North Second Street
Dardanelle, Arkansas 72834
(479) 229-2221

EMERSON COUNTRY STORE

Not far from Danville lies the smaller community of Rover, where one can get one's fishing license set up and acquire bait and the like at the Emerson Country Store. The shop often has fried pies of various flavors available by the register to take with you on your trip to the Fourche River or to tuck in your sack for motorcycle riding on Arkansas Highway 27. Daily hot lunches and anytime cold made to order sandwiches are also available.

19601 Arkansas Highway 27
Rover, Arkansas 72860
(479) 272-4177

MEMORY LANE CAFÉ

In all my travels, I have seen few variations on the possum pie, outside of whether a vanilla layer has been added to the layers of cream cheese, chocolate and whipped cream. At the Memory Lane Café, though, they offer the state's only cherry possum pie – a gorgeously rendered sandy-bottomed cream cheese/whipped cheese pie with cherries between the layers. Pecan, apple and Oreo cream pies as well as fried pies are also in the rotation.

200 North Main Street (Arkansas Highway 10)
Belleville, Arkansas 72824
(479) 493-2414

PAUL'S BAKERY

Originally the Mace's Bakery, Paul Lehnen bought the facility and renamed it after himself in 1959. He and his wife Jo Ann operated what he called "an elaborate doughnut shop" for decades afterwards, showing up for work even into his 70s. Though he passed away in 2012, his family still operates the shop. Of the many pies offered at Paul's, you'll often find double-crusted fruit pies such as raisin, apple and pecan. The butter chess pie (on the front page of this book) is a simple delight.

1800 Main Street
Van Buren, Arkansas 72956
(479) 474-7044

KOPPER KETTLE SMOKEHOUSE

Along US Highway 64 between Van Buren and Alma, you'll find the venerable Kopper Kettle Candies, which has served as the chocolate maker of note for Western Arkansas for three generations. Next door to the shop, there's a log cabin the Greer family had moved to the spot, and in that cabin for the past three decades there's been a restaurant. That eatery, the Kopper Kettle Smokehouse, is a local pie palace.

Kopper Kettle Smokehouse seems to delight in the pies that are at the back of the family cookbook, pies such as the Japanese fruit pie, a dried fruit extravaganza that's rich and somewhat buttery, say like an extravagant raisin funeral pie; the rich, firm

chocolate truffle pie, with that Kopper Kettle Candy flavor; the delectable pecan cream cheese pie, a perfect blending of the Thanksgiving favorite over a firm cream cheese layer; German chocolate with the chocolate and coconut flakes baked right into a firm pecan-nutty pie; so many to choose from. Just be sure to pick up your pie by 2 p.m. Oh, Kopper Kettle Smokehouse also has a one pound BLT, for what that's worth.

6300 Alma Highway (US Highway 64)
(479) 474-9949
Facebook.com/KopperKettle-Smokehouse

LET'S EAT

Tara Way keeps Let's Eat in the family. Her son and daughter are just as invested in the cooking of good food within this teal-walled strip-mall spot as she is – as evidenced by the audience I got the day I walked through the door the first time.

Tara has around 80 different pies she rotates in and out of a pastry case that sits at the back of the single lunchroom. In it are a variety of cheesecakes and pies that vary more often than an Arkansas weathercast. Each day she decides what's going to be in that case the next day, goes to the store for ingredients and prepares those pies fresh. They vary from Samoa coconut cream to cherry delight, peanut butter, banana cream, pineapple icebox, Almond Joy, whatever she feels like.

Of unusual note is the Elvis, a peanut butter pie topped with a layer of banana cream. Like the other pies Tara makes, she has no recipe, she just puts in what feels right. Somehow, she manages to create one delectable pie after another.

Every Friday is Free Pie Friday, where every meal comes with a slice of your choice – which, in addition to the four free days of pie in nearby Fort Smith, one can dine on pie every weekday for free.

208 Collum Lane West
Alma, Arkansas 72921
(479) 632-6322
Facebook.com/AlmaLetsEat

WORKMAN'S I-40 TRAVEL CENTER and HILLBILLY HIDEOUT

In the town of Ozark, you get two pie places for one. Both are housed on the north side of Interstate 40 right off US Highway 23, and both opened in late May 2013.

The first is Workman's I-40 Travel Center. Big, fat double-handed fried pies are available by every register for the truck stop itself – in traditional flavors such as cherry, blueberry, apple and coconut. These big boys are wrapped in plastic and perfect for sliding into a saddlebag or jacket pocket when you're heading somewhere, immensely portable with a crispy but firm crust and plenty of filling within. And yes, that's a bear. There is indeed a stuffed bear in the vestibule. Go see it.

If you turn to your left when you enter the travel center and proceed to the back, not one but two restaurants sit side by side. The first is a hot barbecue bar. The second is Hillbilly Hideout, a collection of booths and tables around a U shaped counter, serving 24 hour diner food. On the far wall, there's a case of pie, local favorites like possum pie and coconut cream, cherry cream cheese meringue pie, cherry nut pie, pecan, egg custard, strawberry cream cheese, you name it.

But there's one pie Hillbilly Hideout does that no one else does: the raccoon pie. Similar to the possum pie, this is a five layer pie with, starting from the bottom, graham cracker crumbs, sweetened cream cheese, blueberry pie filling, lemon custard and

whipped cream. This instant hit is almost always available, but if for some reason it's out, choose something from that case. It's definitely worth it. S save that fried pie from the register for the drive later.

3202 Pence Lane
Ozark, Arkansas 72949
(479) 667-0711
WorkmansTravelCenters.com

SOUTHERN GRILL

Country diner by day, steakhouse by night, Josh Carter's operation opened in 2013 continues to provide an excellent plate of fried pickles as well as a neat selection of pies every day. It's the only place I've found in all of Arkansas that serves a double-crusted cinnamon roll apple pie. The Oreo cream is decadent.

311 West Commercial Street
Ozark, Arkansas 72949
(479) 667-0704
Facebook.com/OzarkSouthernGrill

ALTUS GRAPE FESTIVAL

I have a soft spot in my heart for the Altus Grape Festival. Held on the park in the heart of the town the last weekend of every July, this fest celebrates the crops of wine and table grapes grown in the unique Arkansas viticultural region. Each year there are tastings, winemaking competitions, the grape-on-a-spoon race, and grape stomping contests (which, I am proud to say, I've won three different times). Then there's the grape pie eating contest.

As Jerry Leding iterated with the story of the Ozark Mountain grape pies he and his daughter Sarah make for Gooseberry Handmade Pies in Bentonville (see page 40), grape pies are a labor of love. It can take more than a pound of grapes divested from their seeds to make a single pie. At the festival, eight people compete to see who can eat the most of a grape pie in a minute. In 2014, my daughter entered the competition. At five, she was the youngest competitor. The start was hollered, and the participants dug in – save my daughter, who after a calculated couple of bites stopped cold and watched the others. We cheered her on, but she just sat there as the others gobbled as much pie as possible.

Afterwards, she carried her pie over to me. I asked her why she stopped. She told me she wanted to be able to share the pie with me. We took that pie home and enjoyed it for a few days.

If you'd like to attend, head to Altus during the last Friday and Saturday in July. For more information, call (479) 518-1963 or visit AltusGrapeFest.com.

KOUNTRY KITCHEN GRILL

Housed inside a former Waffle House, Kountry Kitchen Grill is a very brightly colored spot in Clarksville. The restaurant, not far north of exit 55 on Interstate 40, stands alongside US Highway 64 on the west side of town.

This smallish restaurant happens to have a really splendid selection of pies in unexpected flavors. For example, this is the only place in all of Arkansas where I have encountered a Snickerdoodle cookie pie – which is a much thicker slice than you might think. There's also the Orange Dreamsicle pie and a marvelous topped-when-you-order-it possum pie. Other varieties such as mint chocolate chip, apple crumb, strawberry, buttermilk and sweet potato are available, and the range varies from day to day.

2604 West Main Street
Clarksville, Arkansas 72830
(479) 754-2611
Facebook.com/kkgclarksville

DAIRY FREEZE

The Dairy Freeze, one of the last holdouts in a once-popular Arkansas franchise, offers fried pies throughout the year served with a nice dollop of soft serve on top. Peach fried pies are most popular in the summer.

1201 West Main
Clarksville, Arkansas 72830
(479) 754-8009

FAT DAWGZ BBQ and SOMETHING SWEET

On the downtown square in Clarksville, this barbecue and dessert joing open since 2010 offers good smoked meats and great sweet eats. If it's peach season, get the peach pie. Otherwise, that fine slice of peanut butter pie drizzled with dark chocolate syrup is always a good bet. Check the blackboard for extra pies.

121 North Fulton Street
Clarksville, Arkansas 72830
(479) 754-2857

OARK BURGER COMPANY

On the way out of Clarksville heading to Lamar, there's a brand new venture within a convenience store that you need to check up. Fuel up your vehicle and your belly at the Oark Burger Company. Already earning a nickname as the O-B-Co, the two tables and the counter at the north end of the facility tend to fill up with people wanting a crazy burger (mac and cheese burger, anyone?) and a slice of pie. The eatery is run by the brother of Brian Eisele, who operates the famed Oark General Store 20 miles away with his wife, Reagan (see page 58).

The pies are made off-site but are crafted by hand and come in an ever-varying selection, with choices such as blueberry lattice, buttermilk chess and coconut meringue common. Pies can be purchased whole, too.

1100 East Main Street
inside Motion Fuels
Clarksville, Arkansas 72830
(479) 754-0092

Clarksville is home to the annual Johnson County Peach Festival, the oldest continually occurring festival in Arkansas. It began in 1938 and celebrates all things peaches – including with a peach pie eating contest held each year on the courthouse porch.

Additionally when you go, check amongst the food vendors on the square. Usually one or two of the local churches will set up a concession booth, at which you can find beautiful fried peach handpies made right in front of you when you order.

Here's a great way to utilize those fresh peaches.

CARAMEL BOTTOM PEACH PIE
Ashley Lavender

2 Tablespoons butter
2 Tablespoons flour
3/4 cup evaporated milk
1 cup sugar
1/2 teaspoon salt
1 deep dish pie crust
2 cups fresh peaches (about 6-7 medium peaches)
16 ounces whipped topping

Make a paste over the stove with the butter and flour. Add in 3/4 cups evaporated milk, then the sugar and salt. Heat until thickened. Pour into baked pie crust. Refrigerate one hour.

Skin and slice peaches and fold into 2/3rds of the whipped topping. Add to caramel-filled crust. Top with remaining whipped topping. Refrigerate until ready to serve.

SWEET TREATS

No billboards. No internet ads. No advertising at all. Yet somehow, Sweet Treats in Lamar has managed to earn itself a delectable reputation as a fantastic lunchroom and a purveyor of some of the Arkansas River Valley's best pies. Having the current tallest meringue in the entire state doesn't hurt.

Greg and Marie Heiser started the little white and brick restaurant in the former Lamar post office. They had dabbled in catering a bit after Greg's 19 years of working as an electrical engineer came to an end, and set rules when they started the little restaurant – they'd only do it on weekdays and they'd only serve lunch. Greg's mom Donna stepped in to wait tables, Marie's mother Ann joined her in the kitchen, and the couple's sons Chris and Nick jumped in as well.

Everything served at the restaurant is made from scratch on site. Within the kitchen, you won't find a fryer or a grill. There's no cookbook, either. Greg makes the entrées and Marie bakes the pies – which are absolutely as tall as the oven allows and no more, standing several inches above the surface of the custard. There are more pies, too, including a possum pie with an extra vanilla layer, a strawberry cream pie, and two different versions of pecan pie. Up to a dozen different pies on the whiteboard at the end of the restaurant, and they disappear about as quickly as they go up.

As of this writing, the Heisers are remodeling a facility next door, and a move is planned The family has been hinting breakfast or dinner may be added.

5 East Main Street
Lamar, Arkansas 72846
(479) 647-0133

THE OLD SOUTH

The Russellville location for The Old South was built in 1947. As much as today's residents of Russellville would like to believe that it's the one and only, it wasn't alone, and it wasn't the first. That was The Old South in Fort Smith, opened around 1945.

The Old South was a concept restaurant, a franchise created as a turnkey operation. William E. Stell, an Oklahoma-born businessman who created and founded the National Glass and Manufacturing Company in Fort Smith back in 1929, had an idea to begin building a modular restaurant system, complete with the fixtures and fittings his company could provide, paired with furniture and even a menu. Unlike the Streamliner design (which was a contained prefab unit), Stell's idea was for a modular build-on-site system that could be adapted to each location. He employed the help of architect Glenn Pendergrass (he designed the El Chico restaurants around Dallas) to design the concept he envisioned. Stell brought in R. C. Strub from Schwab's in New York City to form a Kansas City-style steakhouse menu. No one knows for certain how many The Old South restaurants were built – but the last restaurant besides the one at Russellville closed in 2005.

The Russellville location was delivered on a contract to Woody Mays of Woody's Classic Inn. It was constructed in just six days and opened on the seventh, April 4th, 1947. As far as anyone knows, it never closed once in the 20th century, operating 24 hours a day. It briefly closed in 2014 due to financial issues, but Russellville natives banded together, held a city-wide yard sale and paid the taxes, allowing the restaurant to continue. While it's no longer a 24-hour restaurant, it still offers grand fried chicken and an eponymous house dressing you can get with your salad or even with an order of fried pickles.

The Old South, like so many restaurants of its era, had a case for pies, and that case is usually full any time you might visit. Of course, it has an excellent possum pie.

1330 East Main Street
Russellville, Arkansas 72801
(479) 968-3789

CAGLE'S MILL

Back in my college days, there were few high-end places to take a date. Of them, two stand out – the now-gone Romedio's Club in Dardanelle and the classic Cagle's Mill in Russellville. It was at the latter that I became acquainted with two dishes – the prime rib, at one point the best in the state, and the possum pie.

Patti Stobaugh with Stoby's once told me she believed possum pie may have originated at Cagle's Mill, and that is possible. It's been on the menu for decades. Of course, back when I went the restaurant was located next to a wall of windows, a row of wooden booths on one side and a salad bar on the other, with the big water wheel right by the concierge desk. Today, Cagle's Mill is a sports bar within the Clarion Hotel. The menu

has changed but the possum pie is still there, with layers of chocolate custard and cream cheese topped with whipped cream and chopped pecans.

Cagle's Mill, in case you were wondering, got its name from the old lumber mill at Russellville on the Arkansas River. Dardanelle Lock and Dam sits over the plot where the original mill once spun.

2407 North Arkansas Avenue
Russellville, Arkansas 72802
(479) 968-4300
CaglesMillRussellville.com

STOBY'S

Speaking of Patti Stobaugh and possum pie, you can grab a slice at Stoby's. This second location of the famed restaurant opened in 1984 (read about its creation on page 259). It's housed in what appears to be a depot, with a real train diner car on the side. A model train runs on a track overhead. Possum pie isn't the only pie in the case at Stoby's. You'll also find peanut butter, chocolate meringue and coconut meringue along with whatever else suites head baker Tina at the time.

405 West Parkway Drive
Russellville, Arkansas 72801
(479) 968-3816
Stobys.com

FELTNER'S WHATTA-BURGER

For day-to-day eats in my college years, the go-to was Feltner's Whatta-Burger. From the moment I first darkened the door during a break in band camp in the summer of 1990 to a week ago (probably a week ago whenever you ready these words), Feltner's felt like home. Originally opened in 1967, the brown painted A-frame with wings has always been packed with hundreds of pieces of memorabilia, which about once a year are swapped out for new décor and a thorough cleaning of the entire building.

Once the provenance of Bob Feltner, an upstanding gentleman who was one of my biggest supporters when I went into radio during my Arkansas Tech days, the restaurant is now in the capable hands of his daughter, Missy Ellis, and her husband Randy. Today, the fourth generation of the family works alongside local high school and college folks, still putting out the famed Whatta-Burger (not affiliated with the national Texas-based chain).

Next to the register, there's a tiered case full of fried pies, perfect for sliding onto your tray when you get your order or just coming up to purchase after you've finished your Sissy Burger. They're perfect with one of the dozen or so flavors of thick milkshakes and those fries that demand dunking in said shakes.

1410 North Arkansas Avenue
Russellville, Arkansas 72801
(479) 968-1410
Whatta-Burger.com

MARY'S KITCHEN

For the most part, the pies at Mary's Kitchen in Russellville are made on order. But from time to time, you might find a bourbon pecan pie in the freezer. Mary Gasaway's operation also makes a delightful coconut cream pie, as well as an old timey fudge pie.

220 East Parkway
Russellville, Arkansas 72801
(479) 498-0737

Mrs. Virginia Tyson was one of my favorite instructors at Arkansas Tech University. She ran me through all her composition classes, and encouraged me to keep writing fiction and poetry even as I slid over into the dark side her husband, Dr. Van Tyson, was more wont to do. Dr. Tyson would eventually become my advisor once I swapped over to a journalism major, and Mrs. Tyson kept up with me. The Tysons would later go on to purchase the *Atkins Chronicle* and have seen it through the end of its original iteration and its re-emergence in the information age.

VIRGINIA TYSON'S MINCEMEAT PIE

Buy nunsuch mincemeat, the kind that's dry in a little box. Crumble it into a medium-sized pot with some water. Peel and cut up an apple into small pieces. Add apple and 1/4 to 1/2 cup sugar or brown sugar (you judge how sweet you want it). Cook it down until it looks like pie filling. Pour into an unbaked pie shell. Cover with a lattice pastry top. Bake at 325 or 350 until the crust looks done. This calls for a lot of personal choices, but it is hard to mess up.

KOUNTRIFIED

One of Russellville's newest restaurants aims to bring back country cooking to Main Street. The restaurant offers homestyle breakfasts and lunches and a pretty good chicken fried steak.

The pies come in the same sort of styles you'd get at the average family gathering – peanut butter, chocolate, possum, and coconut meringue.

2621 West Main Street
Russellville, Arkansas 72801
(479) 967-1505
Facebook.com/
KountrifiedCooking

BUCCANEER RESTAURANT

Dover lies a few miles north of Russellville. There you'll find the Buccaneer Restaurant, a combination burger joint and pizza barn, which happens to serve a rather nifty fried apple pie a la mode.

45 East Camp Street
Dover, Arkansas 72837
(479) 331-9779

ATKINSON'S BLUE DIAMOND CAFÉ

Atkinson's Blue Diamond Café has served Morrilton for more than 30 years. Much of its clientele comes from the nearby Morrilton Packing Company, which manufactures Petit Jean Meats products such as smoked hams, bacon and red weiners.

In 2004, Earle and Pat Eichenberger and Garry and Karen Atkinson purchased the property and gave it the Blue Diamond name. The restaurant offers several specialties, including a signature sandwich called The Shaner with your choice of three meats, two cheeses and what bread you want -- and Bill's Dills, fried pickles battered when you order them. There are also nachos, a daily plate lunch special and plenty of Petit Jean Meats products such as hot dogs and the BLT. Atkinson's also offers the Dandy Dog, a battered and fried Petit Jean hot dog corn dog.

The eatery's dessert selections include a host of ice cream based desserts, brownies and pies – both meringue pies and fried pies you can get with a side of soft serve ice cream.

1800 East Harding Street
Morrilton, Arkansas 72110
(501) 354-4253

MORRILTON DRIVE-INN RESTAURANT

If you can't find something you like at the Morrilton Drive-Inn Restaurant, it's on you. The ordering window is completely surrounded by menu boards listing everything from burgers to Ark-Mex foods to country diner specials and even ice cream. Fried pies are in a basket by the register.

1601 Oak Street
Morrilton, Arkansas 72110
(501) 354-8343

MATHER LODGE RESTAURANT

On the edge of the crest of Petit Jean Mountain near Morrilton, you'll find one of the oldest places to stay in the state. Mather Lodge retains much of the original charm that's been bringing people up the mountain for generations.

In 1921, Dr. T.H. Hardison, the company physician for the Fort Smith Lumber Company, pushed for Congress to accept 80 acres of land in the Seven Hollows section of Petit Jean Mountain as Petit Jean National Park. Though the effort was unsuccessful, it did garner local interest, and in 1923 the state legislature named the donated area Petit Jean State Park. After President Franklin D. Roosevelt's New Deal began in 1933, workers with the Civilian Conservation Corps were sent to Petit Jean, where they constructed several cabins and a lodge between 1933 and 1938. The lodge was named after the head of the national parks system, Stephen Mather.

The most recent renovation of the lodge has been to its restaurant and desk. In 2013, an addition built in the 1970s was removed and the entire wing replaced with new construction that incorporated original stone along with heavy logs and lots of big windows that showcase the remarkable views over the hollows below. The restaurant has been upgraded, and now you can dine at its heavy wooden tables for breakfast, lunch or dinner. The expansion also included a gift shop area, new conference room with audio visual equipment and a large lobby, while the original lobby and gift shop areas have been preserved within the overall structure, creating two comfortable rooms that feature original furnishings and fireplaces.

Tim Schultz - Arkansas Department of Parks and Tourism

The restaurant serves breakfast, lunch and dinner alongside magnificent views, and offers two pies – possum pie and lemon icebox pie – for dessert.

1069 Petit Jean Mountain Road
Morrilton, Arkansas 72110
(501) 727-5604
PetitJeanStatePark.com

MATHER LODGE'S LEMON ICEBOX PIE

1 16-ounce package frozen lemonade concentrate
2 16-ounce tubs whipped topping
2 14-ounce cans sweetened condensed milk
4 graham cracker crusts

Blend concentrate, whipped topping and condensed milk. Pour into pie crust. Chill for one hour. Top with graham cracker crumbs and/or whipped topping if you choose

MUSTANG SALLY'S

Housed in the building that was once home to Rankin's Café, Mustang Sally's opened to serve Perryville in 2012. The plain yellow exterior belies a thoroughly updated interior with plenty of booths and tables for gatherings. Get a fried pie, a fat golden-fried peach or apple pie wrapped up in faux newsprint and brought searing-hot to the table in a basket.

303 West Main Street
Perryville, Arkansas 72126
(501) 889-1501
Facebook.com/
MustangSallysBurgers

PATTICAKES and STOBY'S

The original Stoby's and its eponymous sibling eatery in Russellville are both venerable landmarks in the Arkansas River Valley. The restaurant is the creation of David Stobaugh. Back in 1977, he was about to graduate from the University of Arkansas in Fayetteville with a degree in banking and finance. One day he was at a restaurant, and it occurred to him that running a restaurant was an honest way to make a living – so right out of college, he took a job as a grill cook at Western Sizzlin'. Within a short time he was managing the Danver's location in Conway. He tackled a lot of other opportunities – one of which was pedaling around an ice cream concession on a bike!

One day in 1980, out of work and broke, David walked into Mrs. Smith's Pie Shop on Donaghey and proposed a deal – he'd split the rent with her if she'd let him go into business with her, making sandwiches to go along with her pies. What he didn't count on was the fact that Florence Smith was ready to be done with running a pie shop. She offered him the place, then asked him to hire her – which he did. She worked for him for years afterwards.

Stoby's opened quietly… David had to sell his wife's car just to get enough money to buy produce and meat for the restaurant. But it caught on, and business went so well that David opened the second location, in the old depot at Russellville, in 1984.

Over the years, Stoby's gained great notoriety for its cheese dip, a smooth yellow made with a secret recipe, still one of the most popular items the restaurant has on the menu. It also garnered notice for the pies in the cases at both restaurants, which included derby pie, coconut cream, and possum.

In 2010, David's wife Patti operated PattiCakes Bakery in the building to the west of the depot, initially to make the breads and pies utilized by both restaurants. The bakery took off quickly. A short time later, the operation was moved to a building behind the Conway Stoby's, where it remains today.

The possum pie is just one of many PattiCakes offers. Every day there are several pies in the case, and sometimes even tarts. Pie slices are offered at both of the Stoby's, as well, and are a popular end to any meal.

Stoby's	PattiCakes
805 Donaghey Avenue	2106 Robinson Avenue
Conway, Arkansas 72034	Conway, Arkansas 72034
(501) 327-5447	(501) 205-1969
Stobys.com	PattiCakesBakery.net

CROSS CREEK SANDWICH SHOP

The Cross Creek Sandwich Shop started out as a single counter at the back of Jennifer's Antiques in downtown Conway. Word of great sandwiches, cookies and pie got out, and the restaurant expanded into a couple of different sections of the antique store. Romantic partners of antique lovers first found this place a lovely spot to sit and snack while their other halves browsed; now the restaurant has equal standing. The pies are located in a case to the right of the counter, and come in varieties such as coconut cream and chocolate peanut butter. The chocolate fudge pie, with its chocolate mousse on top and decadently dark chocolate custard on the bottom, is rich and delightful.

1003 Oak Street
Conway, Arkansas 72032
(501) 764-1811
CrossCreekSandwichShop.com

ED'S CUSTOM BAKERY

Ed Bradley left his post in the bakery at Simon's on Front Street back in the 1980s to start his own cake and doughnut place. Ed's Custom Bakery became a classic. In 2016, Joseph Langer purchased the shop and runs it today. The shop still offers doughnuts in the morning and rolls in the evening alongside wedding and birthday cakes and a smattering of pie options including chocolate crusted peanut butter, chocolate cream, lemon meringue, apple, cherry, Key lime, sweet potato, pecan and pumpkin.

256 Oak Street
Conway, Arkansas 72032
(501) 327-2996

JULIE'S SWEET SHOPPE

Despite being in one of Arkansas's most bakery-saturated cities, Julie Goodnight's decision to step out on her own and begin her own bakery has been a successful one. In 2013, Julie left the older shop to tackle a difficult location on US Highway 65 to start her own bakery. Julie's Sweet Shoppe opened and she never looked back. Customers came and the cases were filled time and again with her doughnuts, fried pies, pimento cheese, kolaches, rolls and whole pies, too.

The doughnuts are popular – so much so that in 2018 Food Network declared them the best in the state. But for me, it's all about the pies. I know when I go I can get a glazed and fried pie in so many flavors, including rarer ones such as blackberry and strawberry and raisin. Julie's also offers more than a dozen varieties of whole pies, including a beautifully radiant lemon pie and a substantially thick pecan pie, alongside coconut, banana and chocolate creams, Death By Chocolate and chocolate whip.

201 Skyline Drive #39
Conway, Arkansas 72032
(501) 205-4301
JuliesSweetShoppe.com

HOLLY'S COUNTRY COOKIN'

Locals swear by this lunch-only, weekday-only cafeteria on south Harkrider - by the fried chicken, by the mac and cheese and by the pies. Desserts are in a case by the register. There's always pie, particularly of the meringue and cream variety.

120 Harkrider Street
Conway, Arkansas 72032
(501) 328-9738

Chef William Ginocchio is a culinary instructor at the University of Arkansas Pulaski Technical College Arkansas Culinary School. He's an incredible baker, and I've been blessed many times over to dine on his creations.

BOURBON-CHOCOLATE PECAN TART

Crust
1 cup all-purpose flour
pinch salt
1 Tablespoon granulated sugar
2 Tablespoons cold lard, cut into small cubes (butter can be substituted)
1 egg
1 teaspoon vanilla extract

Tart filling
3 eggs
8 ounces light brown sugar
1 cup molasses
1 teaspoon vanilla extract
2 ounces butter
¼ cup chocolate chips
1 cup pecan pieces

Combine the flour, salt and sugar for the crust in the bowl of a food processor. Pulse until mixed. Add the lard and pulse until it is incorporated into the flour mixture. It should look like peas or small pebbles.

Beat the eggs and vanilla together lightly. Slowly add to the egg mixture while pulsing the processor until the dough comes together into a cohesive ball. Wrap the ball of dough in plastic and refrigerate for 1-2 hours, or until it is chilled and firm, but still malleable. While the dough chills, make the tart filling.

Preheat the oven to 350°F. Beat the eggs with the sugar until creamy, slowly beat in the molasses and vanilla.

Melt the butter in a skillet. Add the bourbon and flambe. Allow the butter and bourbon to cool. Temper the butter and bourbon mixture into the egg mixture.

Roll out the dough between two pieces of parchment. Spray a 10" tart pan with pan release and press the dough into pans. Be careful not to stretch the dough too much.

Sprinkle the chocolate chips evenly in the tart pan. Pour the mix over the top, and sprinkle the pecans evenly over the top of the mixture. Bake at 350°F for approximately 30 minutes, or until the mixture is set.

Yield: 12 servings.

FLAVOURS

A skillet pie? Why yes, you can find one on the border between Maumelle and North Little Rock. But the skillet apple pie at Flavours isn't the only thing exceptional about this eatery. Its people are extraordinary, too.

Fred and Cindy Noonan opened the small space in 2011 as a catering office. But the Noonans had a bigger mission than just feeding people delectable eats. They were out to help adults with developmental disabilities. Through their connections with the Civitans and the Arkansas Down Syndrome Association, the couple began to assemble a staff. In the years to follow, the catering business became a five-day-a-week restaurant, which has ties with the University of Arkansas Pulaski Technical College's Culinary program.

Today, about half the staff at Flavours fall into the categories the Noonans serve with their mission – individuals with developmental disabilities, young adults who have aged out of foster care, and veterans with physical disabilities.

Even without such a strident goal, Flavours is a gratifying place to dine, with a selection of homestyle entrées and some adventurous undertakings, too. The skillet apple pie, however, is in a class of its own – brought plated gorgeously as soon as it comes off the heat, topped with ice cream, measurably spiced. It's a race to the finish to enjoy this wonder before the ice cream fully melts, a race you win, one way or another.

13120 Crystal Hill Suite I
North Little Rock, Arkansas 72113
(501) 920-2247

BOBBY'S CAFÉ

One of the best old-fashioned coconut cream pies I have ever enjoyed still makes frequent appearances on the menu at Bobby's Café in North Little Rock. The creamy custard, dairy cream layer and toasted coconut on top isn't fancy, but it is a delectable classic. Be sure not to fill up on one of the famed Bobby Burgers before you order your slice. Peanut butter and chocolate also appear.

18505 MacArthur Drive
North Little Rock, Arkansas 72118
(501) 851-7888

MICK'S BBQ

Fried pies are on the menu alongside ribs, sandwiches and that sweet and zesty sauce found at Mick's BBQ, a counter-service barbecue stand along Camp Robinson Road just north of Interstate 40. Apple, peach and chocolate are available.

3609 MacArthur Drive
North Little Rock, Arkansas 72118
(501) 791-2773

WINK'S DAIRY BAR

Locals call it Wink's Dairy Bar, but the sign out front says Wink's Malt Stand. Whatever you call it, burgers and ice cream are the stars at this spot on North Little Rock's east side. And when you go, be sure to look in the window and see if one of the grand meringue pies Wink's is available. Worth a bite.

2900 East Washington Avenue
North Little Rock, Arkansas 72114
(501) 945-9025

LINDSEY'S HOSPITALITY HOUSE

The original Lindsey's Bar-B-Que opened in 1956. The creation of D. L. Lindsey, it was a nice little barbecue shack with a great following. In 1989, the restaurant re-opened as Lindsey's Hospitality House at its current location, a block over. Originally just a lunch joint, Lindsey's popularity grew and so did its hours. Today, the restaurant offers up dining and catering and you'll find that great smoked pork, beef and chicken everywhere at local functions.

Lindsey's does some great chicken, and their fried chicken is particularly memorable. But getting it smoked is also a bonus. Let's face it, anything that goes into the smoker at Lindsey's is going to come out glistening, sweating and lightly smoky.

The thing that brought me to Lindsey's the first time and what keeps bringing me back are the pies, because pie. Or pies... because there are so many at Lindsey's - and the selections are noted on the board each day. I have declared the sweet potato pie there one of the best I've ever had, and there's a reason for that. Unlike similar options at Say's and Sim's, the golden orange sweet potato pies at Lindsey's are firm and have a substantial texture. The slices are syrupy and pure, without a reliance on spice to show off the sweet potato's distinct flavors.

The egg custard pie is humble yet speaks to my gullet in a comforting way that makes me feel both redeemed and guilty after I consume my slice. Lindsey's also offers an array of Flywheel fried pies prepared when you order.

207 Curtis Sykes Drive
North Little Rock, Arkansas 72114
 (501) 374-5707
LindseysBBQnMore.com

WHITE PIG INN

The oldest barbecue joint in central Arkansas has been in operation along US Highway 70 since 1920 – three years before there was a US Highway 70, to be precise. The White Pig Inn has been operated by the Seatons from its very beginning. To find the place, look for the big white pig on the sign.

White Pig Inn sells a variety of Flywheel fried pies, unadorned but just the right amount to enjoy after a rack of ribs or an enormous barbecue stuffed baked potato.

5231East Broadway
North Little Rock,
Arkansas 72117
(501) 945-5551
WhitePigInn.com

BJ'S MARKET CAFÉ

One of the more popular places to get pie in Central Arkansas is at the home-food haven in North Little Rock's Prothro Junction neighborhood. BJ's Market Café is a multi-room breakfast and lunch hotspot attached at one end to an actual farmers market, where you can pick up fresh produce, nuts and sundries whenever you like. BJ's always has pie by the slice, with each one written on a big white board posted in each

of the three rooms. Common choices are egg custard, peanut butter, coconut meringue and possum pies. Icebox pies and cream pies of different sorts rotate seasonally. You can view the day's specials, including pie listings on the website.

45 North Plaza
North Little Rock,
Arkansas 72117
(501) 945-8884
BJsMarketCafe.com

LITTLEFIELD'S CAFÉ

Littlefield's Café started out in the old Starlite Diner before moving into a former Pizza Inn location at the north end of the Indian Hills shopping center. Inside, much of the diner aesthetic is contained between blue-painted walls on concrete floors - a bar for solo diners, tables and padded back chairs for two or more. The bar and back are clad in something approximating corrugated tin, and the specials were listed on a blackboard.

The coconut meringue pie is an honest-to-goodness chunk of airy but solid meringue atop a firm coconut custard, all through cool and soothing. The pie selection changes daily; several fried pies, cooked in peanut oil, are also offered.

6929 John F Kennedy Boulevard
North Little Rock, Arkansas 72116
(501) 819-6120

THE HUMBLE CRUMB

The Humble Crumb is a tiny boutique bakery in Sherwood run by three women (Tori Halvorson and Betsy and Ruth Peters) which offers a variety of cakes and pies to its customers. Strawberry, coconut cream and chocolate cream are amongst customer favorites.

110 Loop Road
Sherwood, Arkansas 72120
(501)766-5584
HumbleCrumbBakery.com

Roy Fisher's Steak House was a North Little Rock landmark for more than half a century. Opening in 1947, it served outrageously good fried chicken, salads with a proprietary dressing and a cherry nut pie to die for. While the restaurant changed hands and then closed in 2005, the recipe for that incredible pie lives on. Chef Anne Wood of Honey Pies recreated the pie from this recipe especially for this book.

CHERRY NUT PIE
from Roy Fisher's Steak House

Crust
1 1/4 cup graham cracker crumbs
1/4 cup pecans
1/3 cup butter
1/4 cup sugar

Combine the graham cracker crumbs, chopped pecans, melted butter and sugar and mix well. Press mixture into the bottom of a pie pan. Bake at 350 degrees for 12 minutes. Cool completely.

Filling
1 (8oz) cream cheese, softened
1 (14oz) sweetened condensed milk
1/3 cup lemon juice
1 t. vanilla extract
1/3 cup chopped pecans
1/2 cup of dark sweet cherries, pitted and cut into quarters

In mixing bowl combine cream cheese, sweetened condensed milk, lemon juice and vanilla extract and mix well. Gently stir in pecans and cherries. Pour mixture into cooled crust. Cover and refrigerate for two to four hours before serving.

TWO SISTERS CAFÉ

For those dropping in for lunch or to pick up a meal from Two Sisters Café in Sherwood, there are a number of pies available, from traditional apple and pecan to cherry, chocolate and banana split.

3130 East Kiehl Avenue
Sherwood, Arkansas 72120
(501) 819-0189
TwoSistersCatering.net

THE HOOK

Catfish is always the star at The Hook, a seafood hotspot packed out most nights on the south side of Jacksonville. The pies come by the slice in such flavors as French silk, lemon and coconut cream.

1802 South Arkansas Highway 161
Jacksonville, Arkansas 72076
(501) 982-2700
TheHookJacksonville.com

CHERYL'S DINER

Traditional pies such as apple, chocolate cream and cookies-and-cream are often on the menu at Cheryl's Diner in Cabot, where the daily plate lunch special comes with a bible verse.

211 East Main Street
Cabot, Arkansas 72023
(501) 422-0834
Facebook.com/CherylsDinerCabot

ORIGINAL FRIED PIE SHOP

Jacksonville and Conway are home to outlets for the Texas-based chain The Original Fried Pie shop, which in addition to a selection of cream and fruit pies also offers versions filled with everything from barbecue beef to Tex-Mex beef to chicken.

The Original Fried Pie Shop
1321 T P White Drive
Jacksonville, Arkansas 72076
(501) 985-0508

Burgers, Pies and Fries
2160 Harkrider Street
Conway, Arkansas 72032
(501) 358-6110
TheOriginalFriedPieShop.com

BOBBY'S COUNTRY COOKIN'

Years ago, there was a great little restaurant on 65th Street that only served breakfast and lunch. It was a meat-and-three affair, a country cafeteria where folks would get a quick lunch before going back to work. I grew up just a few miles away from the spot, and visited over the ages.

Funny, then, that one of the closest restaurants to where I live today is the same restaurant, moved to West Little Rock. Bobby's Country Cookin' has a history that goes back a quarter century, a history that includes a move in 1998 from those 65th Street digs to Shackleford Road, where it has remained since.

Little has changed over those years. The neat-as-a-pin lunchroom is crowded with pine tables and chairs, every table covered with a blue and white checkered tablecloth. Locals did expect a big change when Terry and Linda Matyskiela retired and sold the business to Larry and Carol Buttram. Nothing really changed except the tablecloths – which went from green and white to blue and white. The Buttrams have kept the lunch-only menu going, with four daily entrées and a host of sides served cafeteria-style.

At the end of the line, there's a case of desserts, always with at least a couple of sorts of pie. In fact, the feature photo on the cover of my first book, *Arkansas Pie: A Delicious Slice of the Natural State*, is a shot of the cherry cream cheese and chocolate cream pies. Today those pies, along with lemon icebox, Oreo icebox, pecan, strawberry and more can be found in those cases.

But beware – if you arrive during the noon hour, expect a line. The lunchroom will fill up. And get your slice of pie when you get your food, or the slice you want may be gone by the time you make it back to the register.

301 North Shackleford Road # E1
Little Rock, Arkansas 72211
(501) 224-9500
BobbysLR.com

BOBBI D'S SOUTHERN CUISINE

Bobby's Country Cookin' used to be on 65th Street – where Bobbi D's Southern Cuisine is located today. For breakfast, Bobbi's does a buffet to enjoy inside or to take along with you, and for lunch there's always hot specials on the line such as pot roast, orange chicken leg quarters, meatloaf, ribs or whatever seems good and hot appropriate, alongside macaroni and cheese and squash casserole. A small case at the end of the line holds the bounty of individually sliced pieces of cakes and pie. The pies range from pumpkin almond to sweet potato, egg custard, Oreo cream, pecan, apple, cherry, strawberry cream and Key lime – all ready to go on individual plates.

The restaurant is great at down-home eats – but also specializes in upscale treats, receptions, weddings and other catering gigs. There's a second location in Benton.

3201 West 65th Street
Little Rock, Arkansas 72209
(501) 565-1699

1016 West South
Benton, Arkansas 72015
(501) 778-3000

MERCADO SAN JOSE

Southwest Little Rock has a marvelous Hispanic population, and dozens of great restaurants have popped up, making it easy to dine the states and regions of Mexico. Mercado San Jose was one of the first panaderias here, and it still produces some of the most fantastic fruit and cream empanadas in central Arkansas. Try the delectable handheld empanadas de piña, a remarkable treat baked fresh every day.

7411 Geyer Springs Road
Little Rock, Arkansas 72209
(501) 565-4246

THREE SAMS BBQ

The very best place to get any sort of sweet, whether it's cakes or brownies or cookies or pie, in Mabelvale is hands-down Three Sams BBQ. Well beloved for its solidly thick peanut butter pie, the restaurant has earned a following for combining two distinct Arkansas food loves – barbecue and pie – in one location.

Fire destroyed the original building in March 2016, but the community rallied to get it back. The local Shriners loaned Sammy and Annette Jones a food trailer, which enabled them to keep selling barbecue sandwiches throughout the 19 months it took to rebuild. The doors reopened in October 2017. Today, the meringue and pecan pies are in a case by the kitchen door under individual glass domes, and those hefty icebox-style pies, including peanut butter pie, are in the fridge.

10508 Mann Road
Mabelvale, Arkansas 72103
(501) 407-0345

HB'S BAR-B-Q

For generations, The Shack served a remarkable, memorable barbecue to downtown visitors. When it was displaced and closed, several different individuals laid claim to the legacy. HB's Bar-B-Q on Lancaster in southwest Little Rock probably has the best claim. HB's was started in 1961 by HB and Madlyn Slaughter. Their son and daughter-in-law, Bruce and Judi Slaughter, still run the place. After all these years, it's still cash-only. From time to time you'll find a pan-style chocolate pie available, but you're far more likely to encounter fried pies to enjoy.

6010 Lancaster Road
Little Rock, Arkansas 72209
(501) 565-1930

SIM'S BAR-B-QUE

The very first barbecue I can clearly remember came in a paper boat tucked tight in two layers of aluminum foil and a paper sack, with a paper wrapped stack of white bread. The sauce was tangy and thin and it left an indelible mark on my tongue.

That flavor, that scent and that experience were all part of growing up, whether it was my mom picking up a pound for a weekday dinner or grabbing a sandwich while out on Geyer Springs road. It's the flavor of a slice of white bread that's been used to mop the last of that thin sauce out of the bottom of that aluminum foil. It's the flavor of Sim's Bar-B-Que.

Allen and Amelia Sims started the place back in 1937. It wasn't much, just meat and sauce and white bread and later beans. Later they sold to Ron Settlers, who incorporated the business. And it grew. It grew from 33rd Street to Barrow Road to Geyer Springs Road. The locations thrive for the same reason I still visit. That flavor, unlike any other Arkansas barbecue joint's sauce, is unique. It's just a few herbs and some sweetener, I am told, but it's more than that and everyone knows it. It's thin like Carolina barbecue but sweet instead of bitter, with a strong flavor of vinegar throughout.

Like everything else Sim's does, the recipe for the sweet potato pie they offer is a secret. I know it's made by Percy Walker and by members of his family. Percy still has the Barrow Road location. Now, I have had more than my share of sweet potato pies over the years, but this one is different. It's spicy. That's right. It has a whole lot of spice to it. It eats like a savory, almost, with just enough sweetness to call it dessert. Smooth as custard. And it's not dolled up with whipped cream or ice cream or any of that nonsense. Best of all, the pie has essentially remained the same over the past

several decades -- a spice-packed smooth concoction packed into a simple flour crust.

1307 Barrow Road
Little Rock, Arkansas 72204
(501) 224-2057

2415 Broadway Street
Little Rock, Arkansas 72206
(501) 732-6868

7601 Geyer Springs Road
Little Rock, Arkansas 72209
(501) 562-8844
SimsBBQAR.com

COTHAM'S IN THE CITY

Cotham's Mercantile, which stood on the edge of a bayou in Scott for 100 years before burning to its stilts in 2017, began as a general mercantile in 1917. Over the years, it spent time as a military commissary and even once served as Scott's local jail. In 1984, owners Bill and Suzy Cotham created an Arkansas icon, adding a single table to the store for area farmers who wanted to sit down and enjoy their lunch, rather than eating their wax paper-wrapped bologna sandwiches on the front porch. It was soon discovered by local politicians such as David Pryor and Bill Clinton, who found the 20-minute drive from downtown Little Rock the perfect distance to escape the state's capitol for a respite and a bite. It wasn't long before more tables were brought in, and the moniker "where the elite come to eat" was tacked on.

Larry Griffin and his nephew Jon bought Cotham's Mercantile in 1996 and opened Cotham's in the City three years later on the corner of Third and Victory. While the original restaurant was sold to Scotty McNair in 2001, Jon Griffin still owns and runs Cotham's in the City. Unlike its country sibling, Cotham's in the City grew its own culture. The oversized, multi-level lunchroom is festooned with generations of political memorabilia and yard signs, covering all ends of the spectrum. The restaurant is only open weekdays for lunch, but on those days you can enjoy the daily meat-and-three or the famed 17-ounce Hubcap Burger with a side of double dipped oversized onion rings. Finish off your meal with an apple, apricot, peach, cherry or chocolate fried pie served with whipped cream.

1401 West Third Street
Little Rock, Arkansas 72201
(501) 370-9177
Cothams.com

BRIDGES

Bridges at The Doubletree is a relatively new arrival on the Little Rock dining scene. Housed next door to Robinson Center, the restaurant offers a great opportunity for dinner-and-a-show for productions at the recently and gorgeously renovated facility, as well as a great place to grab a nightcap afterwards. End-of-meal or end-of-the-night offerings includes cordials, cognacs, coffee beverages and a choice of Arkansas handpies in apple, peach or cherry, served with a scoop of locally-created Loblolly Creamery's fantastic Double Vanilla ice cream.

424 West Markham Street
Little Rock, Arkansas 72201
(501) 508-8156
BridgesLR.com

CAPITOL SMOKEHOUSE AND GRILL

The lunchroom at Capitol Smokehouse and Grill is small and tight, but it packs out. Candy Wilkerson and her husband Doug bought the former Mr. Mason's, which had become very well known over the years for its fantastic barbecue. They continue to share that barbecue goodness today alongside a fine selection of sides, including an

excellent squash casserole. For dessert, there's some of the best banana pudding you've ever tried in your life.. But if you ask Candy nicely (and still some left), she will pull a slice of chocolate cream or coconut cream pie out of the case for you. Both are light and sweet. During the holidays, the Wilkersons also offer pecan pies, not to be missed.

915 West Capitol Avenue
Little Rock, Arkansas 72201
(501) 372-4227
CapitolSmokehouseAndGrill.com

DAVE'S PLACE

I recall my first Key lime pie - the tartness, the smoothness and the simplicity. It was Key lime juice from a bottle, sweetened condensed milk from a can, a graham cracker crust, not much more. The first time I took a bite of the Key lime pie at Dave's Place in downtown Little Rock, that was the sensation I got – that no frills, delectably baked homestyle favorite amongst the dessert offerings at this downtown mainstay restaurant, a favorite for judges and attorneys who argue at the Pulaski County Courthouse nearby. Most folks know Dave's for its lunches, but on Friday nights the joint hops with sweet jazz from the younger of the two Dave Williams, while the older of the two whips up more substantial fare from wherever he has the whim to try, be it German, Cajun, Mediterranean, Italian or whatnot.

210 Center Street
Little Rock, Arkansas 72201
(501) 372-3283
DavesPlaceRestaurant.com

ONE ELEVEN AT THE CAPITAL and CAPITAL BAR AND GRILL

Pies have always been on the menu at the eateries within the Capital Hotel. The edifice, lauded as the "front porch of the South," is home to two distinct restaurants with different aesthetics.

Michelin star, James Beard award-winning Chef Joël Antunes helms One Eleven at The Capital, the successor to the original high-end restaurant at the hotel, Ashley's. Joël has sculpted his own place on the Little Rock culinary scene, serving a variety of gorgeous locally-sourced delicacies with high emphasis on flavor and design.

Pastry chef Matt Dunn plated for me one of One Eleven's specialties – a blueberry tart with honey thyme housemade ice cream. Pie never looked so elegant.

Across the hallway you'll find the Capital Bar and Grill, which amongst its daily Southern specials, robust sandwiches and charcuterie, offers a solitary pie – a bourbon pecan pie with vanilla ice cream. Usually this pie stands alone – but during the month of February, CBG offers different pie slices every day, from ancho chile fudge to brandied cherry to malted walnut to good old fashioned sweet potato.

One Eleven at the Capital
111 West Markham Street
Little Rock, Arkansas 72201
(501) 370-7011
OneElevenattheCapital.com

Capital Bar and Grill
111 West Markham Street
Little Rock, Arkansas 72201
(501) 370-7013
CapitalBarandGrill.com

278

BEA BLESSED BAKERY and GARDEN SQUARE CAFÉ

Bea Blessed Bakery offers a number of individual-sized treats in the Ottenheimer Market Hall within Little Rock's famed River Market District. The little shop offers heritage cookies, tea cakes and cobblers, alongside gorgeous little hand-pies and individual peach and apple lattice-topped tarts.

The Garden Square Café in the Ottenheimer Market Hall keeps in its case a variety of sweet snacks, including sliced pecan and apple pies.

400 President Clinton Avenue inside the Ottenheimer Market Hall
Little Rock, Arkansas 72201
(501) 244-2622

DEMPSEY BAKERY

Little Rock is home to a gluten-free bakery that makes pies on occasion – and which always has gluten-free and even gluten-free egg-free pie crusts in its take home case. The bakery is a labor of love for Paula Dempsey, who decided with her family in 2008 to shut down the longstanding Dempsey Film Company and open a place where those with gluten allergies could dine without worry.

The move came after the first member of the family was diagnosed with health issues requiring a gluten-free diet. As more members of the family were found to have the genetic condition that prevented gluten consumption, Paula saw it as a reason to create something special for those who needed another option. Today the restaurant serves not only cakes and pies but bread, sandwiches, soups and other lunchtime eats, as well as its expertly stocked take and make case.

323 South Cross Street
Little Rock, Arkansas 72201
(501) 375-2257
DempseyBakery.com

The newest restaurant in this book hasn't even opened yet. But no one doubts that Cathead's Diner – a southern fusion eatery going into the Paint Factory in Little Rock's blossoming East Village – will become another culinary destination. Headlined by the effervescent Kelli Marks and the consummate chef Donnie Ferneau, the new space will serve barbecue and daydreams, as evidenced by the reports of "hangover kits" of doughnuts, Bloody Marys and Southern staples as a standard menu item.

Kelli, who helmed the much missed Sweet Love Bakery, will not only create outrageous doughnuts but cakes and pies as well. The multi-year winner of the Say It Ain't Say's Sweet Potato Pie contest (see page 280) whipped up one of the many pies that may be spotted in the new space, the winning entry from the 2017 competition.

SINFULLY SWEET SWEET POTATO PIE

This recipe makes a large pie- 10" or a deep dish 9" with three layers, a deep purple potato custard, topped with a light purple cheesecake, finished with a white cream topping ~ Kelli

Crust:

3 1/2 cups all-purpose flour	2 egg yolks
1/2 cup melted butter	2 tbs. lemon juice
1/2 cup shortening	1 tsp. salt
5 tbs. vodka (if no vodka, water works	1 tbs. sugar
almost as well)	1/4 cup ground toasted pecans

Combine flour, sugar, salt, and shortening in to bowl of stand mixer. Combine until small chunks of shortening are seen. Add egg yolks while mixing, followed by lemon juice, vodka, lemon juice and melted butter. Mix until crust comes together in a ball.

Roll out between two layers of plastic wrap. Once the desired thickness, sprinkle pecans over the crust. Roll crust once more to push pecans into the crust. Use the bottom layer of plastic wrap to pick up the crust and turn it into the pie tin.

Filling:

Purple sweet potatoes	1 tsp. vanilla
(enough for 1 1/2 cups)	1/4 tsp. salt
Honey	1/4 tsp. cinnamon
Sea salt	1/8 tsp. ginger
1/2 cup granulated sugar	1/2 tsp allspice
1/2 cup brown sugar	2 tbs. bourbon
2 eggs	1/2 cup heavy cream
6 tbs. butter melted	1 1/2 tsp. corn starch

Peel sweet potatoes. Make sure to select ones that have the purple skin and flesh. Some purple sweet potatoes have white flesh. Cube potatoes into about 1/2-inch pieces and lay out on a sheet pan.

Peel sweet potatoes. Make sure to select ones that have the purple skin and flesh. Some purple sweet potatoes have white flesh. Cube potatoes into about 1/2-inch pieces and lay out on a sheet pan.

Drizzle with a small amount of honey and sprinkle with sea salt. Roast until potatoes are soft to the touch, about 30 minutes.

Place all ingredients into a blender. Blend on high until no lumps remain. If color is not as purple as you'd like, add a few tablespoons of ube powder (needed for cheese-cake layer) or add a few drops purple food color. Pour into unbaked crust. Bake at 350° for 30 minutes. Cover edges of crust with aluminum foil to keep crust from getting too brown. While baking, make cheesecake layer. It will be added on top of this and baked again. Make sure to leave room for it.

Cheesecake layer:

8 oz cream cheese	1/4 cup whipping cream
1/4 cup granulated sugar	2 tbs. ube powder (available at Asian
1 egg	food stores)
1/4 cup sour cream	

Beat cream cheese until soft, add sugar until combined, add sour cream and egg. Finish with whipping cream and ube powder. If a deeper color is desired, add another tbs. of ube powder or a few drops of purple food color. Pour on top of pie and bake for another 20 minutes.

Whipped cheesecake topping (optional):

5 oz heavy cream (by weight)	1/2 tsp nutmeg
3 oz granulated sugar (by weight)	1/4 tsp salt
8 oz cream cheese (by weight)	1 tsp. vanilla
1 tsp. cinnamon	

Whip heavy cream and sugar on medium until peaks begin to form. Add cold cream cheese a tablespoon at a time until incorporated. Scrape bowl, add cinnamon, nutmeg, salt, and vanilla, beat about 1 minute longer until no big lumps are visible. Spread or pipe on the top of the cooled pie.

The first Sunday of every December, the Mosaic Templars Cultural Center welcomes all for an open house and celebration. The event is centered around the Say It Ain't Say's Sweet Potato Pie contest, where both professional and amateur bakers spar to see who can create the most magnificent sweet potato pie (the recipe for the 2017 winner by Kelli Marks is on page 278).

The contest is a tribute to the man dubbed the Sweet Potato King of Arkansas. Robert "Say" McIntosh got his nickname for taking every opportunity he could to voice his opinion. He gained a magnificent reputation in the 1970s for taking toys to underprivileged black children at Christmas here in Little Rock, and he's been connected to the holiday ever since. Say's famed sweet potato pie dates back to 1962. The gorgeously bright and glowing pie is smooth, sweet and marvelously tangy.

To find details about the annual event, visit MosaicTemplarsCenter.com.

DORA MAY PEARSON'S SWEET POTATO PIE

David Franks contributes this delectable sweet potato pie recipe.

3 eggs	1/2 teaspoon ginger
1 cup brown sugar	1/2 teaspoon. nutmeg
2 Tablespoons melted butter	1 1/2 cup cooked, mashed sweet potato
(salted is fine)	1 C. milk
1/4 cup lemon juice	9" crust (unbaked pastry or pre-baked
1 teaspoon cinnamon	gingersnap)

Preheat oven to 375° F. Beat eggs; beat in remaining ingredients in order. Pour into crust; bake at 375° until center is done—c. 50-60 minutes.

NOTE: This usually overfills a 9" gingersnap crust; a pastry crust with a high edge should be fine.

Gingersnap pie crust:

1 3/4 cup crushed gingersnaps   ¼ cup melted butter
2 Tablespoons dark brown sugar

Preheat oven to 425° F. Mix all ingredients together. Press into 9" pie pan; even out by pressing with second pie pan. Bake at 425° for 10-15 minutes. (Watch carefully for burning.) Cool, then refrigerate for an hour. Brush with egg white before filling.

SANDY'S HOMEPLACE CAFÉ

Sandy's Homeplace Café is out in the heart of east Little Rock's industrial district. The little yellow house sandwiched in-between larger operations is a good place to catch a no-frills buffet lunch. Sandy's gorgeously rustic pecan pie is not to be missed.

1710 East 15th Street
Little Rock, Arkansas 72202
(501) 375-3216

CIAO ITALIAN RESTAURANT

One of Little Rock's oldest Italian joints offers Key lime pie direct from Key West, Florida, with pies flown in twice a week offered both as whole slices and "just a bite" half slices.

405 West 7th Street
Little Rock, Arkansas 72201
(501) 372-0238
CiaoItalianRestaurant.com

COMMUNITY BAKERY

Ralph Hinson first opened it in 1947 in North Little Rock. It's been in Little Rock proper since 1952 and at its current location at 12th and Main since 1993. The bakery (along with its sister location on Shackleford Road) offers a wide selection of pies: pecan, cherry, apple and pumpkin to chocolate cream, lemon cream, sweet potato, French silk and even Boston cream (though, the last isn't technically a pie). The French silk is unusual in having no whipped cream on top. Instead, it is dense but delectable solid chocolate, light enough to enjoy with a fork, strong enough to convince you this is the pie you need.

1200 Main Street
Little Rock, Arkansas 72202
(501) 375-7105
CommunityBakery.com

270 South Shackleford Road
Little Rock, Arkansas 72211
(501) 224-1656

SOUTH ON MAIN

Chef Matthew Bell opened South on Main in 2013, which instantly became the SoMa District's hot dining spot. The former Juanita's location features a thrust stage in the center of its dining area, a gorgeous bar and notes of Little Rock's 21st century hipster vibe. The food is gorgeously plated southern fare with clear aesthetics.

Most desserts come in a Mason jar. The pie slices often available are callbacks to traditional sweets – like Thin Mint chocolate cream pie, coconut buttermilk and strawberry.

1304 Main Street
Little Rock, Arkansas 72202
(501) 244-9660

TRADITIONAL PIE BAKE-OFF AND RECIPE SWAP

Grav Weldon

Each year, The Root Café in Little Rock's SoMa District holds a friendly competition where dozens of cooks bring out their most delicious and creative efforts to see who will bring home the title. After the judging, the community gets to sample all the efforts. The event is held in conjunction with the Arkansas Literary Festival.

APRIL'S FAMILY KITCHEN

April's Family Kitchen is a frequent guest to the farmers market at Little Rock's Bernice Garden, a private art garden open to all visitors along Main Street in Little Rock's SoMa District. The market happens every Sunday through the harvest months.

At April's Family Kitchen booth, you can often find pecan, sunflower and the unique heritage recipe Navy Bean pie alongside the kitchen's packaged parboiled yellow, Spanish and browned rices. Advance orders recommended.

To order products from April's Family Kitchen, call (870) 636-0990.
The Bernice Garden is located at 1401 South Main in Little Rock.

CAFÉ BOSSA NOVA and ROSALIA FAMILY BAKERY

Café Bossa Nova's four layer delight has at its base a sandy bottom (flour, butter and pecan crust), a cream cheese layer, a chocolate layer and a whipped cream layer on top. The only two differences between this and a regular possum pie is the cocoa dusted on top and the name.

It's an absolutely divine slice of pie, but as you can imagine, Rosalia has even better pies in her arsenal. Case in point - this lemon meringue pie, with a crisp and clean-cut custard and a floofy, caramelized meringue top. Even on a dense bed of graham cracker crust, the lemon shines without reservation. It is lick-the-plate good.

Best of all, you aren't limited to having your pie at the restaurant. Dan and Rosalia Monroe opened Rosalia's Family Bakery next door in 2010. It's the only Brazilian Bakery in the state. Choose from a half dozen different oversized (11" diameter) pies in the case.

Café Bossa Nova
2701 Kavanaugh Boulevard #105
Little Rock, Arkansas 72205
(501) 614-6682
CafeBossaNova.com

Rosalia Family Bakery
2701 Kavanaugh Boulevard #101
Little Rock, Arkansas 72205
(501) 319-7035
RosaliasFamilyBakery.com

THE PIZZERIA IN THE HEIGHTS

Woodfired pizzas star at The Pizzeria in the Heights, also known as Pizzeria Santa Lucia. Operating out of a historic grocery in Little Rock's prestigious Heights neighborhood, the eatery has also earned note for its pie of the day, which varies all over the place. Varieties such as Choco-Nut, brown butter pecan, Flutternutter, Vanilla Cream and French apple a la mode have been sighted.

4910 Kavanaugh Boulevard
Little Rock, Arkansas 72207
(501) 551-1388
Pizzeria-SantaLucia.com

BURGE'S IN THE HEIGHTS

Alden Burge came to Arkansas in 1953. He brought his family up from Shreveport, bought a home and went to work in the oil fields nearby. Mr. Burge loved to barbecue, and he built his smoker in the backyard and got to smoking. He started cooking up smoked chickens, beans and coleslaw to sell at high school football games. In 1962, Burge was offered the chance to buy a little dairyette at the intersection of Highway 82 and Highway 29. He, his wife and their three kids jumped in to create this family-run barbecue joint. The place became well known for its smoked hams and turkeys -- which some folks passing through would take with them -- and for smoking goat and serving peppermint ice cream on Independence Day.

The Burge family bought the restaurant on R Street in Little Rock in 1974. Alden's son Jack Burge ran the restaurant until 2009, when he encouraged customer Jeff Voyles to buy it off him so he could retire. Jeff, who had spent 20 years as an investment broker, thought about it for about a year and a half before agreeing.

The restaurant is well known for a hot turkey melt, for burgers and for a turkey salad locals call "turkey crack," a cold secret blend of smoked turkey and other ingredients that's hard to resist. The fried Flywheel pies are fried on-site, dusted with sugar and set in a hot case by the register. Apple, peach and chocolate are the favorites.

5920 R Street
Little Rock, Arkansas 72207
(501) 666-1660
SmokedTurkeys.com

McBRIDE'S CAFÉ AND BAKERY

This family-run lunch counter on the bottom floor of the Baptist Health Rehab and Physical Therapy building on the Baptist Health complex. The counter serves an ever-varying selection of sandwiches, soups and desserts, including four-layer delight, peanut butter pie, lemon icebox pie, coconut meringue and more.

9501 Baptist Health Drive Suite 105
Little Rock, Arkansas 72205-6247
(501) 227-7701

MILFORD TRACK

Likely the absolutely most secret place to dine on pie in the entire city (if not the state) happens to be within the Plaza 2 building in the vast Westlake business office complex off Shackleford, just west of I-630. Milford Track is on the ground floor. You cannot access it from outside. Instead, you must pass through the front doors of the building and go downstairs. The restaurant is covered in world photography and occupied by a classic pinball machine and a 60-year-old jukebox in the other corner. Orders come in on what appears to be an old modified wall pay phone. The view outside is gorgeous, overlooking a pond.

Pies and cheesecakes are available by the slice, whole if you order in advance. While the pecan pies are magnificent in their own right, it's the rustic apple pie that has drawn my attention.

10809 Executive Center Drive, Plaza 2 (ground floor)
Little Rock, Arkansas 72211
(501) 223-2257
Milford-Track.com

IZZY'S

Izzy's opened far west of the heart of Little Rock way back in 1985. Over the years it has earned a reputation for its overreaching menu of sandwiches, hot plates, pizzas, tamales, cheese dip and the veritable kitchen sink, and for its marvelous array of hand-selected tea blends. The restaurant's owners also incorporate honey harvested from its own apiary, cultivated from bee-friendly plants in the restaurant's bee and butterfly garden. There are two pies on the menu: a lemon icebox pie with a pleasing zing, and a raspberry cream cheese pie on a walnut crust. Ask for a tea pairing.

5601 Ranch Drive
Little Rock, Arkansas 72223
(501) 868-4311
IzzysLittleRock.com

CAJUN'S WHARF, CAPERS and COPPER GRILL

Three Little Rock restaurants share the same couple of pies. All three of these places begin with the letter C, and all under the auspices of Chef Mary Beth Ringgold, named in 2018 to Arkansas's Food Hall of Fame as one of the state's top proprietors.

The restaurants – Cajun's Wharf, Capers and Copper Grill – each have their own geography. Cajun's, open for more than 40 years now, is on the riverfront in the Riverdale Design District west of downtown. Caper's lies on Arkansas Highway 10 in what used to be far West Little Rock (and which development has now surrounded). And Copper Grill sits on the south side of the River Market District.

I am rarely ever surprised by a pie. But this one deserves a special measure of notice. From top to bottom, it's a fluffy almost meringue-like cloud drizzled with vanilla over a pungently rich golden lime custard on a coat of darkest chocolate atop a dense graham cracker crust. The same pie is on the regular menu at Caper's and Cajun's Wharf and sometimes appears at Copper Grill as well. A laudable coconut cream pie with a similarly rich custard is also available. Share this one.

Cajun's Wharf
2400 Cantrell Road
Little Rock, Arkansas 72202
(501) 375-5351
CajunsWharf.com

Copper Grill
300 East Third Street # 101
Little Rock, Arkansas 72201
(501) 375-3333
CopperGrillLR.com

Caper's
14502 Cantrell Road
Little Rock, Arkansas 72223
(501) 868-7600
CapersRestaurant.com

TRIO'S RESTAURANT

Capi Peck is a fourth generation member of Arkansas's hospitality community. Her folks owned the Sam Peck Hotel, with its well-respected restaurant and delights. She opened Trio's Restaurant, the vanguard of Little Rock's westward movement, in 1986.

Capi continues to evolve the International-al-meets-American menu the eatery offers with continuous self-education, including frequent trips out of country (she speaks fluent Spanish). She serves on the Little Rock Board of Directors, works with groups to showcase local and regional farms and produce, and keeps a full calendar of food events. The restaurant she runs with partner Brent Peterson still offers some of the best from the original Sam Peck Hotel, including the famed Peck salad. It also offers one of Arkansas's best pies, a raspberry cream pie that I have seen people fight over. The crushed raspberries provide the perfect tart counterpoint to the exquisitely light, sweet cream underneath.

8201 Cantrell Road # 100
Little Rock, Arkansas 72227
(501) 221-3330
TriosRestaurant.com

LOCAL LIME

Lime. Just pure and simple lime. That's what you taste when you bite into the Key lime pie at Local Lime in Little Rock's Promenade on Chenal. Scott McGehee's taco palace goes simple for this gorgeous dessert, with a fresh lime custard topped with hand whipped cream on a graham cracker crust. Good with tequila.

17809 Chenal Parkway
Little Rock, Arkansas 72223
(501) 448-2226
LocalLimeTaco.com

FRANKE'S CAFETERIA

In Little Rock, you can find two restaurants owned by the same family, that dates back to 1919. Franke's was originally a bakery run by C.A. Franke that served up doughnuts downtown. Five years later, the first Franke's Cafeteria was opened. Today two locations remain. The extensive cafeteria line bears everything from congealed salads to roasts of beef, fried chicken, baked fish, sides, rolls, pies and beverages, all plated by white-clad staff.

Franke's has so many pies: pecan, sweet potato, pumpkin, egg custard, lemon meringue, brownie, banana cream, chocolate cream, lemon cream, coconut cream, strawberries and cream, and more. The cinnamon custard pie is, at this time, the only one of its sort offered at an Arkansas restaurant. It's similar to a tiramisu without the ladyfingers, layers of different degrees of custard interlaced with cinnamon. Get a cup of coffee to enjoy with this one. Pay after you dine, before you head out the door.

11121 North Rodney Parham Road
Little Rock, Arkansas 72212
(501) 225-4487
FrankesCafeteria.com

Regions Center Building
400 West Capitol Avenue
Little Rock, Arkansas 72201
(501) 372-1919

DELICIOUS TEMPTATIONS

Pie with your breakfast? Yes please. Because honestly, there's no better way to complete a meal of Eggs Temptation and potato casserole with orange spice tea than with a slice of delectably boozy bourbon pecan pie. The excellently made, buttery, gooey pie comes out in a long slender wedge, the perfect amount to conclude a lovely meal. You may also want to come back and try the caramel fudge pie.

11220 North Rodney Parham Road #8
Little Rock, Arkansas 72212
(501) 225-6893
BreakfastInLittleRock.com

Youth Homes, Incorporated has published a number of cookbooks over the years. Back in the 1980s, the private agency that works to rehabilitate severely disturbed teenagers in central Arkansas, operated a tearoom and gift shop known as the Yellow Daisy. This recipe comes from *Lunch at the Yellow Daisy II*, published by Youth Homes, Inc. in 1982.

FRANKE'S EGG CUSTARD PIE

1 ½ cup sugar
2 Tablespoons melted Oleo (margarine)
dash salt

1 teaspoon nutmeg
1 2/3 cup whole milk
4 eggs

Mix all ingredients well and pour into a 9-inch unbaked pie shell. Bake 7 minutes at 425 degrees, then 50 minutes at 325 degrees

DIANE'S GOURMET LUXURIES

West Little Rock residents have been dropping in at Diane's Gourmet Luxuries for years to pick up the perfect take and make entrées, sides and desserts that make them shine when entertaining at home. Open since 1969, Diane Knight's shop is packed one side with gourmet gifts and the other with delicacies and remarkable quickly-heated dishes and appetizers, perfect for parties. Her quiches are extraordinary.

When it comes to dessert, Diane's goes for simple but perfect – which means, of course, there are always pies available. Double-crusted cherry and apple pies are always excellent choices to take home from the case right by the register.

11121 North Rodney Parham Road # 20B
Little Rock, Arkansas 72212
(501) 224-2639
Dianes-Gourmet.com

TERRI-LYNN'S BBQ AND DELI

Terri-Lynn's BBQ and Deli is a Little Rock neighborhood secret. Since 1960, patrons have lined up for lunch five days a week to enjoy some of Little Rock's most underrated smoked meats, definitive deviled eggs and two delectable pies.

The restaurant was opened in 1959 by Harry Giberson and his wife, Mary. The couple named the deli for their daughter, Terri Lynn, who was just two months old. The deli on Little Rock's far west side was known for potato salad, coleslaw and succulent smoked meats. The Gibersons ran the deli until Harry passed away in 1986, and Mary sold the operation to Jim and Sharon Brooks. They brought the deli and smokehouse into the 21st century, passing it on to Aaron and Kristin Hether a few years ago.

Despite the years, the restaurant still manages to serve a large number of people from a single dining room - though locals know ordering ahead and picking lunch up to go is the way to do things. Like the majority of Little Rock's barbecue-serving establishments, Terri-Lynn's offers the triumvirate of 'cue, cheese dip and pie.

While the desserts in the case may vary, Terri-Lynn's always has pecan pie and a chocolate chess pie - which you can doll up with a squirt of whipped cream. The pecan pie is a thick syrup-filled slice of autumn, and the chocolate chess is just sinful - one of the best chocolate chess pies out there.

10102 North Rodney Parham # 2
Little Rock, Arkansas 72227
(501) 227-6371
TerriLynns.com

LAZY PETE'S FISH
AND SHRIMP

On west Little Rock's Bowman Curve, Lazy Pete's offers fried shrimp, crawfish, catfish and other Creole and Southern delicacies. Fried apple, peach and chocolate pies are available, as are slices of pecan and Key lime.

200 North Bowman Road #9
Little Rock, Arkansas 72211
(501) 907-6453
LazyPetes.com

ALLEY OOPS

Gary Duke and Jeffrey Chapman run a restaurant that's been part of Little Rock's food scene for more than 30 years. Alley-Oops, originally located at the corner of Kanis and Shackleford, now sits at the end of a strip mall at Kanis and Bowman. Enter the glass doors, then pull the original wooden doors from the older shack the restaurant once lived in, to open. The eatery is well known for po'boy sandwiches, plate lunches and burgers, and for a cheese dip often augmented with fried onions.

Gary Duke shares his recipes often on local TV station KATV, including those for the two famed pies the restaurant always offers – chess pie and chocolate chess pie, which have been featured on the websites of Serious Eats and Food Network.

11900 Kanis Road
Little Rock, Arkansas 72211
(501) 221-9400
AlleyOopsLR.com

CHOCOLATE CHESS PIE

1½ cups sugar
3 tablespoons cocoa
3 beaten eggs
5 tablespoons evaporated milk

2 teaspoons apple cider vinegar
1 tablespoon vanilla extract
4 tablespoons melted butter
1 flour-and-butter blind-baked pie crust

Sift together sugar and cocoa. Beat together eggs, milk, vinegar, vanilla and butter. Add sugar and cocoa and incorporate. Pour into pie crust and bake at 350 degrees for 35 minutes or until surface begins to form bubbly pits and is firm.

HONEY PIES

There's a reason I wanted to end with Honey Pies. Sharon Woodson's adorable bake shop in west Little Rock opened the summer of 2016. Her husband, Lance, had convinced her to transition out of her former job and, when she finally left that business, worked her into something new.

"We thought that we were going to be this cute little tiny pie shop," says Sharon. "I was going to bake and run the register in the afternoons and it was going to just be the cutest little thing you ever did see." But that's not how Honey Pies has turned out. After an almost immediate surge in popularity, Sharon found out this little shop was going to be something rather big.

"We didn't know we'd become a full-blown bakery. We're adding new things every single day. We really want to give the customers what they're asking for."

Within a year, Honey Pies went from pastries to breakfast, then on to lunches. But the pies are still what initially draw customers through the door. The big seller is the chocolate fudge brownie pie – a pie that's honestly a cross between chocolate chess pie and the best parts of a brownie, especially the crispy crust on top.

Every day Sharon, Chef Anne Wood and the Honey Pies crew create pies large and small, alongside quiche, banana pudding, soup and sandwiches, gourmet coffee beverages created from Leiva's Coffee and espresso from Onyx Coffee Labs. The pies, the bakery, it all comes out of love. There are always a half dozen different pies in slices, whole pies and mini-pies, in flavors such as caramel apple, S'mores, possum, and pecan The crust (which you can also purchase) and the recipes are handed down through time.

"I was always at my grandmother's house. It was my safe haven," says Sharon. "She loved to cook. I was five years old, standing on a stool in the kitchen, washing dishes while she was making things and putting things in the oven."

Honey Pies offers an oasis for pie in a busy city, for lunch or even breakfast, slices and whole pies to enjoy in the shop or at home. Sharon wants you to stop by.

"We definitely want to be the place where you come by yourself or meet a friend and sit and visit and have a slice of pie."

315 North Bowman Road, Suite 14
Little Rock, Arkansas 72211
(501) 613-7950
MyHoneyPies.com

MAINE BLACK AND BLUE BERRY PIE

This recipe was kindly shared by Marilyn Foltz Whisenhant.

3 cups blueberries, rinsed and dried
3 cups blackberries, rinsed and dried
1/4 cup to 1 cup sugar depending on tartness of berries
1 teaspoon grated lemon zest
3 Tablespoons cornstarch
1/4 cup heavy cream
1 egg white, beaten with 1 teaspoon water
sugar

Preheat oven to 425 decrees. Line pie plate with pastry. In a large bowl combine berries, sugar, cornstarch and lemon zest. Toss gently to mix. Spoon filling into pastry shell. Dampen rime of pastry with a little of the egg white mixture. Cover with the top pastry. Cut an 8 inch X in the center. Fold back points from center and seal triangle points to pastry with egg white mixture to create a square in the center of the pie. Fold under and crimp edges. Brush top with remaining egg mixture and sprinkle with sugar.

Place foil or drip pan on oven rack below pie. Bake 15 minutes at 425; lower oven to 350 degrees. Cover pie lightly with foil and bake 30 minutes more. Spoon the heavy cream into the center. Return pie to oven and bake 15 minutes longer.

BLUEBERRY BANANA CREAM PIE

My friend Keith Dixon makes this pie, from a recipe he learned from his mom.

1 large prepared graham cracker crust in 8 or 9 inch pie pan
2 large bananas, peeled and sliced
1 cup powdered sugar
1/2 container whipped topping
8 oz. cream cheese
1 teaspoon vanilla (optional)
1 can blueberry pie filling
1 can blueberries (optional)

Line bottom of crust with bananas. Blend together cream cheese, vanilla, sugar, and whipped topping. Place the cream cheese mixture on top of bananas. If using canned blueberries, drain well and stir into blueberry filling. Place the blueberry filling on top of the cream cheese mixture. Chill for two hours before serving.

ACKNOWLEDGMENTS

What's crazier than admitting you're writing a book on pie? Admitting you're writing another book on pie. I've toodled with the idea of this book for years, but with *Make Room For Pie: A Delicious Slice of the Natural State* coming to fruition on the Arkansas Educational Television Network, the time was right to revisit the idea, thoroughly. It wouldn't have come about without a significant number of individuals, for which I offer my sincere appreciation.

To Sara Willis, Mona Dixon, Mark Herbst, Courtney Pledger, and the Arkansas Educational Television Network Foundation, thanks so much for germinating a project through nearly two years of thought, hustle and action. Making the transition from behind the camera to its frontside was a hell of a leap, but you all had confidence in the stories I was ready to share. Special thanks once over to Sara Willis, who spun all sorts of advice that kept me on track.

To Larry Foley and Hayot Tuychiev and the *Make Room For Pie* crew, for bringing the concept to the screen and showing me the need to evolve the this book into reality.

To the Arkansas Department of Parks and Tourism, the Arkansas Hospitality Association and the tourism industry who assisted with lodging, contacts and promotion.

To Sharon and Lance Woodson and Anne Wood, for the pep talks and support and pie creations and above all the open door. To Ruthie Pepler and family for safe haven and encouragement.

To Rhys Harper, who pulled my butt out of the fire when the software went kaput on me, and who converted my progress so I didn't have to utterly start over.

To Mary Jo Tennison-Willis, who read through the whole mess and assured me I had not entirely lost my mind or grammar skills.

To Mike and Caren Walloch, for covering the car of my daughter when I needed to be on the road or absorbed in the writing of this book. Hunter is also grateful.

To my mom, Kitty Waldon, for making sure I could concentrate on preparing this book, supporting me and allowing me to make this happen. I would not have been able to do this without her.

To Grav Weldon, for the cups of iced coffee and plates of steak, washing my socks, patiently listening to me voice my thoughts and feeding the cats and the kid.

And to Arkansas's piemakers, restaurateurs, bakers, truck stop attendants, front of the house and back of the house folks who allowed me the run of their dining rooms and kitchens with my camera and who provided me with kindness and hospitality.

PIE PLACES
(recipes listed in blue)

ABOUT THE AUTHOR

Kat Robinson is a food historian and travel writer based in Little Rock. She is the author of three previous travel dining guides: *Arkansas Pie: A Delicious Slice of the Natural State* (2012), *Classic Eateries of the Ozarks and Arkansas River Valley* (2013) and *Classic Eateries of the Arkansas Delta* (2014). She is also the host of the Arkansas Educational Television Network program *Make Room For Pie: A Delicious Slice of The Natural State.* She is a committee member of the Arkansas Food Hall of Fame and the Arkansas fellow to the Southern Food and Beverage Museum, as well as the 2011 Arkansas Department of Parks and Tourism Henry Award winner for Media Support.

Her work appears in regional and national publications including Food Network, Forbes Travel Guide, Serious Eats, AAA Magazines and AY Magazine, among others. While she writes on food and travel subjects throughout the United States, she is best known for her ever-expanding knowledge of Arkansas food history and restaurant culture, all of which she explores on her 1200+ article website, Tie Dye Travels (TieDyeTravels.com).

Ask for Arkansas food recommendations by tweeting and following Kat on Twitter @TieDyeTravels.

For updates and more information on pie in Arkansas, please visit ArkansasPie.com.

CPSIA information can be obtained
at www.ICGtesting.com
Printed in the USA
BVHW02s0255020418
512179BV00015BB/336/P